P9-CMO-142

Religion
&
Contemporary Society

Religion & Contemporary Society

Edited by HAROLD STAHMER

The Macmillan Company, New York
Collier-Macmillan Limited, London

First Printing

The Macmillan Company, New York
Collier-Macmillan Canada Ltd., Toronto, Ontario
DIVISIONS OF THE CROWELL-COLLIER PUBLISHING COMPANY

DESIGNED BY IRENE KEAN
Printed in the United States of America

Library of Congress catalog card number: 63-15052

Acknowledgment

The editor is especially indebted to his colleague, Ursula Niebuhr, The Danforth Foundation, the contributors, his students in Religion 25, and to Miriam Buck for her clerical assistance. This book is the first of several publications honoring the Seventy-fifth Anniversary of Barnard College (1889–1964). It is appropriate that it should go to press on the eve of the retirement of President Millicent Carey McIntosh, whose support and interest throughout this venture are greatly appreciated.

Contents

Introduction

THE essays in this collection were originally presented in lecture form in a course entitled "Religion and Contemporary Society," given at Barnard College. Professor Ursula Niebuhr began this course seven years ago, assisted by occasional outside speakers, all experts in their particular fields. Through a generous five-year grant from The Danforth Foundation, we have been able to maintain this consistently high standard of lectures designed to introduce students to the phenomenon known as American piety. Rather than present an analysis of American religious life from a single perspective, whether it be that of a single confessional viewpoint or the methodology of the social sciences, it was felt desirable to have students listen to eminent representatives of each of the three major religious traditions as well as experts in the fields of church and state, religion and education, and religion and politics. This pluralistic approach represents an attempt at a fair and objective presentation of an exceedingly complex subject. While the approach is largely descriptive, the reader will soon recognize the particularly normative concerns of each writer. In this way it is hoped that students of the subject will obtain both a sense of authentic religion within the Judeo-Christian tradition as well as a feeling for the unique character of American religious life.

I

The common concern throughout these essays is with the paradoxical character of American piety as expressed in the now classic phrase "America is at once the most religious and the most secular of nations." Against the background of seventeenth-century Puritan theology with its stress upon the transcendent and critical role of religion over society stands the contemporary tendency to identify prophetic and critical religion with the prevailing aims and norms of American culture. The tendency to identify the critical, judgmental, and prophetic character of our Judaeo-Christian tradition with secular interests must inevitably result in a loss of vitality, direction, and identity, both with respect to our American values and national sense of purpose, as well as affect the creative sense of historical responsibility inherent in our religious heritage.

The first collection of essays discusses the Judeo-Christian tradition, and not only reflects the uniquely pluralistic character of our American religious heritage but also suggests in outline form those elements we Americans have regarded as the sacred ingredients of this heritage. In almost every other Western nation, religious pluralism resulted from what Father John Courtney Murray has described as "a disruption or decay of a previously existent religious unity." In America, religious pluralism is part of the uniqueness of her social character. Any appreciation of our national character must begin with a recognition of this uniquely American phenomenon. Perhaps because of the affinity of our religious heritage with the very structure of our social character, we Americans have often tended to identify the two, thereby contributing greatly to the paradoxical character of American piety referred to above.

In sharp contrast to this stands Renan's characterization of the true Israelite as one "torn with discontent and possessed with a passionate thirst for the future." Historically, this applies to the Christian's dilemma as it does to the Jew's. The preoccupation of the Jew with the prophetic character of history, and the Christian's sense of a completed and normative cosmic scheme within time and history, reflect the significance of what theologians refer to as "eschatology," or a concern for the determinative role in the historical present of what has been promised at the end of history. The traditional uneasiness on the part of Jews and Christians with respect to the *status quo* and with the proneness of the secular mind to exalt the present at the expense of the lessons of a sacred sense of history accounts for the concern reflected in these essays for the state of contemporary American religious life. Arthur Cohen's essay on eschatology illustrates the historic tendency to identify the City of God with the City of Man, and shows how it is possible to speak of secular eschatologies completely devoid of their sacred impetus. In summary it may be said that the sense of historical urgency and responsibility arising from the tension between the temporal and the Eternal constitute essential and decisive qualities of the Western religious temperament. The dramatic interaction of the sacred and the secular ought to serve as constant reminders that our religious allegiances and responsibilities impinge upon, but are not identical with, our sense of national purpose.

The first set of essays serves as a background against which one can appraise those later lectures devoted to the curious and complex intermingling of religious and social issues on the contemporary scene. Admittedly, the concerns of this book are with the social implications of religion in America today. The specific social issues that seemed of paramount concern to students of religion in the years 1960–1961 involved questions of church and state, religion and education, and the religious factor in politics, as evidenced by John Wicklein's analysis of the 1960 presidential campaign. The summary analysis of the contemporary religious situation in America by Reinhold Niebuhr is a suitable conclusion to those issues discussed in earlier essays. Niebuhr's remarks remind us of our larger international obligations in a time of ideological conflict and threat of nuclear catastrophe.

Finally it may be admitted that many readers might well have chosen other issues as being far more important for the cause of "true religion." As these essays go to press, two events of tremendous significance are being vigorously debated throughout the nation. I refer first to the controversy surrounding the June 25, 1962, Supreme Court ruling which held that the reading of a twenty-two-word prayer at the start of each day in the New York public schools is a violation of that clause in the First Amendment which prohibits "an establishment of religion." Although delivered in the fall of 1961, Professor Jones's discussion of this issue anticipates in many respects the inevitability of that decision. The second issue is related to the "prayer crusade" by Dr. Martin Luther King and his associates in Albany, Georgia. As his group suggests, the outcome and consequences of their action will not be decided for quite some time. The response of local Negro groups in other southern communities will undoubtedly affect the historical significance of this crusade.

Because religion is bound to be an important factor in any period of social transformation and upheaval, it is inevitably a source of distress and unhappiness for many of our people. For others, it is a means of hope and liberation. These essays are offered as an attempt to make the reading public aware of the significant role of religion in the transformation of American society today.

HAROLD STAHMER

Barnard College
Columbia University

May 2, 1962

PART ONE

Reflections on the History of Jewish Religious Thought

ARTHUR A. COHEN

I: The Biblical and Rabbinic Foundations

JUDAISM begins with the end of the Bible. It is a post-biblical reality. It is as well a reality that matures its distinctive historical forms and finds its articulate voice in the period after the emergence of Christianity and after its abasement by the armies of Rome.[1]

Rabbinic Judaism (135 B.C.E.–1035 C.E.) is founded upon characteristic emphases of biblical faith. Where it differs from biblical Judaism is not in the substance of its thought, but in its forms and method—not in the characteristic problems that emerge in the relationship between man and God, or the community and God, but in the attitudes and approaches by which

[1] This is true even though historical events were to oblige Judaism to come to terms with both Rome and Christendom, with the temporal state and the temporal church.

the rabbinic mind seeks to concretize and to transmit that substance and that relation. Rabbinic Judaism is, therefore, a process of rationalizing the biblical encounter with the Holy. Whether one describe this process of rationalization as pneumatic, organic, eschatological, or any number of similarly arbitrary and confusing descriptions, what remains is that abundantly simple and abundantly arduous reality that the West has called theology. Jews are uncomfortable with the theory and practice of theological thinking; they avoid it; they misconstrue it; they evade it; but inevitably they are theologians and they have produced theology. Can it be true that the wonder, concern, commitment, and faith the Word of God arouses in the Jew is other than theology? Could it be that the building of that monumental witness to the divine-human meeting that is Torah be other than theology? It matters not to theologians that theological thinkers are unaware that they are theologizing when they respond to the Word of God, but it is no less theology for their innocence. It is proper, therefore, that theology be the task of the rabbis, that to them—the second, and third, and fourth, and millennial community of witnesses to the covenant made with God on Sinai—should have fallen the task of taking what was clear and evident to the Patriarchs, the Judges, the Kings, and the Prophets, and sustain their experience as the marker and criterion for those who are seized anew by God, but have not the historical memory to refine, winnow, and examine their experience of Him. The Rabbis performed this service for Israel. They could perform it, however, only because their work was founded upon the work of the Bible and their word was a witness and commentary upon the biblical Word of God.

The Bible is formed out of a vivid apprehension of the holiness of God, its rich foreboding, its mysterious manifestation, its breaking upon and forming of the religious consciousness of the ancient Hebrew. Yehezkel Kaufmann's magisterial *The Religion of Israel* has described the biblical matrix that confirms Rudolf Otto's earlier analysis of the idea of the Holy; Kaufmann has defined a position that runs counter to a tradition of more than a hundred years of biblical criticism. Where traditional biblical criticism was to argue that a natural continuity existed between pagan and Israelite religion, Kaufmann has affirmed (and, we believe, demonstrated) that "Israelite religion was an original creation of the people of Israel." The Bible is not derivative; it is not a mere articulation and culling of pagan mythologies already disseminated among the tribes who inhabited Palestine prior to the days of its conquest. Pagan religion was not merely a mythological presence that melted away before the conquering troops of Joshua; nor was it the vanquished culture, which in its very defeat penetrated and transformed those who had conquered it.

The Bible is not a document whose exalted moments are late (the work of zealot priests returned from the Babylonian exile or prophetic reformers); rather the essential *realia* of Biblical religion are all early, however reticent and concealed they seem at first viewing. For the essential ideas are not first present as ideas, but as experience. It matters little whether the ideas are fully formed and articulate or inchoate and unfashioned, for what is crucial is that a unique and preempting God chose a people and that that people accepted its service. What comes first is God and Israel, no longer gods and men.

Our concern here is not to expound Kaufmann's views (for that one must read Kaufmann), but to suggest rather the connection between the pristine and spontaneous religious genius of the Hebrew Bible, and the rabbinic mind that worked upon it and fashioned the postexilic Judaism that is substantially the Judaism of our day. The Bible is a refracted and refracting document. It is never fully open, for God is never wholly present, and never completely closed, for the presence of God is ever new and renewed through it. It is proper, then, to describe it as a document eminently anthropomorphic (in that man always sees in God that which God has already given to man) and theomorphic (in that God always offers to man that which man has already sought from God).

Such anthropomorphism (or, as it has been more meaningfully called by Abraham Joshua Heschel, "anthropopathetism") presents the image of God as a translation of his mystery into the accessible dimensions of human passions and actions. What is crucial is not the biblical translation of the revealed God into man apotheosized or deified; but rather, as Heschel has noted, that the Bible is God's anthropology—that God reads man in God's terms in precisely the same sense in which man reads God in man's terms. What results is not anthropomorphism in the manner in which the Eleatic philosopher Xenophanes ridiculed it:

> If oxen and horses or lambs had hands, and could paint with their hands, and produce works of art as men do, horses would paint the forms of the Gods like horses, and oxen like oxen, and make their bodies in the image of their several kinds.

For what Xenophanes misses is precisely the significance of the *numinous*, the incommensurability of the Other; not merely the transcendence of God, but the utter otherness of God, the impassable dissimilarity of God and man. And yet not even mere dissimilarity, for God cannot be "other" unless he be "like." "Other" and "like" are terms of contrariety—they can be defined only in intimate relation. It is impossible to speak of that which is "other" unless one acknowledges at the same time a reality which is "like." God, therefore, is not only dissimilarity and otherness—for if he were wholly "other" he could not be apprehended, and if we were wholly unlike, he could not have created us (a reverse Anselmian proof). God assumes the forms of time that he might be fulfilled in time, that the abundant possibilities of his person be actualized and history and historic times afforded the medium of divine actualization.

The rabbinic rationalization of the biblical *numen* consists in the translation of the mysterious, the momentous, into a consistent experience that man is capable not only of preserving but also of transmitting. Surely it cannot be that man can live face to face with God at all times. As much as God is available to man at all times, his presence is not his immediacy—he is there, but he cannot be immediate (as theologians of the I and Thou would have him). This is only to say that the numinal encounter must be rationalized, not for God's sake, but for man's. The moralization of the numen (which Otto has so brilliantly described) consists in the effort to sacramentalize, perhaps routinize, man's obedience toward God.

This process of rationalization is indispensable for "the history of salvation," for it permits the self-revelation of God to be incorporated into the movement of history. The moralization of the "idea" of God is not, however, to be interpreted as a suppression of the numinous or its supercession by something else (which would result not in the preservation of God, but of a "God-substitute"), but rather a reinfusion, a recharging of the experience of God with new meaning. The rabbinic tradition is therefore a process that could not have taken place without the revelation of God in Scripture, without the awesome experience of the *numen*. But since it is also *tradition* it is a process of receiving the Word of God, defining its hegemony and dominion over the people of Israel, and establishing the *sancta* which guarantee its transmission through history.

Thus, the rabbinic tradition begins where the Bible ends. But it begins where the Bible ends in such fashion as to make unmistakably clear that at no point can it dispense with what the Bible has given. The rabbinic age is a vast, capacious, and comprehensive millennium. It begins with the rededication of the Temple under the Maccabees in 135 B.C.E., and extends until the close of the era of the Gaonim in 1035 C.E., when the transfer of the center of the Jewish Diaspora from Babylon westward to Europe, takes place. During the compass of this millennium, Judaism was permanently marked by a number of critical and interconnected historical events: first, the founding of the Hasmonean Dynasty which began with the successful rebellion of the Maccabees against Antiochus IV Epiphanes in 135 B.C.E. It was during this period that the three characteristic sects of Judaism, the Sadducees, the Pharisees, and the Essenes, emerged. The second crucial event was the triumphant imposition of Roman authority upon Palestine, culminating in the destruction of the Temple in 70 C.E. by the Emperor Titus. The third crucial event was the establishment, shortly after the destruction of the Temple, of the first rabbinical academy at Jabneh on the coast of Palestine. Fourth, the final decimation of Jewish life in Palestine, following the Jewish rebellion against Hadrian in 135, resulted in the expulsion of all Jews from the immediate vicinity of Jerusalem; the subsequent abandonment of Palestine as a center of Jewish studies; the transfer (in the fifth major event) of the focus of Jewish life and worship from Palestine to Babylon and the founding of two great academies of Jewish study, those of Sura and Pumbeditha.

The internal history of Judaism, responding as it did to such impressive historical events, was one of conservation and maturation. This process of inner expression resulted in the development of a comprehensive system of conduct and the formulation of directive principles for the structuring of conduct. The rabbinic mind (a strange and precarious hypostasis) was not, it would appear, preoccupied with theology. This view has been emphatically presented and passionately defended by centuries of Jewish exegetes; indeed, during the productive centuries of Jewish philosophy from the tenth century to its decline in the early fifteenth century, the opponents of philosophic speculation consistently cited the rabbinic age as evidence that Judaism did not require "theology" in order to serve God. The rabbinic age was adduced as a model of pristine Jewish piety, the exemplar of religious life conducted independently of the requirements of theology. But the theology that such exegetes oppose was not Jewish theology as such, but modes of theology that prevailed in the Christian and Moslem world and that it rightly felt were inappropriate to the requirements of the Jewish community. This is only to say that it opposed erroneous theology (the superficial definition of error being an atmospheric and temperamental disjunction between Jewish and alien modes of thought). Unfortunately, it did not understand what theology entailed, for, very much like the Molière character, it was speaking theology all the time without ever knowing it. The rabbis of Mishnaic and Talmudic times were certainly theologians—that is to say, they had only one object of preoccupation; that object and He alone seized and held their imagination and intellect; to Him above all else were they committed and only in Him did they believe; for Him and for no other did they weave the tapestry of the commandments that He might be exalted; for His sake only were they prepared to suffer and die. If this is not theology, then theology is not understood, for theology is nothing less than having God as the single object of human concern. Moreover, such human concern is only partially served by the operation of the reason. The Bible documents the foundations of God's relation to man, and asks of man that certain relations be reciprocally established. It is on this basis of revelation that theology undertakes its work. All that theology undertakes—ever, always, and continually—is to deepen the understanding of what it is God has said and done with man.

The rabbis were in one sense hopelessly naïve and in another eminently sophisticated. Their naïveté consisted in the fact that they imagined there was a necessary and indispensable correlation between God's will and human action; between divine concern and human response. Their naïveté was most profound; indeed, it was naïve only in the sense in which it was not modern (and it should be added that most of the corruptions of contemporary religion arise from the insistence that it be made modern before it can be made true). One of the characteristic emphases of the rabbinic mind, however, is its preoccupation not with contemporaneity, where contemporaneity refers to the conditions of a post-Temple exilic society, but with the concerns of truth as witnessed to by the biblical text and concretized in the rabbinic literature. Their naïveté was therefore most profound but "unmodern." Its hallmark was the constant search for a relation between divine cause and human effect. As a result, the rabbis projected a series of polar concepts or contrarieties that arise out of the immediacy of history and that require rationalization and absorption by religious tradition—such concepts as providence and history; prescience and freedom; punishment and mercy; the obligations of performing the commandments as they are transmitted and exceeding the letter of the commandments as they are transmitted; of performing within the ambit of the act while, at the same time, retaining a vivid awareness that no act is complete unless directed to the service of God who transcends all human limits.

The rabbis were poignantly aware of the incommensurability of faith and formula; nevertheless, they did not believe that faith could be sustained without formula. Judaism became, in consequence, a religion of formula, a religion of formula under the pressure of the needs of conservation, on the one hand, and an atmosphere of religious freedom and mercurial creativity, on the other. Not the formula, but the dialectic of human action and passion defined the center of rabbinic Judaism.

At the same time that one acknowledges the naïveté of the rabbis, one is obliged to recognize their sagacity and sophistication. They did not bother to demonstrate what they were wholly persuaded could not be demonstrated; moreover, the very injunction to forego speculation about the Divinity itself arose less from the feeling that such would be desirable (however morally pernicious) than from the conviction that it would be an arrogant and irrelevant inquiry (and hence morally pernicious). How could the rabbis formulate a doctrine of *fides ut intelligam* when, in fact, they drew no distinction between faith and understanding. The act of faith was for them an act of coming to know and trust God. Faith was knowledge, and what was given as knowledge (knowledge of the only significant object—the person and wishes of God) was faith. It is understandable, therefore, that however much the rabbis may have been disturbed by the insinuations of Hellenistic philosophizing, they did not find it necessary to exert themselves in formal argument on such problems as the nature and attributes of God, the relation of providence to human freedom, or the presence of evil in a world created by a gracious God. This is not to say that they were unaware of these problems, for the homiletic and exegetic literature they produced abound in examples that exhibit their sensitivity to such theological questions. In spite of such recognition, however, they considered it more pertinent for man to concentrate upon the activity at hand, the living of life with maximum concern for justice, mercy, humility, and right conduct.

Rabbinic theology can be described, as Solomon Schechter has observed, as "a complicated arrangement of theological checks and balances." The rabbis begin with certain "givens," with experienced realities about which they have no questions —the creation of the world, the gift of the Torah to Israel, the giving of the Land (Palestine) to the Israelites of the desert that they might inhabit it and fashion there "a kingdom of priests and a holy nation." These are urgent and factual data for Jewish faith. Beyond these, the God who created, revealed, and bequeathed is a God of mercy and justice, a gracious father who concerns himself with the action of his creatures, who gives them instruction and reproof, and who delivers to their keeping and transmission a regimen of conduct that inspirits right action and inhibits their impulse to waywardness and irresponsibility.

The theology of the rabbinic world is a pragmatic theology —the very fact of its being theology, however, makes its pragmatism somewhat less experimental than might be expected. It is pragmatic in the especial sense that Jewish law was never developed or imposed independently of the capacity of the community to sustain, observe, and transmit it. Its pragmatism is manifest in the entire range and expanse of the dialectic that refined the method and principles of Jewish law. It is a pragmatism, however, that is finally dependent upon a cluster of primary realities available only to faith. These primary realities are, as Max Kadushin has so brilliantly defined them in *Organic Thinking*, the love of God, the justice of God, the preeminence of the Torah, and the centrality of the community of Israel. As realities, they are first felt and savored, experienced as specific acts of graciousness, charity, and affection—they are living realities because the Bible witnesses to their life. It is only against the background of the inheritance of the Bible that this congerie of experience becomes patterned and organized, mutually coherent and transitive in implication. It is the passage from experience into concepts that gives to rabbinic tradition its peculiarly organic character. Divine love and justice, the giving of the Torah, and the election of Israel are interwoven and connected, reticulated by subtler and more obscurely felt concepts (suffering, purity, mission, holiness, sanctification, desecration, and so on), and out of this network of intelligible interconnection there emerges that organic complex that may be called Judaism.

The primary experiences that texture and define the faith of Israel are not readily recognizable as theological. They would be considered by academic Christian theology to be secondary, not primary, theological concepts. If one speaks of the love or justice of God or the preeminence of Torah and Israel, conventional theology would consider these possible but surely not self-evident deductions from the "essential" nature of God. The rabbis, however, felt themselves proscribed from speculating about God's "essential" nature—the nature which preexisted Creation. The essential God they could not know; to persist in the effort to apprehend such essence rabbinic tradition advisedly considered an enterprise that leads to madness, apostasy, and death. Rather the rabbis concerned themselves with the "empirical" given, with what it is that man has before him, and what it is that man is charged by God to do for His own and man's sake.

What rational theology would consider prior questions—God's existence, nature, attributes, and relations—rabbinic theology considers posterior to the evident fact that he did reveal himself, disclose his existence, manifest his nature, allude to his attributes, and define his relations with men. The factuality of revelation makes all questions of rational theology posterior to the content of revelation—love, justice, grace, and election.

The polarities that Christian theology developed in its *ressentiment* (both high and low *ressentiment*) toward Judaism—law and grace, justice and love, distance and incarnation—are meaningless to Judaism. They are the devisings of forensic theology that serve to elucidate the foundations of Christian experience, but touch not at all the reality of Jewish experience. We may be agitated by the genius of St. Paul, but we are agitated less by what he says against us as Jews than by what he says against us all as human beings. For the pretensions of the Law that Paul despises are the pretensions of any human institution that purports to be divine when it is only human. The Law of Israel is, however, not only human (which is to say that it bows not to the natural proclivities and inclinations of men) and it is not only divine (which is to say that being also human, it cannot be sufficiently divine). The Law is, as is all revelation, the perfection of God entrusted to the deficiency of men—as such, the Law is divine and human, perfect and corrupt, righteous and guilty, loving and possessive. The Law is the fragile gift of God. But, lastly and finally and ultimately, the God who gives the Torah to the Jews is not a principle of order and origin, but the living source from whom life proceeds and upon whom it depends.

The bequest of the rabbinic tradition is therefore a liturgy of life, a discipline of variety and coherence. And this properly is what may be referred to as the "catholicity" of Israel. The catholicity of Israel may be defined as a consensus whereby the community acknowledges the authority of tradition, and transmits that tradition from one generation to the next. It is not a consensus that carries with it the obligatory authority Paul Tillich might describe as a "demonic absolutization of the relative." Jewish tradition is under no illusion that it has *every* answer; but it does believe that it has those answers that are important. It does not claim to absolutize a historic moment. It does claim to insist that what is given in Scripture is the foundation of a liturgy of life and a discipline that might well become the consensus not only of Judaism but also of mankind. As such, it exercises not only an internal catholic claim upon the visible community of Israel but also a claim upon the invisible community of those who stand near it in conviction but distant from it in explicit practice and faith.

II: The Concerns of Medieval Jewish Thought

The Judaism of the Middle Ages was a Judaism of transition and adaptation. It lasted vastly longer than the medieval cultures of Christendom, though not quite so long as the medieval culture of Islam, which only in the nineteenth century commenced to give way before the erosions of change. Throughout the Middle Ages, the Jews, unlike Moslems and Christians, were a sufferance community. They were appointed to separation from the nations of the world not by means of self-abasement and self-denigration; rather, they saw themselves appointed to separation, on the one hand, by virtue of a providential judgment God and Israel has passed upon the nations; similarly, and for legal, cultural, and theological reasons, they were placed by Islam and Christendom in a position of enforced separation.

The sufferance community of Israel was a voluntaristic community. The conviction that only by maintaining the purity and pristine character of Jewish faith in the exile would it be possible to fulfill its obligations to God demanded, so Israel understood, self-imposed isolation and *hauteur* before the world. In the same sense, therefore, in which the rabbinic age served to rationalize the revealed word of Scripture into law and teaching, the medieval tradition of the Jews was confronted with the task of rationalizing the law and teaching of the rabbinic age in such a way as to communicate and argue it before Christianity and Islam.

But why the challenge of Islam? Islam burst upon the world in 622, and in the succeeding two hundred years established itself throughout the Near East, North Africa, the outermost limits of continental Europe, and the far-flung missionary outposts of Asia. Early Islam had physical power, but it had no history. It had to acquire history, and with history it had to acquire a theology. In order to justify Mohammed's claim to be not merely the founder of a radical sect but also the consummation of the providence of God begun with Moses and completed according to the Christian dispensation with Jesus Christ, it became necessary for Islam to insist that there was yet a third stage, a penultimate stage, which embodied both Moses and Jesus and brought them to fulfillment in Mohammed. As a result, it became necessary for Islam to read itself back into the history of faith, to adapt and take over to itself the tradition of Judaism and Christianity, and to make it an indispensable portion of the teaching of the prophet. Islam sought to acquire a sacred history and make itself the fulfillment of that history.

Islam incorporated Judaism and Christianity into the doctrine of Islam, acquiring thereby a sacred pedigree while at the same time adopting the philosophic traditions of Greece that it might defend its pedigree before the attacks of both Christianity and Judaism.

The Greek philosophic tradition, primarily Plato, the neo-Platonists, and the Hellenistic schools of Alexandria, were well known to the fathers of the church. By the ninth century, however, nearly two centuries after the rise of Islam, the philosophic tradition of Greece had been all but lost or forgotten by Western Christianity. It was only in the late eleventh and twelfth centuries that new translations of Greek sources, mediated by Jewish and Arabic translators, became abundantly available once more to Latin Christendom. Islam enjoyed, therefore, for several centuries the all but uncontested opportunity of employing Greek philosophy to interpret and justify its sacred lineage before the world.

1. SAADYA BEN-JOSEF (892–942)

Judaism, however, was not threatened directly by Islam. It was agitated by its own heresy. Under the leadership of Anan ben David (c. 770), there arose in Baghdad the sect of the Karaites. Basing their dissent from rabbinic Judaism upon the repudiation of the meaning and justification of the oral law, the Karaites returned to a biblical fundamentalism that claimed that any tradition that could not be fully documented in Scripture was neither authentic nor binding. The Karaites, protected by the secular power of Islam (which was not unduly dismayed by the discomfiting of Judaism), defined a challenge to rabbinic Judaism. At the same moment that the speculative dogmatics of the Islamic Mutazilites was being directed against the orthodox defenders of the oral tradition (*hadith*) of Islam, the Judaism of the Islamic world was being challenged. Indeed, the danger of Karaism might have been greater had it been capable of developing a theology equal to its biblicism. As matters turned out, Karaism had succeeded more in directing the hostility of the poor Jews of Persia against the established centers of Jewish authority than in sharpening a new theological thrust. Moreover, in the effort to perpetuate their small numbers the Karaites developed a liturgy and tradition that by the tenth century was no less elaborate and demanding than the rabbinism it opposed. Karaism was but a drop of poison easily diffused in the congenial medium of Islam. It may be conjectured that the concern of the rabbinites was less that the oral law might be overwhelmed by Karaism than that its sources of authority, once weakened and compromised by Karaism, might finally give way to the assaults of the rationalism of Islamic theology.

The orthodox of Islam, no less than the orthodox of Israel, were dismayed by the intellectual and spiritual license that prevailed. The world of Islam was tolerant, if not hospitable, to Christian, Jew, Zoroastrian, Indian philosophers, Manicheans, as well as schools and disciplines within Islam. Indeed, the ferment was so intense, that one Moslem historian, Al-Hum'aydi, records the experience of a companion in Baghdad in the tenth century:

One of the Spanish theologians—Abu Omar Ahmad ibn Muhammad ibn Sa'di—visited Baghdad. . . . Upon his return he met a famous scholar of Kairuwan, Abu Muhammad ibn Abi Za'yd, who asked him whether he had had an opportunity of attending, during his stay in Baghdad, one of the assemblies of the Kalam. "Yes," he answered, "I attended twice, but I refused to go there a third time." —Why? —"For this simple reason which you will appreciate: At the first meeting there were present not only people of various Islamic sects but also unbelievers, Magians, materialists, atheists, Jews and Christians; in short, unbelievers of all kinds. Each group had its own leader whose task it was to defend its views, and every time one of the leaders entered the room, his followers rose to their feet and remained standing until he took his seat. . . . One of the unbelievers rose and said to the assembly: 'We are meeting here for a discussion. Its conditions are known to all. You, Moslems, are not allowed to argue from your books and prophetic traditions, since we deny both. Everybody, therefore, has to limit himself to rational arguments.' The whole assembly applauded these words. So you can imagine," Ibn Sa'di concluded, "that after these words I decided to withdraw. They proposed to me that I should attend another meeting in a different hall, but I found the same calamity there." [2]

The calamity to which our Islamic historian refers was the willingness of medieval Islam to countenance philosophic argument cut off from its roots in revelation. Islamic liberality of intellect—which has timid approximation in twelfth century Christian Europe—was threatening not only to Orthodox Moslems but to rabbinite Jews. It was to the double thrust of Islamic rationalism and Karaite heresy that Saadya ben-Josef (892–942) addressed himself.

Saadya, the most distinguished legist and theologian of his age, determined to take the issues posed by Islamic rationalism and employ them in the defense of Judaism. His famous work, *The Book of Doctrines and Beliefs* (933), does not project a philosophic system; however, it does succeed in interpreting Judaism in the light of reason. The conflict, so Saadya understood it, was not between faith and reason properly employed, but rather between faith and pseudoreason, that is, reason

[2] Saadya Gaon, *The Book of Doctrines and Beliefs*, edited by Alexander Altmann, Introduction, East and West Library (Oxford, 1946), pp. 13–14.

masquerading as common sense. The average man is misguided if he imagines that common sense can ever successfully illuminate and justify the foundations of faith. Common sense is a most febrile and inadequate instrument of apprehension, for common sense will most often instruct man to draw improper conclusions from his experiences. The conflict between faith and common sense is real, because common sense is a source of error and confusion. There is, on the contrary, no conflict of faith and educated reason.

Judaism, Saadya argues, is rational if it be recognized that the universe conforms to the order of God. God cannot act against his nature, which is composed preeminently of order and reason; hence to conclude that faith is opposed to reason is to concede that one has improper faith and erroneous reason. *The Book of Doctrines and Beliefs* proceeds from such preliminary argument to an examination of the specific doctrines of Jewish faith—not to rationalize or explain them, but to demonstrate rather that they are, properly understood, only the conformance of nature, reason, and divinity. The task of philosophy is not to combat the presumptive insufficiencies of faith, but so to purify the statement and communication of faith that its compatibility with reason becomes clear. Reason is to be purified of its admixture of common sense and doubt that it might be exalted and made worthy of faith. The usual argument of faith seeking the justification of reason is inverted; reason is purged that it might be illumined by faith.

Saadya's argument is characteristic of medieval Jewish thought. There was little doubt on the part of Jewish scholasticism that faith, properly understood, could comport, agree, and conform with all the requirements of reason. The problem was that the reason of man is corrupt; philosophy is accordingly assigned the task of educating reason to apprehend the decretals of faith.

2. BAHYA BEN JOSEF IBN PAKUDA (C. 1080–1156)

Of all the thinkers of the medieval synagogue, undoubtedly the most mysterious was Bahya ibn Pakuda, judge in the Jewish civil court of Saragossa, Spain. Unlike Saadya, Bahya was not a rationalist concerned with establishing the conformance of reason to faith. Nor was he agitated, as was Saadya, by the external challenge of Islam to Judaism. His concern, shaped as it was by currents of Islamic mysticism, was rather the rooting of faith in the understanding of the heart.

Bahya commences his masterwork, *The Duties of the Heart*, with the assumption that the problem of disbelief arises from the fact that most of man's life is lived not in the light of reason, but rather in the twilight of the heart. It becomes necessary, if there is to be right faith, that the obligations of the heart be submitted to the structuring order of reason, that the heart be rationalized. Bahya is concerned lest the heart be surrendered to unreason and passion, rather than that reason be purged of the heart. The few moments of man's life in which reason pursues a course independent of the heart are unnatural and indecisive. Indeed, were the same degree of scrutiny that reason gives to the refinement of argument turned to an inquiry into the grounds of the heart, it might be discovered that the "reasons" the heart gives for faith are purer than those reason gives the heart. Unlike Saadya, the argument of Bahya is a formal exposition of Jewish faith beginning with an examination of the opening declaration of Jewish faith—the "Hear, O Israel"—and proceeding through a patterning of Jewish observance with the laws of the heart. In appropriating characteristic emphases of Islamic mysticism, Bahya is able to counter the temptation of drawing Jews to the rationalism within Islam and Judaism. *The Duties of the Heart* is constructed in order to support and reaffirm in more sophisticated terms the belief of those who are anxious to persevere in their faith, to effect a closer union with God, and seek defense against the assaults of a pretentious reason.

3. JEHUDAH HALEVI (C. 1085–1140)

Reason has always been the opponent of unreason. It was centuries, however, before it became the opponent of revelation. That revelation should be construed as unreason and opposed for that fact represents a novelty of the modern perspective. It was no surprise to some that philosophy would one day come to polarize faith so radically as to threaten its very foundations. It is in anticipation of this condition that Jehudah Halevi early set out to arraign philosophy before its ultimate judge and to vindicate revelation before it became obscured.

Jehudah Halevi and his masterpiece, *The Kuzari*, are undeniably a perplexity to our age. There is something in his life and work that threatens a world of caution and equanimity—a spirit of recklessness and daring, of intensity and passion that dislocates the ordered world which modern Judaism seeks to ensure for itself. The medieval Jew who would abandon fame and reputation late in life to make a dangerous and solitary pilgrimage from Spain to Jerusalem is not a reasonable man, however heroic and admirable his conduct. The example of a life, single and mute, is less dangerous, however, than a work that has the daring to claim before royalty the unrivaled truth of a people despised, lowly, and oppressed. Where Maimonides would mention Christianity and Islam with circumspection, self-conscious and respectful, speaking with forebearance and tact, Jehudah Halevi will reduce their positions with dispatch, discharge their proponents, and set before man the only true challenge and the only real alternatives: the truth of Israel or the truth of philosophy.

It is apparent that Jehudah Halevi was not satisfied with the efforts of his antecedents to justify tradition before the bar of reason. It was somehow, in his view, unbefitting for the highest to be justified by the less exalted. It is not that Halevi rejects philosophy. He does not. He rejects Christianity and Islam. On the contrary, philosophy is for him the only real alternative to Judaism, and hence its only authentic opponent.

The Kuzari, which Jehudah Halevi composed about 1130 in Spain, was written, he informs us, with the view of stating the arguments and replies that might be brought to bear against the attacks of philosophers, the followers of other religions, and Jewish sectarians. It is a work of apologetics, but it is immediately apparent that it is not an example of traditional apologetics. Its apologetics differs profoundly from that of classic Christian apologia in the nature of the argument and the form of the dialogue. The work is only superficially apologetic, for the normal conditions of a genuine apologia and an open victory do not obtain. The contestants do not meet in open contest. Israel does not win after having vanquished its opponents in face-to-face argument. It wins because it can make a stronger appeal to one seeking for tradition and an authenticated faith. The fact that the philosopher and the Jew never formally debate, that none of the religious representatives confront one another and expose their claims and differences does not prevent the victory of the rabbi from being profound. The apologetics cannot be the discourse of argument. At stake is precisely what Judaism cannot and moreover will not argue: what would be lost if it resorted to argument. Argument presupposes certain common concepts, a common body of discourse, sources of proof, and principles of analysis available to all participants. To admit the existence of such a framework would imply that a religion of revelation and a philosophic teaching enjoy parity. Were reason to prevail and conquest by rational argument to arbitrate the victory, Judaism would lose, for it cannot offer argument on this order. It can testify only to its history and its life. It is, however, this very testimony, and not the testimony of argument, that Bulan, King of the Khazars of South Russia, wishes to hear.

It should be recalled that the king is not perplexed by a problem of doctrine. The tradition Halevi adopts in defining the conditions of the dialogue is explicit: Bulan was beset by repeated dreams in which an angel informed him that "Thy way of thinking is indeed pleasing to the Creator, but not thy way of acting." Since the thoughts of the king are pleasing, obviously the remedy of thought which the Muslim rationalists or the efforts of Saadya and his followers deemed primary, was irrelevant. The argument is weighted against the philosopher. The philosopher can recommend a life of acts that follow thought, that are its consequence, rather than its motive or source. Since the philosopher pronounced God perfect, complete, fulfilled, without need or desire for man, the task of man is to adjust himself to the indifference of God and to become as like to His perfections as he is able. The philosopher must rise above the limitations of flesh, cultivate wisdom and understanding, become as one with the emanation of God, the so-called Active Intellect of the neo-Platonists. With stoic calm the philosopher demonstrates the irrelevance of the king's concern, for to speak of "the pleasing" to God is improper. The pleasing is really the *ataraxia* of man. The king acknowledges the truth of the philosopher's discourse but ignores it. Why? Precisely because the question the king has posed assumed exactly what the philosopher begins by denying—the philosopher denies that there is favor or disfavor in God's nature, whereas the king assumes that there is, else he would not have been instructed to seek the pleasing.

The philosopher is dismissed. The Christian and Muslim are then called. Each in turn is rejected as being either incoherent or else founded upon a prior tradition to which both make consistent appeal for legitimation of their antiquity. The king finally decides that if both traditions depend upon a prior one, let that community, even if it is "of low station, few in number, and generally despised," be called to testify. A rabbi, representative of the Jews, enters and is questioned. He answers as follows: "We believe in the God of Abraham, Isaac, and Jacob, who led the children of Israel out of Egypt with signs and miracles; who fed them in the desert and gave them the Land, after having made them traverse the sea and the Jordan in a miraculous way; who sent Moses with His law, and subsequently thousands of prophets, who confirmed His law by promise to the observant and threats to the disobedient. Our belief is comprised in the Torah—a very large domain."

Though the king is stunned by the directness and uncompromising character of the rabbi's assertion, he is not satisfied. He asks whether it would not have been more proper for the rabbi to have commenced with a description of God and his attributes. Such a question is patently rhetorical, for the king has already rebuked those who began in this manner. The rabbi properly rejoins that such questions are relevant only if one is a philosopher who wishes order and proof, reasonableness and system—and even in such a case, Halevi adds, philosophers cavil and disagree. If the king, however, is truly interested in right conduct pleasing to God and has called the rabbi because there lingers on, as tracings in the clay of history, the ancient activity of God in Israel, presumably he wishes to hear of the attestations that God has spoken and revealed. The king is pleased with the rabbi's rebuke of philosophy, adding that such a rebuke is more to the point than his opening statement. The rabbi answers: "Surely the beginning of my speech was just the proof, and so evident that it requires no other argument."

It is clear that the rabbi does not choose to argue, nor is he of the opinion that argument is pertinent. Argument is presumably relevant if one wishes to refine principles or press the virtues of conception and speculative doctrine—but before argument, Israel wavers and bends. It has no argument. It makes declarations that are confirmed by nothing other than axiomatic assumptions common to men of faith seeking right conduct: that God does not deceive, that He chooses to act in public rather than secretly, that He addresses history and selects in it the particularity through which to channel His address. He selects from history chosen vessels and instruments through which to confide His Word and through which to advance its truth and dominion. God is the Lord of history and, in Israel, He is manifest most clearly and distinctly. To the discourse of philosophy, Halevi responds with the declaration of acts.

This is not simply theological empiricism. Halevi is no unsophisticated biblical fundamentalist; he does not stand pat on the biblical word—for God is the Lord, not of the single moment or the single epoch, but of history. Holy history is, however, profoundly different from the history of discrete events. Halevi is unwilling to make philosophy the arbiter of history. To do so inevitably means to turn reason to the consideration of each doctrine and contention as though it were discrete and separate. Reason is inescapably partitive, examining each element and moment with absolute attention. Reason compels each moment to bear the weight of history—testing it for truth or error, meaning or triviality. The historical consciousness of faith rejects the single moment and discerns only the line and sweep of providence, the ongoing movement and articulation of the whole. It rejects the analytic dissolution of the totality. Its concern is the essential mark that touches and distinguishes every moment—the mark of the divine. This, Halevi makes clear in his reassertion that all and sufficient proof is given in the rabbi's opening declaration of faith. If one grants that God is and acts, then testimony consists not in the reconstruction of the divine nature, but in the record of acts —that He discomfited Pharoah, led Israel from Egypt, revealed Himself to Moses, and disclosed the Torah. The rest, as Halevi makes clear in his expansion of this remark, is the record of Israel in "personal experience" and "through uninterrupted tradition."

The Kuzari is perhaps the most profoundly contemporary production of medieval Jewish thought. It is contemporary, by contrast to the works of Saadya Gaon, because it raises considerations that are peculiarly apt to the situation of "the despised and lowly" in Israel throughout history. Where Saadya seeks to meet the challenge of rationalist criticism in Islam or the Karaite critique of tradition by demonstrating that what is thought irrational is rational, that what appears to be unclear reflects unclarity in the thinker and not in the thought, that tradition can be refined of inconsistency and opaqueness by applying to it the methods of careful and judicious reason, Halevi says something different. If Judaism were merely reasonable, it would be nothing, for philosophy inevitably would be more reasonable. Speculation cannot justify divine truth—it must always oppose it, because when divine truth is submitted to the instrumentality of speculative reason its mystery is dissolved and superseded.

Halevi does not say that Judaism is absurd. The temptation of both "existentialists" and "anti-existentialists" will be to make of such a view something comparable to the "credo quia absurdum est" of Tertullian. Nothing of the kind. Halevi does not say Judaism is absurd or paradoxical. Absurdity and paradox emerge only if one allows philosophy to submit sacred history to the criteria of nonreligious criticism. Religion is always obscure to the nonreligious. It is obscurantist, obtuse, and unclear. This fact cannot be denied, nor should it prove embarrassing. Only faith can enter into faith (perhaps this is the only paradox that is tolerable); only Halevi, accepting the acts of God as real acts, can speak clearly and convincingly— for he assumes that God acts and that His acts are real and meaningful.

The task of Halevi is not to make Judaism clear and reasonable to the philosopher. The philosopher is never met directly. The philosopher is heard at second hand, through the words and reports of the king who sees philosophy as the only plausible alternative to the faith of Israel. Halevi is aware, however, that as long as it is the king who is addressed (this paradigmatic figure who wields power on earth as God, in tradition, exercises regal dominion over all the earth) he alone is it worthy to convince to believe. Halevi is not interested in converting the philosopher, for the philosopher is independent of history. The king, however, who wishes right action and commands his subjects to right action—he is to be won. Since the king has received from God (in whom he believes even before the rabbi encounters him) the signal disclosure that He is concerned with man, that human action is meaningful to Him, the task of the rabbi is to make clear that the life of Israel, not the thought of philosophy, will render the king acceptable. The king, the man of power and acts, is important. It is he, and with him all men, whom Halevi must rescue from philosophy.

The apologetics of *The Kuzari* is unique in two senses: it is the only work of medieval Judaism to make unambiguously clear that traditional Judaism is the only truth, and it argues this conviction by exhibiting the rightness of that which God has done for Israel and of the life lived by Israel for God.

4. MOSES BEN MAIMON (1135–1204)

The appearance of *The Guide for the Perplexed* by Moses Maimonides in 1190 is intended for the perplexed. This monumental work, however, is not written for the many, but for the few; not for the instruction of the traditionally educated, but only for the philosophically trained; not directed to perplexities that undermine popular faith, but to the perfection of faith and the transformation of naïve belief into certain knowledge. The perplexed, to whom Maimonides addressed *The Guide*, are already wiser than the conventional wise, for they seek to clarify by reason what Scripture has already vouchsafed to faith.

Many works of medieval Jewish thought commence with an acknowledgment that their speculations are forbidden by traditional teaching. Saadya makes mention of the fact that the Mishnah had defined the limits human inquiry must not transgress. His rationalization was that his reflections are circumscribed by the evidence of Scripture, that he has no intention of exploring the mysteries, but only of defining what is necessary for the preservation of faith against the insurgent questions of alien philosophy and religion. Saadya is not seeking, by reason, to explore a *terra incognita*, but, as he himself suggests, to mark more clearly the path Scripture had already charted. Maimonides, acknowledging the same interdiction, supplies a somewhat different and revelatory justification:

God knows that I hesitated very much before writing on the subjects contained in this work, since they are profound mysteries; they are topics which, since the time of our captivity have not been treated by our scholars as far as we possess their writings; how then shall I know to make a beginning and discuss them? But I rely on two precedents: first, to similar cases our Sages applied the verse, "It is time to do something in honor of the Lord: for they have made void thy Law" (Ps. CXIX:126). Secondly, they have said, "Let all thy acts be guided by pure intentions." . . . Lastly, when I have a difficult subject before me—when I find the road narrow, and can see no other way of teaching a well established truth except by pleasing one intelligent man and displeasing ten thousand fools—I prefer to address myself to the one man and to take no notice whatever of the condemnation of the multitude; I prefer to extricate that intelligent man from his embarrassment and show him the cause of his perplexity, so that he may attain perfection and be at peace.

Since Maimonides writes without precedent—the oral teaching of the mysteries having been forgotten and its adepts having disappeared—the right understanding of scriptural language is assumed to have been forgotten. In the confused popular understanding of Scripture the nature of God is misconstrued; He is thought to possess corporeality, attributes, characteristics that resemble the perceptible dimensions of human flesh and sensibility. While Scripture might seem to support such misconstructions, its subtler meaning, hidden beneath the husk of language, indicates precisely the opposite. The law is made void by misunderstanding; the sensitive mind is perplexed by the grossness of contradiction between scriptural statement and the barest reasonings of common sense. To do something for the Lord is to do something to correct the misapprehensions of the uninstructed. Even if the prejudices of the common mind are disturbed and the simplicities of their anthropomorphisms dismissed, better that one man be brought to perfection than that ten thousand should be comforted by folly. Maimonides did not tolerate the self-satisfaction of delusion. Error was error. No matter whom its chastisement harmed, error must be removed.

With all its apparent forthrightness and preoccupation with the extirpation of error, Maimonides cautions that *The Guide for the Perplexed* was directed to the few, to be taught only to individuals, to be communicated only under conditions of maximum circumspection and care.

The Guide for the Perplexed is called a work of philosophy. Loosely speaking, this is justifiable. The characteristic marks of a philosophic work, by contrast to a work of theological exposition or religious exegesis, are present. *The Guide* assumes that those who read it are familiar with the foundations of logic and natural philosophy, that they are concerned with founding knowledge upon rational principles. Moreover, the subject matter of *The Guide* would apparently indicate that it is none other than a work of philosophy: it is directed to the proper exposition of physics and metaphysics. It is clear, however, as Leo Strauss has brilliantly argued, that *The Guide* is not a work of philosophy, as philosophy was commonly understood in the Middle Ages.

It is between Plato and Aristotle that the philosophic pendulum of the Judeo-Islamic Age swings. Historical scholarship, too much influenced by the role Aristotle comes to play in Christian scholasticism, assumes that the situation of medieval Judaism was similar to that of Christian scholasticism. It was not. Where it is impossible for a Christian to become adept at the statement and interpretation of Christian doctrine without considerable philosophic training, this is not true of Judaism. The Jew becomes master of Judaism by the study of Torah and its commentaries. Where Christianity is formed out of dogmatic definitions of the divine nature and its persons (which involve distinctions in the notions of substance and attribute as well as the complications of metapsychology), Jewish life is founded on the consequences of divine revelation, its instructions regarding the ordering of the whole of life, the principles whereby obedience and conduct are ordered. The Jew could know nothing of philosophy and be a faithful and instructed Jew. The Torah did not have to be justified by philosophic argument; precisely the reverse is true: the study of philosophy had to be justified by Torah.

Revelation in Judaism is addressed not to faith as in Christianity—the mystery is not what God reveals, but *that* he reveals. The fact of revelation is the mystery. Once the fact of revelation is acknowledged, its content is accepted *pro forma.* For Christianity it is less the fact that God reveals—such is known and accepted on the evidence of Hebrew Scripture—than what he reveals. The mystery of Christianity, which turns its historical statement to the faculty of faith, is that what is postulated by revelation defies reason. The fact of the "divine absurdity" makes of the Christian community an order founded upon a body of irrational facts. It is unavoidable that the history of the definition of Christian mysteries should mature a tradition in which analysis, philosophic inquiry, speculative distinction, and synthesis should become crucial.

Judaism possesses a document, not a doctrine; a code, not a system of conceptual definitions of mystery. Revelation created in Judaism a social order that defined the obligations and duties of man to God, explored the consequences of behavior, and adjusted the limits and freedom within which human action could occur. Revelation could be considered, therefore, a perfect law. The task of the loyal philosopher was, as a result, not to explore revelation with principles that are independent and contradictory to revelation, but to make revelation the ground and arbiter of philosophy.

If revelation is addressed to man, it must pass through a medium that effects its translation from the divine intellect to the civil order. In this, as well, Scripture supplies the paradigm to the philosopher-king of Plato, for the prophet is he through whom revelation is transmitted. The problem of prophecy, already central for Islam, is crucial for Judaism, for not only the greatest of prophets, Moses, but a line of prophets establishes the chain of tradition, and upon the wisdom of the prophet rests the wisdom of Judaism. If true "philosophy" consists in the understanding of revelation, then the philosopher and the prophet are equally the consequence and spokesmen of revelation. The issue is not, as some students have queried, whether Maimonides considered himself to possess the spirit of prophecy or to be a prophet, but whether he considered himself a *failasûf*. If he was a philosopher, thus understood, he enjoyed the perfections of the prophet.

It is equally clear that Maimonides did not regard himself a philosopher in the accepted sense of being an adherent of the methods and conclusions of Aristotle. To the wrong opinions of philosophy are not opposed a true philosophy or a religious philosophy, but "our opinion" or the opinion of "the community of the adherents of the law" or the convictions of those who believe in accordance with the "law of our teacher Moses." It would appear that in this Maimonides is orthodox and traditional, that *The Guide* is merely an effort to articulate the foundations of Torah in opposition to the invidious questions of critics of Judaism and philosophic opponents of revealed religion. Maimonides would then stand in the line of Saadya Gaon, a brilliant and penetrating apologete, one who made reason serve the ends of revelation.

Such a view is insufficient. *The Guide for the Perplexed* is not a work of philosophy. Its investigation is not an independent speculative account of physics and metaphysics. It is not a work of apologetics, for it does not contrast, except incidentally or by way of exposition, the doctrines of Judaism with those of either Islam or Christianity. It is not a work of theology or religious philosophy, for such terms would be meaningless to the medieval thinker (however much they may serve us retrospectively in our attempts to categorize and describe him). It does not have the intention of combating false opinion or ignorance, except to the extent that the views developed illumine confusion or substitute right opinion for false. Explicitly, Maimonides states that though the work will profit those who have not studied philosophy, their profit will be accidental. Those whose profit will be profound are those "whose studies have brought him [them] into collision with religion." They are not those whose "minds are confused with false notions and perverse methods." Presumably the collision of speculation and religion to which Maimonides addresses his *Guide* is one that has not yet produced fixed and inflexible convictions. The student who qualifies, as both perplexed and yet open to correction, confused and yet available to right opinion, must be young and tractable. It is not unusual that Maimonides should have dedicated and intended the *Guide* for his favorite student, Joseph ibn Aknin. Yet clearly the communication was not to be kept private or secret, as Maimonides had authorized before his death in 1204 that Ibn Tibbon commence translation of the work from Arabic into Hebrew for the benefit of Provençal and Spanish Jewry.

The *Guide* is thus addressed to the young thinker who has "studied philosophy and acquired sound knowledge, and who, while firm in religious matters, is perplexed and bewildered." What is the perplexity and bewilderment? It is clearly not philosophy that has bewildered him, for it is stated that he is unshaken in religious convictions. Presumably, then, two philosophies must contradict each other—a philosophy whose principles are grounded in reason and a philosophy whose principles are grounded elsewhere. If, as Maimonides tells us, he intended to compose *The Guide* in order to explore the sciences of physics and metaphysics as they are disclosed by the scriptural account of creation and that *locus classicus* of Hebrew metaphysics, the mystery of the chariots of Ezekiel, then the contest is between nonrevealed philosophy and the right understanding of philosophy as it is disclosed by Scripture. The conflict that produces perplexity can also yield to disbelief. It is interesting to observe that where Saadya Gaon devotes considerable attention to the problem of doubt, the problem of doubt is hardly mentioned, as such, in *The Guide*. Presumably the perplexity of the initiated is not the perplexity of doubt. Where Saadya assumed that doubt arises from the conflict of apodictic religious statement and the assaults of external speculative question, perplexity arises only at that point at which man has already begun to think speculatively.

Maimonides begins where Saadya leaves off. The issue of doubt is culturally motivated—a consequence of conflict among absolute and exclusive doctrines. It becomes for Maimonides, however, something more—it is the peculiar hazard of the speculative mind. It no longer assails the common mind, the religious teacher, the Talmudist, the simple believer. Those latter required but the statement of the end of the argument, the bare conclusions. It is sufficient to tell them that God is incorporeal, that His unity is without analogy to the world, that the creation out of nothing is effected neither by the arguments of the Aristotelians on behalf of the eternity of the world nor of the Muslim orthodox theologians who make the world utterly dependent upon God's unpredictable will and design. It is sufficient to instruct the masses with the *Mishneh Torah*, Maimonides' great and enduring summary of Talmudic law—to teach them, in the discourse of its first treatise, *The Book of Knowledge*, the consequences of philosophic argument, not its principles or method.

What is dangerous then? Why the circumspection and care? Maimonides, with frequency and diligence, recites throughout *The Guide* the cautionary admonitions of Scripture and the Rabbis: Do not teach metaphysics (*Maaseh Merkabah*) except to the skilled; do not teach it to more than one student at a time; always teach it *viva voce;* do not disclose more than the chief rubrics; do not detail the secret wisdom. Metaphysics is dangerous!

The paradox emerges here: if metaphysics is constituted by the study of the significances of Ezekiel's symbolic description of the divine chariot, the heavenly beings, the *cherubim* and *ophanim*, if these opening chapters of the prophetic book contain all the secrets of esoteric wisdom, how does one account for the rest of *The Guide?* The true subject of metaphysics covers but the briefest span of *The Guide*. It is prefaced by an introduction that affirms that it "is the pin upon which all hangs, and the pillar upon which everything rests." It is concluded with the affirmation that nothing more will be spoken in the remainder of the work about such sublime and terrifying mysteries. Yet before it, there was an elaborate and subtle investigation of problems that would normally be considered issues of traditional metaphysics. Maimonides quotes frequently from Aristotle's *Metaphysics* in precisely those sections where he disclaims that metaphysics is being discussed. Moreover, at the conclusion of his discussion of "true metaphysics," the metaphysics of Ezekiel's vision, he introduces the concluding discussion of providence and the institutions of Torah and its commandments.

The danger of "true metaphysics" lies not in its substance but in its method. Were man to be instructed in the inner secrets of creation or ushered into the mysteries of heaven prematurely, he would, as Maimonides often states, suffer the fate of the three recorded in the Talmud who stormed heaven and were thrust out in madness, confusion, and death. The one who survived, Rabbi Akiba, survived only because he acknowledged the limitations of human knowledge, the confines of human wisdom, the superficies beyond which the human mind cannot travel. Maimonides himself does not travel beyond these limits. Even when he explores the mysteries of the chariot of Ezekiel he acknowledges that he proceeds without inspiration, that only reason guides him, and that its limitations guard him from transgression.

Presumably what precedes and follows the study of the "true metaphysics" of Scripture are preliminary and consequential to it. The metaphysics of the philosophers would appear then to be merely preliminary to the metaphysics of revelation, what God revealed in cryptic and metaphoric language to the philosopher. Where for Aristotle and the Kalam the issue of God's incorporeality and relation to the world are primary issues of metaphysics, they are, to a revealed metaphysics, but preliminary questions to be resolved and ordered before the major exploration can proceed. Moreover, if the highest wisdom is that which is disclosed by the prophets Moses, Ezekiel, and Isaiah, it is proper that the nature of prophecy should be defined before the content of most profound prophecy is disclosed.

It is true that the metaphysics disclosed by Scripture—the inner order of the heavens that is symbolically spoken of by

Ezekiel and Isaiah—is the highest order of truth; yet God must make such truth accessible to man. Obviously, not all men can be metaphysicans. Maimonides has made this clear: a man must be disposed by habit, ability, preparation, leisure, moral excellence, and the variety of natural perfections with which training and capacity may endow him to become a metaphysician. These qualities of perfection are found preeminently among the prophets. Among alternative definitions of the prophet, that of the philospher is accepted in full. If a person "perfect in his intellectual and moral faculties" prepares himself to be a prophet, he cannot help becoming one. This, with the single provision that God wills that he be a prophet. In the end the arguments of philosophy are submitted to the evidence of Scripture, for in the end whatever man is able to become, it is God who chooses or rejects, employs or discards. It is on this note that the second part of *The Guide* ends.

The concluding section of *The Guide* opens with the exposition of the mysteries of the visions of Ezekiel, the true metaphysics. It then proceeds, apparently inexplicably, to the consideration of the seeming meaninglessness of creation where evil is present. Evil, however, is an illusion before God. It is the consequence of man's imperfection, his surrender to flesh and the debilitating impact of matter, which, like a veil, separates man's soul from the divine influence. The will of God is that man become perfect, for only in perfection can man imitate, in the manner of limitation and imagery, the divine life. Man can become like to God only through a perfection that is like to God. Only in knowledge, the perfection that detaches man from the preoccupations of flesh and self-preservation, can God be contemplated. To this end God makes available Torah: that it perfect man's body and thereby discipline the harm of man's flesh and sensuality. It makes available, as well, commandments that order the soul. These perfections serve only to socialize man, to structure his relations to nature and his fellow. If these were the only perfections, why then the striving for knowledge?

The Torah prepares man for his highest perfection, but in obedience to the explicit measure of Torah the last perfection is not gained—for the last perfection is the perfection of wisdom and prophecy:

> The fourth kind of perfection is the true perfection of man; the possession of the highest intellectual faculties; the possession of such notions which lead to true metaphysical opinions regarding God. With this perfection man has gained his final object; it gives him true human perfection; it remains to him alone; it gives him immortality, and on its account he is called man. Examine the first three kinds of perfection; you will find that, if you possess them, they are not your property, but the property of others. . . . The last kind of perfection is exclusively yours; no one else owns any part of it.

The last perfection, to whose attainment all that precedes has been directed, is the perfection of the mind. It is to the few, the trained, the skilled, the intellectually perfect upon whom prophecy falls, to whom Torah is revealed, to whom even the highest of mysteries, the secrets of heaven are disclosed. The wise are few and alone; yet theirs is true perfection.

Maimonides sought to resolve a fundamental paradox of religion and philosophy: if truth consists in the right understanding of Scripture, while at the same time being too dangerous to be made public, an inevitably esoteric doctrine results. Truth is not to be made available. On the other hand, only such truth can make man wise and perfect. The paradox is one that can neither be escaped nor resolved. The conclusion of *The Guide for the Perplexed* is the identification of the wise man (the true philosopher) and the prophet. If the goal of the intellectually trained and competent youth is to seek, by right instruction and clarity of understanding, the attainment of prophetic wisdom, perfection becomes synonymous with disengaged individuality. It is not suggested that Maimonides enjoyed the conditions of the perfection he admired. His own words record the involvement of his days, and his own writing indicates his preoccupation with the events of the hour and the crises through which Jewry passed. There is a difference, however, between the record of immediacy and the ideal that is bequeathed to posterity. Where the *Mishneh Torah* illustrates Maimonides' concern for making the ordinance of

Torah easily accessible to all Israel, it is at the same time a work in which the methods of metaphysics and the perfection of man is not described. The *Mishneh Torah* is a socializing work, designed to effect the achievement of those lesser perfections society demands for the realization of harmony and continuity. The ideal is, however, reserved to the few.

CONCLUSION AND PROLOGUE

What has passed is but the barest sketch of the unfolding of medieval Jewish thought. But four thinkers have been discussed, and of these, two have received preponderant attention, undoubtedly because they are correctly regarded as having had the most substantial and enduring influence upon the subsequent course of Jewish religious thinking. To this constellation of thinkers innumerable others might have been added, many of whom are well known to general and Jewish tradition—Ibn Gabirol, Ibn Ezra, Nahmanides, Hasdai Crescas, Gersonides, Joseph Albo, to name but a few.

The characteristic styles and emphases of Jewish philosophy—those that endure and challenge contemporary formulations of Jewish thought are well reflected by the work of Saadya, Jehudah Halevi, Maimonides (and Bahya, whom we regard in much the same way as Meister Eckardt is regarded by Christians—as an orthodox mutant, who speaks tangentially, but profoundly to the whole of his tradition).

The transition from medieval thought to contemporary Judaism will be, of necessity, foreshortened. The decline of Jewish philosophy in the fourteenth century is an immense disaster, whose nature and implications can only be sketched. What has resulted from this enforced disaster can be read in the often aimless, often powerful restoration of theological concern in twentieth century Judaism.

III: Notes on the Predicament of Modern Jewish Theology (1783 to the Present)

It should be clear that this is an uneven essay—a hopelessly uneven essay. It is not shaped by the desire to communicate general information or by a constant interest in a limited number of problems. There is no *general* information about Judaism, and Judaism has no sharply delimited and well-marked problems. The inadequacy of this reprise of Jewish thought—since it is recognized and admitted as inadequate—is consciously contrived. It is inadequate precisely because its author is very much concerned with certain specific notions and a rather limited body of intellectual history. A historian might well communicate information and attend to problems, but it should be clear that the author of the present essay is no historian (as any conscientious scholar will be quick to point out). The author is a theologian and not in the slightest unhappy about the fact. He is a theologian in the very simple sense that he has found himself deeply and utterly absorbed by a single object of preeminent concern: the word and action of God. He cannot be an "abstract" theologian dealing with God in the manner in which the theoretical physicist or the pure mathematician can deal with realities of whose existence he is uncertain and whose properties are merely hypothesized in order to test behavior under artificial conditions. No biblical theologian can be abstract. If he is a Jewish theologian, he is first and foremost a theologian of the God of the Bible. Only subsequently in his pursuit of God does he come upon the history of God's action in those ages that succeed the initial speaking of his word. The theologian is then obligated to be more than a "pure" theologian (what human activity is even theoretically pure?). He becomes perforce a historian, a philosopher, an exegete, a politician—he becomes all things in order better to be what he actually is, a theologian.

Now that the author of this essay has been described, it is

somewhat easier to explain why this essay is unbalanced; why the opening section of this essay which deals with biblical and rabbinic Judaism is seriously (even though schematically) theological; why the second section of this essay, although it emphasizes the impact of Islam and Karaism on Jewish thought, centers its attention on but two thinkers, Jehudah Halevi and Maimonides; and why in this closing discussion we shall hardly discuss thinkers at all, although there are an abundance of thinkers whose work might be considered.

Since I have made clear that I understand myself as a theologian—or more properly as one who wishes to become and remain a theologian—I am obligated to make clear why I do not wish to rehearse here the history of modern Jewish thought, why I vigorously disqualify it, however much I acknowledge it, why I choose to ignore it here although elsewhere I have devoted considerable space to its exposition. Is it just to ignore Moses Mendelssohn, Naḥman Krochmal, Samson Raphael Hirsch, Hermann Cohen, Leo Baeck, Franz Rosenzweig, Martin Buber, Mordecai M. Kaplan, Abraham Joshua Heschel, and the host of younger Jewish thinkers among whom I would occasionally be numbered? Or are there perhaps more serious reasons for wishing to address myself here to the general difficulties that confront modern Jewish thought rather than to the particular approaches that have been defined in the nearly two centuries that have passed since Moses Mendelssohn wrote his epoch-making *Jerusalem* (1783)?

It is not easy to isolate the dominant characteristics that define the continuity of biblical and medieval Jewish thought. The common cultural traits of Jewish life in Mishanic and Talmudic times, the age of the Gaonim, and the dispersion of the medieval Jew throughout Christian Europe and Islam are innumerable. Since this is not, however, a rehearsal of social and cultural history, we are not concerned here with the impact of historical events upon intellectual and theological tradition. Clearly, although a continuity might be affirmed in the social and cultural life of the Jews of Talmudic times with that of medieval Jewry, the same continuity cannot be affirmed of medieval and modern Jewry.

Medieval Jewry was preeminently concerned with remaining obedient to the faith of Israel. Its social and cultural life, as well as its intellectual tradition, was primarily motivated by its preoccupation with keeping faith with its ancestral tradition. However challenged and tempted by adversity to disaffection from Judaism, the medieval Jew, by and large, preserved Judaism for the modern Jew. Moreover, it may be said that the intellectual tradition that he created in order to ensure his faith against erosion of confidence and belief was less an effort to rationalize the course of historical events and his unfavorable predicament than an attempt to apprehend more clearly the foundations of his faith that he might live the more happy and secure in its service.

The tradition of Jewish thought that the modern Jew has matured differs from the medieval in crucial respects: it is overwhelmed by the historical, fashioned and ordered by impulses that are external to it; it is concerned with rationalizing the continued existence of the Jew amid a culture and society that appear to have no further need of him; it defines the obligations of loyalty and endurance in terms that are fixed by the norms and standards of natural cultures and nations; it is impelled by a wholly secularized messianism whose ideology is less dependent upon the prophetic morality of Scripture and rabbinic tradition than upon the moral "enlightenment" the Protestant Reformation introduced into European thought and culture.

The modern Jew has cut himself loose from his supernatural moorings. Whatever the Counter Reformation within Judaism that resulted from the thought of Franz Rosenzweig (1886–1929), and Martin Buber (1878—), it has been insufficient to arrest the movement toward an atomization and radical individualizing of the Jewish obligation to Judaism. According to many, the central problem of contemporary Judaism—the problem that explains the emergence of Jewish Reform in the early nineteenth century in Germany and the rise of "historical" conservative Judaism in the later nineteenth century is the loss and abandonment of the traditional authority of Jewish Law. It has always seemed to us that such a view is a misapprehension of the fundamental religious problem. The problem of contemporary Judaism is not the failure of authority, but the sapping of obedience.

What is the source of authority in religion? It is first and last the authority of the God who speaks and acts. Nothing less and little more! The God who reveals Himself as incomparably creative, powerful, and gracious has sufficient authority to compel man. The religious community, the *ecclesia*, the *bet din* (religious court), the secular instrumentalities of police and state have only secondary power before the power of God. They can succeed at best only in enforcing outward conformity to the requirements of civil society. They can do little to compel the obedience of the authentic heart and mind of man. Such obedience only the inclination of God toward man and the reciprocated action of man toward God can ensure. Clearly societies can transmit the illusion of obedience toward authority in ages when state and church reinforce each other, but can it be imagined that the dogmatic affirmations of church can compel the disobedient heart in ages when church is not supported by the ministering consensus of culture and the supporting devices of law and censure? Does excommunication or *herem* function in a time when men find other ways of serving or disserving God than by obedience to tradition and dogma? Indeed they avail not, for they are not (nor have they ever been) sufficient instruments of authority. The wholeness and unity of a religious community or its fragmentation and dissolution do not suggest the breakdown of authority, only the alteration and loss of the desire to obey.

Who is obeyed, whose law is regnant, whose teaching is heard if not the person, law, and teaching of God? And if there is disobedience it is because that person, law, and teaching has lost something of its power to instruct and incline the will of man. The obedience of earlier ages of Jewish history and the disobedience of the present age is insufficiently understood, if examined from the viewpoint that has become commonplace in such discussions. It is not only that modern science, secular language and culture, the nation state, the nonhieratic and heterogeneous society have superseded the closed society of the Middle Ages. Undoubtedly the emergence in the late seventeenth and eighteenth centuries of such sociocultural phenomena have served to weaken the cohesiveness and order of traditional religion; but still more these have successfully attached and overwhelmed the ancient foundations of the religious mind, because the categories of religious faith had been rendered suspect from other quarters.

The predicament of modern Jewish thought—its abundance of cliché and its genuine deficiency of power—may be rationalized by an appeal to historical exigency. The emergence of the Jew into the modern world has been neither leisurely nor sanguine. It has been necessary to invent numerous artificial devices and accommodations to stay the tide of assimilation, indifference, and sheer boredom (a necessity Judaism shares with other Western religions confronted by similarly widespread disbelief). It has been necessary to fashion appeals to the historic Jewish conscience that rest upon sentiment, nostalgia, and lofty preachment. And indeed at the present moment it may be noted that the tragic and joyous fortuities of the death of millions of Jews during World War II and in its aftermath the emergence of the State of Israel have succeeded, where an earlier rhetoric had failed, to return Jews to their ancestral culture and tradition. None of this, however, is religion—this shifting of numbers, this quantification of strength and weakness, this dependence upon historical fortune, this urge to reidentification. None of these would have been recognizable factors in the decision of Johanan ben Zakkai to establish an academy for the conservation of Torah in the days immediately following the destruction of the Temple or the decision of Maimonides to couple an exhausting medical practice with endless years of philosophic and Talmudic study or the decision of the Hasidic dynast Israel Baal Shem Tov to found a new order of religious community in seventeenth century Eastern Europe. Undoubtedly all these religious personalities were concerned with the conduct and perseverance of the Jew; all of them were moved by the events of history to contemplate their impact for good or ill upon their people. Indeed, they shared a primary concern that the people of Israel endure, a concern rooted in the conviction that it should endure because it was a holy people.

The essential dimension of Israel upon which the major

thinkers of the German-Jewish renaissance of the early twentieth century—Hermann Cohen (1842–1918), Leo Baeck (1874–1956), Franz Rosenzweig, and Martin Buber—agree is that it is the holiness of the Jewish people that defines its uniqueness, that this holiness is always precariously present and evanescent, that this holiness is founded upon a specific comprehension of the relation of the Word and action of God to the community in whom, upon whom, and through whom He acts. Though there is an occasional temptation in such thinkers as Franz Rosenzweig to make the holiness of Israel into a substantive racialism, this danger is counteracted and overwhelmed by the insistence of general secular culture that the Jew be wholly naturalized, that all assumptions of providential election and uniqueness be put aside (as though what God has done can be undone because men decide that it is no longer useful or prudent) as unbefitting a free and equal society. Both extremes are equally mistaken. Rosenzweig is mistaken for eternalizing the Jew, abstracting him from the totality of the historical *passio* through which he passes in company with all men, transforming liturgy into a sort of mystery play in which all nature and time are gathered up and etherealized. But the naturalizers of Jewish tradition—the company of Mordecai M. Kaplan (1881–)—are equally mistaken in accepting the inheritance of history as a given fact without sustaining a sense of the vocational condition that enables the modern world to inherit the culture of the Jew alone of all ancient cultures of the Western world. Indeed, the polarities of those views that utterly eternalize the Jew or utterly naturalize him are wrong, for they forget (as indeed the thinkers of medieval Judaism never forgot) that God alone mediates between eternity and time, providence and history.

It is thus to God that Jewish thought must finally turn if it is to be Jewish thinking. It cannot be (as it was in the early days of the Jewish *Aufklärung* of the late eighteenth and nineteenth centuries) a thinking about the Jew in migration from tradition to emancipation—a thinking that drew artificial distinctions between universally rational moral principles and sectarian revelation (as in Moses Mendelssohn) or between material stages of Jewish history and their enduring spiritual form (as in Naḥman Krochmal) or between the devices and temptations of secular culture and the prophetic morality of Israel (as in all the Kantian moralists of German Reform Judaism). All such distinctions were designed to rationalize a crisis within the natural unfolding of the Jewish people—its emergence from privacy and sequestration into an ostensibly neutral (but still Christian) public order. The most theologically sensitive modern Jewish thinkers (Rosenzweig, Buber, Schechter, Heschel, and others) are all aware that what is crucial is how God and Israel are related, that this relation alone is the locus of Jewish thought, that to the understanding of this relation all proper Jewish thought is to be turned.

Such thinking about the relation of God and Israel is theological thinking. It is not *halakhic* thinking, for thinking about the Law is a sufficient and ongoing enterprise for which theological questions are both preliminary (and therefore indispensable) and methodologically independent (and therefore irrelevant). Nor is theological thinking a reflection upon the history of Judaism and Jewish culture, for history is an action that can be interpreted independently of the role God plays within it and can therefore be studied wholly independently of the theologoumenon. Nor is theological thinking to be confused with biblical exegesis or with homiletics or with social action or with liturgical studies or, indeed, with any of the multitude of human inquiries that can be developed upon lines and principles wholly independent of the speech and action of God. And yet, conversely, all these modes of religious inquiry and performance—*halakhah*, history, exegesis, homiletics, social action, liturgy—may become theology in the proper sense. At that moment at which all of these are pursued in such a manner as to yield a clearer, more sharply defined, more intelligible apprehension of what it is that God bestows and expects from men, then these, too, become theological activities.

There has been an absence of Jewish theology in the modern world because the Jew has been (justly or unjustly is beside the point) preoccupied with understanding himself and enduring with the knowledge gained from self-understanding. The Jewish intellectual enterprise has been an all too natural undertaking. It has inquired after God last, not first. The rebirth of theological thinking that is upon us in recent decades has come from those who have inquired of God first, not last—and so it must ever be.

Our Roman Catholic Heritage

WALTER J. ONG, S.J.

In this chapter I propose to examine the Roman Catholic heritage, which forms now a major part of our American tradition, selectively but from the inside. This is not a course in Catholic teaching, nor even an outline of all Catholic teaching. It is more like a tour of the Catholic mind, a tour in which we can examine items of special interest or meaning for our times but in which we shall have to pass by many things. We shall, however, try to conduct the tour not externally or superficially but rather through the inside of the Catholic consciousness, for it is only in interior perspectives that the church can be effectively grasped.

THE CHURCH AND CHRIST

In speaking of the church and Christ we can do no better than to start with the fact that the Catholic Church is a mystery, and that, although she has certain marks by which she can be surely identified, she considers herself a mystery. This is perhaps worth saying in present-day America because in contrast with other religious groups, Roman Catholics do place an emphasis on natural law and natural reason. This is, however, only by contrast with other groups because these things are, of course, secondary for a Catholic. At the beginning, in first place, is faith.

The faith by which a Roman Catholic adheres to God and to the church is a mystery. Faith, for a Catholic, is something man can reason toward. That is to say, the activities of natural reason are not irrelevant to faith. They have something to do with faith. Nevertheless, it is the defined doctrine of the Roman Catholic Church that one cannot reason his way into faith. This is quite impossible.

At this point I should like to suggest one little perspective concerning the obedience which the Catholic Church demands (and which is really not so ominous as it is sometimes made out to be). This obedience itself, which is so distinctively Catholic, is a kind of seal of the mystery of the church, a hint of the mystery which the church is. Obedience is given in the last analysis to persons, not to things, and the fact that the Catholic Church demands the kind of obedience which she does—which is the kind of obedience one gives to one's mother and ultimately to one's father—this fact suggests that she herself participates in a kind of personality. Now, persons themselves are mysteries. Jesus Christ Himself is a mystery. And the obedience which we give to another person, putting ourselves at his beck and call, is in the last analysis a kind of mysterious thing because it is personal. Indeed, in its total commitment of one person to another, obedience touches the relation of one person to another at the very quick.

What do I mean by a mystery? A mystery is not something that you cannot get into. It is rather something that you cannot get out of. A mystery is something which we can understand in part, but never entirely—something which continually entices our minds further and further, but without offering ever to be completely and totally exhausted.

A person, as suggested, is a kind of mystery, and when we consider our relations to another person we can get an insight into what we mean by mystery. When you know another person, there really is no point at which you can say: I now know absolutely everything there is to know about this other person. There is always a little more that you can learn. This is true even with regard to oneself—one can always learn a little bit more about oneself. The connection of mystery with person is so profound as to suggest that what is mysterious is always likely to have a personal cast, to be felt in terms of the personal. We might walk into a dark forest somewhere and feel that the forest is very mysterious. Is this not rather tantamount to feeling that somewhere here in the forest there is some*one* whom we cannot quite find, or even whom we really *might* find? We tend to personalize what is mysterious, and perhaps the reason is that a person (or the personal) is, in the last analysis, the ultimate mystery. A person is someone we know, and yet someone we do not quite know. This persistent mixture of the unknown with the known is found even in myself as I am present to myself as well as in other persons.

However this may be, the Roman Catholic Church is quite aware that she is a mystery. She has reflected on this fact for a couple of thousand years now and as a result of this reflection is able to state certain aspects of her own mysteriousness more fully than she could do at an earlier period. As the church reflects upon herself and upon the revelation which she communicates from God to men, the explicitness of her treatment, both of the revelation and of herself, increases. As she gains time, she can make more things clear. She can explain more. But explicitness never becomes complete. The Roman Catholic Church will never reach the point where she has said the last word she has to say about her teachings. She knows she will never reach this point. All she can do at any given point is say more, explain more.

This is one of the aspects of the mysteriousness of the church that we ought to keep in mind. Her dogma remains the same from generation to generation, and yet it becomes more and more explicit. It is impossible, you see, that a statement of any sizable body of truth, say, 100,000 years from today should coincide exactly, word for word, with the statement of that same body of truth today. A hundred thousand years from now the people uttering this truth will know many more things than we know. They will have accumulated and sifted through much more experience. Consequently, anything they state will give off a kind of resonance echoing this total body of truth which they know. Approached out of new awarenesses, even a basic kind of truth will show up in a richer context, with new facets exposed. This is not to say, of course, that people a hundred thousand years from now will not know what we know. They will know it, but they will know it together with a lot of other things which will tend to make themselves felt when they state their knowledge of things that we know.

To make my point clearer, we can take the example of a child and an adult. If you ask a little ten-year-old to state his relation to his father and his mother, or, since you really cannot ask him the question that way, if you ask him who this is, he'll say "My daddy," or "My mommy." And what do you think about him? What do you think about her? "I love him," or "I love her." By plying him with further questions you can pull out aspects of his attitude towards his father or mother which will show you what he understands of this relationship. And yet, if you ask him, later on, when he is thirty or forty years old, to explain this same earlier childhood relationship to his father or mother, he will state these same relationships in a quite different context and in a different way. You can imagine what the same child would say further of the same relationships if he becomes a depth psychologist and you ask him again when he is sixty years old about his childhood relationship to his father and his mother. In each case, you see, the individual is talking about the same thing, but as he grows older and gains experience he knows more, and the other things that he knows cannot help but show up when he talks about these things that he knew as part of himself at the very beginning of his life.

So the Catholic Church learns to be more and more articulate about herself. Yet she remains forever to some degree a profound mystery.

I mention the church's mysteriousness in speaking on the subject of the Church and Christ because the real reason why the church is a mystery and why she considers herself a mystery is her relationship with Christ. She communicates to men the revelation which God made through Jesus Christ. She is both part of Christ's revelation and an organ of His revelation, a revelation ultimately concerned with the interior mysteries of God's own personal life.

Jesus Christ is the Word Incarnate. He is both these things, the Word and Incarnate, and we have to keep both of them alive in our thinking about Him. He is the Word of God—from other associated points of view, the truth of God, the voice of God, the manifestation of God. And yet He is at the same time Incarnate, set within the physical history of our created universe. The Catholic Church belongs to Christ under both these aspects. She belongs to Him as the Word of God, and she belongs to Him as the Word Incarnate, but she belongs to Him most particularly because of His Incarnation. It is through His Incarnation that the church was instituted.

We must remember that in a certain sense all of our words, all words pronounced or heard by human beings, are incarnate. That is to say, although they may refer to things outside time and space, the actual conception of mental words, the conception of a truth in our mind, as well as the expression of sensible words, takes place in a here and now, always in one historical moment. This "here" and "now" of the ordinary human words which we conceive corresponds in a way to the "here" and "now" of Christ's humanity. The church is connected with Jesus Christ through his Incarnation and this connection is brought out by the fact she speaks of herself, considers herself the Mystical Body of Christ, a kind of mysterious protraction of Jesus Christ through time and space down to our day, in which her membership of assignable, physically existing individuals is an effective counterpart of Jesus' physical human body. The foundations for the doctrine of the Mystical Body, of course, are Scriptural. They will be found in the Epistle to the Ephesians (1:22–23; 2:19–22; 4:1–16; 5:22–23) and in the First Epistle to the Corinthians (12:12–31), the principal texts on which this doctrine is founded, but there are supporting texts also in the Epistle to the Romans (12:4–5) and in Colossians (1:17–20).

What do I mean by the Incarnation? Let us take a brief, drastically simplified view of what happened to effect the Incarnation.

In Catholic teaching there is one God, but in this one God, there are three Persons. It is Catholic teaching that we can reason to the existence of one God, although this is to be done not from what we do not know about things, as people used to try to do particularly in the seventeenth, eighteenth, and nineteenth centuries, but from what we *do* know about things around us; i.e., from the fact that things change, and so on. We can reason to the existence of one God, but we could never find out, according to Catholic teaching, by our natural reason that there are three Persons in God. Reason gets us to God's nature, which is by comparison with the Persons in God a somewhat exterior thing, from our point of view. The Persons are the utter interior of God, the secret, *the* great secret within God that Jesus Christ came to reveal.

These Three are real persons, Father, Son, and Holy Spirit. Each is different from the others as I am personally different from you. We know this from the Scriptures because Jesus, who is the Son, speaks to the Father and calls Him "Thou" or "You," and he speaks to the Father about the Holy Spirit as a third Person. Thus to the Father, the Son is "You" and the Holy Spirit is "You"; to the Son the Father is "You" and the Holy Spirit is "You"; and to the Holy Spirit the Father is "You" and the Son is "You." Each of these *You's* is to be taken in the singular number, of course. Father, Son, and Holy Spirit are each really a different Person. And yet they are united in a way in which it is quite impossible for us to be united with another person.

To put it briefly, somewhat dramatically, we can say this about the union of these Three. You will never know by your natural powers what it feels like to be me, nor I what it feels like to be you. You might of course say in such a case, "Thank God!" I do not know what it feels like to be you simply because we are different persons. And you do not know what it feels like to be anyone else either—except yourself. And no one else knows what you experience in being you. You are alone and I am alone in what the Jesuit poet Gerard Manley Hopkins speaks of as "my selfbeing, . . . that taste of myself, of *I* and *me* above and in all things which is more distinctive than the taste of ale or alum." Even your father and mother, although marriage is the closest union of human beings in this world, even they are subject to the same law—your father does not know the experience which your mother has in being the person she is, and so your mother does not know the experience your father has in being the person he is. Persons in love would like to know this of one another, but even man and wife can never find out.

In the case of the three Persons in God, although they are personally distinct, completely distinct from one another as persons, there is only one nature because there is only one God, one numerical nature. The unity of the three divine Persons is not merely a matter of an abstract nature such as men share with one another—human nature—but rather a matter of one numerical existing nature. As a result, although each one of the divine Persons preserves inviolably his own personal identity, each one of them knows what it means to be each of the other two. This is a kind of maximum of personal intercommunion and love which remains for always an inviolable mystery. And just because Catholics believe in it (many Protestants believe in it, too), does not mean that we understand it. We understand some things about it. We can go pretty far in explaining certain of its aspects and consequences, but there remains in it something irreducibly mysterious.

God, the one true God, Yahweh Elohim, exists for all eternity in these three Persons whom until the revelation given through Jesus Christ He kept a secret to Himself, because the presence of these three Persons does not show in what God creates outside Himself, although His nature does show in what He creates. That is, from created things His existence, the unity of His nature, His goodness, His omniscience, and so on, can be reasoned to, if with some effort. But in created things, the existence of the Persons does not show. It is made known by special revelation through Christ.

These three Persons exist of course from all eternity in the Godhead. Now at a certain point in time, to redeem mankind from sin, as the result of a free decision of God and to show His love for us, one of these three Persons, the Second Person, the Son or Word, became one of us, taking to Himself a human nature. This is what we mean by the Incarnation: the taking of a human nature by the second Person of the Blessed Trinity. The Son became man, the Word was made flesh—of course without ceasing to be God. He was conceived in the womb of Mary, conceived without the aid of a human father. Jesus Christ has only one Father. The fact that God the Father is His Father from eternity suffices, we might say, for His human paternity, too.

When the Son became man, He took to Himself a complete human nature, not only (as some people might think) a human body but also a human soul, because the body is not just a machine. Our bodies are ourselves and our souls are ourselves. They are ourselves in somewhat different ways, but both of these are ourselves. If someone strikes my body, I tell him he has struck me. The body and the soul which gives us consciousness belong together and to have a complete human nature, to be a complete human being, God the Son had to have a human soul and body both. But He did not become another Person; it is quite impossible for one person to become another person. After the Incarnation He was still one Person, but now with two natures, two principles of operation: the divine principle of operation and the human principle of operation. The ways in which these two natures are related is a matter of interest for theological speculation which you can go into at your leisure some time. People have been working on this for some two thousand years now, and, in this as in other matters, while all Catholic theologians agree on the basic things, there are many things on which they do not agree.

We can get across rather simply in effect what we mean when we say that Jesus Christ, the second Person of the Blessed Trinity, is one Person. We can get this across even to people who are not very mature, in a very simple way. Were we to have with us today Jesus Christ present in His visible human nature as He was present in Palestine around the year 3 to 4 B.C. up until around 30 or 33 A.D.—if this historic Jesus Christ were here, and a Catholic addressing Him were to say to Him "I love you," this "You" whom he addresses as a real man is the same "You" as the Second Person of the Blessed Trinity, who is God Himself. Speaking to Jesus, he is speaking to one

"Thou" or "You" who is both God and man. It is a matter of your use of this "Thou" or "You." That is why little children, who could not possibly define a person, never use the word in their vocabulary and cannot follow any detailed explanation of such things as person and nature, still know very really what is meant when they are told that Jesus Christ is God and Man. They know this You, this Person, because they pray to Him. They call Him "You" when they think of Him as man; they call Him the same "You" when they think of Him as God.

This, then, is what we mean by the Incarnation. But the implications of the Incarnation are countless. The presence of God among us through the Incarnation is more than a presence in the ordinary sense of this term. It is a revelation of God by the very fact that the Son is also the Word of God. These names, Son and Word, are both His proper names, which He has in the Scripture. He is the Son of God and He is the Word of God. Later names which are given to Him, such as the Light of Light, are not proper in the sense in which these names are proper. The two names, Son and Word, are very mysteriously interlocked in ways you might later investigate, particularly from the point of view of phenomenological analysis, but I can only indicate here that recognition that the Second Person of the Blessed Trinity is Word and is Son dates from the very earliest days of Christian history.

That which constitutes Him Son also constitutes Him Word. One can see something of what this is by reflecting on the fact that any son is to some extent an image of his father. He is a kind of "other" for his father. When the Second Person of the Blessed Trinity became man, took to Himself a historical human nature, He was thenceforth a human being as well as God, One who is related to us, and descended as man from the same human stock we are descended from.

Because His very Person is a word, a manifestation, *the* Word of God, Jesus' very presence among us is a revelation to us, even when He is silent. This is a thing which is of great significance. Christians have always meditated on the fact that Jesus Christ spent most of His life of thirty-three years or more in virtual silence. We have no record of the early things which

He said, with very, very few exceptions. His public life of teaching by preaching occupied roughly only the last three years of His existence on this earth before His death.

St. Augustine of Hippo was one of those who liked to think about this silence of the Word. He liked to think about the *Verbum infans. Verbum* is the Latin for Word, and *infans*, which gives us our English word *infant*, in Latin means non-speaking. The *Verbum infans* is the Word which does not talk —in the human way of talking. God, the second Person of the Blessed Trinity, gives us divine revelation first by His presence. Of course, secondly He also gives us divine revelation by His explicit verbal teaching. He did not come to earth and walk around as other men while saying nothing about His Father. Rather, He talked about God, about Himself, about His Father, about the Holy Spirit, about man's duties, about eternal life. In addition to being simply present among men, He talked about these things explicitly, so that his explicit teaching and preaching is also a manifestation or revelation of God. The Catholic Church continues as the Mystical Body of Christ and she continues the teachings of Jesus in this same way in the world both by her presence and by her explicit declarations or teachings concerning what He manifested.

When we get to the subject of explicit teachings it is time to say a little more about the matter of authority in the church. *Authority* sounds to many of us today like a horrible word. It really is not so bad. If you look at the term *auctor* in Latin, around which our concept of "authority" is built, you find that it comes from the word *augeo*, which means to increase or to augment. Words in this line of descent are akin to the Sanskrit word *vaksh*, which is in turn akin to and at the root of our English word "wax" in the sense in which we use this word when we talk of the "waxing" and the "waning" of the moon. When we say in a somewhat archaic fashion that "he waxed strong," we are using a concept closely allied to the root meanings out of which has developed our term "authority."

When we think of the authority of the Catholic Church— and I am speaking now from "inside"—we should think of it by analogy with the authority in the family. Let us not forget that a family is an authoritarian structure, and that it has to be.

If it is not, the children are likely to end up in insane asylums. The need for authority is that serious. The family has to be an authoritarian structure. Every psychologist knows this. But, on the other hand, if someone were to ask you to describe your relations to your family, and you describe these relations entirely in terms of an authoritarian structure, you are also in a pretty bad way. And you are likely also to be headed for the insane asylum. The Catholic Church is authoritarian, but this is not all she is. She is authoritarian within a certain context, and the context is a context of love, just as in a family. A father and mother have to tell their children what to do, but these commands are all within a context of love. Authority in the family must include some element of love, or it is not what it should be. This is the way authority looks inside the Catholic Church too. Sometimes authority is hard to take, even though it does include love. But even when it is hard, we can take it if love is there and if we have made this love our own by giving our love in return to God and to His church.

The way you feel in your family is simply "at home." This is the dominant Catholic feeling with regard to the church, and with regard to those beings who inhabit the universe within and outside the church. A member of the Roman Catholic Church should ordinarily feel that he or she "belongs," that he or she is surrounded by love and by its inevitable complement, responsibility.

Father Gerard Manley Hopkins, the English poet, says that grace comes to man, "not out of His bliss," that is, not out of God's eternal happiness, not directly out of heaven, but through history, through Jesus Christ in history. The Roman Catholic Church, therefore, is not abstract. She is not purely spiritual. The way she considers herself is connected with the fact that she derives from the Incarnation. She is, as we have noted, the Mystical Body of Christ, made up of flesh-and-blood members who, sinners though they are, through their assimilation to Christ by baptism and by adherence to an authority externally identifiable in the Pope and Bishops, with Christ Himself as its head, are an extension of Christ's own personal presence in the history of our globe. The Roman Catholic Church considers herself not only as an interior but also as an exterior phenomenon; if you wish, an interior and an exterior fact. In a way she is invisible, but she is also visible. The basic reason for this is that Jesus Christ was Himself not only an interior consciousness but also visible and tangible. The church is, in a certain way, tangible.

Some have said that the church was invisible only. This was one of the Protestant positions taken in the sixteenth century. A Catholic would reply to this that if you make out the church to be invisible only you set in movement a line of thought which is going to drive you or your successors, in years to come, to deny the Incarnation. Catholics would point to the fact that the movements which began in the sixteenth century denying the existence of a visible church have matured today in doctrines such as those of the Unitarians and others who deny the truth that God Himself has become visible as man in the Person of Jesus Christ.

The church, then, considers herself as something physical, visible, tangible in her members as well as something involving their interior state of soul. She recognizes herself in the verifiable unity which her members interiorly and exteriorly profess and which is centered around the visible head of the church on earth, the Pope, the Bishop of Rome, as well as around her divine head, at present invisible to us, Jesus Christ, true God and true man.

THE CHURCH AND HISTORY

We have seen that the Roman Catholic Church regards herself as an extension of the Incarnate Word of God, as His Mystical Body, and hence, as present not only to the interior world of the individual heart but also to the visible, audible, tangible, sensible world. Since the church is visible and otherwise sensible, she is very definitely involved in the history of this material evolving universe in which we know we live. She is in time. In *Four Quartets* T. S. Eliot says "only through time, time is conquered." When he speaks this way, a Roman Catholic can certainly underwrite his words. Of course, the church is not only in history, but she is also in a sense out of it. She is not quite settled in history. She will not let people, all of us who live in history, be quite at our ease. She stands in judgment on history, for man's actions through time call for judgment before God.

In treating the Catholic Church and history, we must underline the fact that in the beginning there was no perfect primitive Christianity which was later corrupted by the church. This used to be a line which certain Protestants took, but it is losing favor even among Protestants today. From the very beginning, Christian doctrine had to be incorporated in a particular culture. This was originally the culture of the Hebrew people which Almighty God had particularized in a way in which no other culture has ever been particularized. Catholic doctrine is always incorporated in a particular culture. Although Catholic doctrine is not to be identified with any particular culture, there is no abstract Catholicism. It is impossible for us to conceive what abstract Christianity could be. The church uses unchanging principles, but at the same time there is no purely abstract position that the church takes any more than there is a purely abstract position which you can take. You may take a position, and a true one, on an abstract subject, but you do it for personal reasons, if you really search your heart, and within a context provided by historical developments. Even abstractions are arrived at through development in time. This is not to say that you are not led by truth, but it is to say that because you are here now, you are led by *this* truth, rather than by *that* truth.

From the very earliest ages the church has considered herself Catholic. The term *Catholic* is of considerable importance. *Catholic* is a word derived from the Greek. Often it is translated by the Latin-rooted word *universal*, but the Catholic Church herself has not much favored this Latin word, even in Latin-dominated cultures. (You must remember that there are other rites in the Roman Catholic Church besides the Latin rite. There are Roman Catholics who use Greek and other languages as their liturgical languages.) Even in the West, where Latin has been the dominant language, the Roman Catholic Church talks of herself not as the universal church, but as the Catholic Church.

There must be a reason for this preference. And indeed there is, for we can detect a significant difference between the meaning of the Greek word *katholikos*, which in its English form is *catholic* and the Latin word *universalis*, which gives us in English *universal*. *Universal*, if we look to its etymology, is based upon two concepts, that of one, *unum*, connected with our terms *unity*, *union*, and so on, and that of *vertere*, "to turn." Something which is universal is at root something which "includes" or encloses all its inferiors. We often define a universal idea as an idea which encompasses all of the things in a particular class. But if you "include" or enclose something, you also appear to exclude something. If you describe a line around a center to get something which is universal and "inclusive," everything that lies outside the line which you draw, you have excluded. I think it is because of this fact that the church has shied away a bit from this term *universal* and preferred the term *katholikos* with its derivatives to designate her nature and her presence in time and in civilization. *Katholikos* comes from two Greek words: *kata* and *holos* and it means at root "through the whole."

The term *katholikos* does not have a negative aspect as *universal* does. *Universal* has a negative turn because while it includes things, it does so by excluding others. This notion of exclusion is negative. *Universal* is also by the same token abstractive in bearing, hinting at selective withdrawal. Abstract concepts or ideas are the sort of things readily thought of as "universals," the antitheses of what is "concrete." When, however, you say that the church is Catholic (through-the-whole) there are no particular bounds, and there is not this gesture toward abstraction. The implications remain positive and concrete. If the whole is enlarged, the church enlarges too.

If by being present "through the whole" the Catholic Church is present in a way which is not at all negative and which is utterly "concrete," she is by the same token, however, always found within one or another specific culture, which is as a whole never entirely Catholic itself. It thus becomes a serious problem to know in some instances just what is the church's teaching and what is an accretion or a context for this teaching in a particular situation. When, for instance, we look at church-state doctrines in terms of Spanish culture, we are looking at a mixture. This is one particular culture in which the church has existed and to which she has addressed herself, but you have to watch that you separate what is typically Spanish from what is typically Catholic.

The church's institutions have all been set up in history, but they are of two kinds. First, there are those set up by Jesus Christ during His lifetime on earth or those established before their deaths by the Apostles (who had been in immediate face-to-face contact with Him). These are things such as the episcopacy, the Papacy, the sacraments. Even they were necessarily set up in particular historical circumstances, and thus call for interpretation to distinguish what in them is by God's will truly Catholic or destined to be "through-the-whole" and what is particular to the Jewish or Hellenic culture of Jesus' day. The Catholic Church is the living organ, the extension of Christ Himself, His Mystical Body, able to give such interpretations —which themselves, however, are always in a concrete historical cultural setting and thus will always need further interpretation.

Second, there are the institutions which have been set up by the church in the course of her life in response to various historical circumstances. These two types of institutions are of course very closely connected, for both are present to us through concrete history, if in somewhat different ways.

Indeed, the second type of institutions, those set up by the church, can grow more or less directly out of the institutions set up by Jesus Himself or His Apostles, so that it is not always easy even to separate type two from type one and to decide that this particular institution was or was not instituted by Christ Himself, or was or was not instituted by the church later on. Whether a particular Christian institution was instituted by Jesus Christ personally during His life on this earth is not always clear from purely historical evidence and is ultimately a dogmatic question, so that for a Catholic the only one who can really settle it is the church herself. If the church does not decide when such matters are not historically clear, Catholic theologians continue to argue among themselves.

Some things can be settled historically from the Gospels or from elsewhere, but many of them cannot, because our written records and other records are incomplete. The Scriptures themselves tell us that they themselves are incomplete, for you will remember how at the end of the Fourth Gospel we read that the whole world would not be large enough to include all the books which would have to be written if you were to say all that Jesus did.

An example of the way in which institutions are established by Christ and then grow in history can be seen in the case of the Papacy. Roman Catholics believe that the Papacy was instituted by Jesus Christ, and they have very good Scriptural foundation for this. There is the passage (Matthew 16:18–19) where the supremacy was promised to Peter, and then there is another one (John 21:15–17) in which it was confirmed. But you see, when we talk about the Papacy in the early days of the church, we have to remember that it cannot possibly look just like the Papacy today. Conditions of communications, for instance, made it impossible for early Christians even to conceive of centralization of the church which was as effective as the centralization which we today take for granted. In earlier days, people couldn't imagine virtually instantaneous communication across great distances over the surfaces of the earth. Consequently, when they speak of the unity of the church, and when they think of the Bishop of Rome as the head of the church, they are going to think of this in a somewhat different historical format from that which we might at present tend to imagine. When we find in the early ages of the church that things were not so centrally organized as they are now, this does not distress a Catholic who believes in the supremacy of the Bishop of Rome from the very beginning, because this particular condition of supremacy in one civilization will look quite different from what it looks like in another.

From these necessarily sketchy remarks about the inseparability of the church from history, we can move now to the effect of history on the church. One of the great effects of history on the church, perhaps in a way the central effect, is the gradual explication, the gradual unfolding, the greater and greater explanation of the revelation which was given to the church originally. Here we must get one thing straight regarding the church's access to revelation. The church never receives any new revelation from Jesus Christ now. The most that a Council of the Church or the Pope can do is to declare that, explicitly or implicitly, this or that particular item was in the original revelation, which the church received by the time of the death of the last Apostle. This has rather interesting consequences because there have been individuals who have lived long after apostolic times and who say that they have received revelations from God directly. Perhaps they have. What is the church's attitude toward these persons? Well, she lets them alone. If their purported revelation attracts no great public attention, God can manifest Himself to individuals privately, and whether He does or not is no public concern of the church. But suppose there begins to be a public stir in connection with a private revelation, as happened in the seventeenth century, when the woman who is now known as St. Margaret Mary Alacoque received certain private revelations reportedly from Jesus Christ, who manifested to her in visions His love for mankind through the symbolism of His human heart. These revelations became publicly known and after a time created a certain public stir. Again in the nineteenth century the revelations which were received by Bernadette Soubirous at Lourdes attracted similar large-scale public attention.

The church is ordinarily suspicious of these claims to private revelation, for many of them are clearly neurotic or psychotic in origin or are even deliberate frauds. But this is not necessarily always so. If devotions start to grow up around these private revelations, the church investigates to see whether this revelation contradicts anything in the church's teaching. If the private revelation contradicts the public revelation that God has already made to all men through Jesus Christ and His church, the church immediately knows that the purported private revelation cannot be true, that there is something wrong, because God does not contradict Himself. She applies here the rule which Jesus Christ himself gives in the Scriptures, "by their fruits you shall know them," to see what these revelations lead to.

If she finds that the people gathering around a person who says he or she has had a private revelation remain within the church, work with other people, and practice the virtues of faith, hope and charity, then she takes a more benign view and equivalently says, "Well, this is all right, at least to the extent that the devotions growing up around this private manifestation obviously help persons to live a good religious life." This is what she said about the revelations to Margaret Mary in the seventeenth century and the revelations to Bernadette in the nineteenth century. The church says that the devotions have proved religiously helpful, that they do no harm, that on the contrary, they do positive good to people spiritually. This is the first thing she is interested in. There is at Lourdes, of course, a board of physicians that investigates reputed cures there and gives its judgment as to whether a reported cure can be accounted for by natural forces or not. Of the physicians on this board many are not Catholics at all or even believers. But the church is not interested in the miracles simply as spectacular happenings. She is interested in the miracles only in their relation to spiritual life. Moreover, she does not regard such miracles or any private visions as public revelation, as adding anything at all to the truths committed to her by Christ.

No Catholic has to believe in any of the miracles at Lourdes or those reported any place else within recent times. Nor does a Catholic have to believe that any particular post-Apostolic private revelations actually took place. Such revelations are not objects of Catholic faith. A Catholic should not of course make public remarks holding Lourdes up to ridicule, since the church has approved Lourdes to the extent that she says that people are helped in their religious life when they go there to pray. I can attest to the fact personally that one is helped. It is a tremendous thing to be at Lourdes with hundreds and thousands of other persons all saying together in a succession of different languages, aloud: "I believe in God," and the rest of the creed. It is a tremendous thing religiously, and consequently a Catholic would be lacking in charity if he were to make light of the devotions there. But he does not have to accept the claims of a private revelation as a matter of faith at all. He can judge such claims as he would judge anything else. He must look into them and see what the reports are based on, what the evidence is. I mention this to point up the fact that the revelation which Catholics must subscribe to, must believe in by faith, dates from Jesus' own time on earth, being completed with the death of the last Apostle. Further revelations are not objects of faith.

But as the church reflects upon the revelation which was given to her in the beginning and which was concluded with the time of Christ, she discovers further things about it. Dogma can be made more and more explicit, can be developed by reflection and comparison with the new knowledge man acquires. But it can never be made totally explicit. Ten thousand or even a million years from now the Catholic Church will still not have said the last word about dogma. Questions will continue to arise which have not arisen before, and, applied to the church's teaching, will yield answers and awarenesses which we do not have today. The teaching of the Catholic Church is inexhaustible and in its totality quite ineffable in human words. Because it is the divine message, although it can in part be stated, and stated truly and accurately in abstract formulae, such formulae can never exhaust its whole truth. God's revelation was not conveyed to man or received by man simply in terms of abstract principles, of abstract statements. It was conveyed and is received in the God-Man Jesus Christ and in His church. Since you cannot get around what you believe in entirely by statements, abstract statements, this belief must be in something, or rather in someone concrete, in the church, in Jesus Christ.

There are dogmatic formulae worded with extreme care, which the church states in her creeds, in her various councils and in the encyclicals of the Popes. Against those who have suggested that these formulae at any given time only approximate the truth, the church has insisted that at any given state of development what she says about divine revelation is completely, totally, and literally true. But it is not all that can be said. It represents what can be said about the initial revelation from where the church stands at one particular moment in history. We can see so much now and maybe we will see more at a later point. The view that dogmatic formulae miss the truth slightly is an oversimplification and distortion of the delicate relationship between dogmatic declarations and the totality of revelation which is really Jesus Christ Himself, God Himself, as well as man.

There is another oversimplification of this relationship, that which says that dogmatic statements represent emotional states, i.e., that when the Catholic Church says there are three Persons in God this corresponds only to some sort of human feeling. This is not true either. A Catholic recognizes in this statement a statement which is literally true. It contains a mystery, something difficult to explain, but something nevertheless which the dogmatic statement really enters into. Of course the statement fails to say all that can be said about the subject. Since all that can be said about the subject is never said, while the Catholic hold on truth involves assent to these statements, this hold is not simply a matter of such dogmatic statements, but is a hold achieved through and with and in Jesus Christ within the church, which is the Mystical Body of Christ.

The hold on truth here is comparable, in a way, to the kind of hold I have on the truth of another person. When I know another person, I know him not merely in terms of abstract statements. I can bring abstract statements to bear on the situation, but none of them quite get round it, they don't encompass it. I can say that he is tall, twenty-five years old, well-educated, the son of son-and-so and so-and-so, and so on, making statements which are true, and true about him. But such statements do not encompass him or my knowledge of him as a person. The knowledge which is the knowledge of faith within the Catholic Church is comparable to my knowledge of him as a person, for it is had through Jesus Christ, and extends, of course, to the Father in the Holy Spirit.

There is a very mysterious dimension in this hold that the church has on truth. That is because it is a knowledge enjoyed not only through a person, but also through that particular Person who is the very Word of God. Jesus Christ's own Person had a special reference to truth itself because His personal name has special reference to truth. His name is the Word. This is not the name of the Father, nor of the Holy Spirit.

An example will illustrate how the Catholic Church, put in possession of a truth by Jesus Christ, the Word of God, during His mortal life on earth, gradually develops a more explicit understanding of the truth and comes to learn its relationship to other things as man's knowledge of the universe develops. The example we can look at has to do with nothing less than the revealed truth that there are three Persons in God. The Scriptures nowhere say explicitly just this, that there are three Persons in God, for they do not have a term for *person*, this being a concept which the people in Jesus' own culture did not use.

You can, however, know a person and speak with him and love him intimately without using the term *person* at all, and certainly without being able to define the term, as it is an extremely difficult thing to define. Children know what persons are, although they do not use the term *person*. The church at the beginning was in a condition in some ways like that of the intellectually inexperienced child. In the New Testament Jesus says that He and the Father are one and allows Himself to be addressed by the Apostle Thomas as God. But He also refers to His Father as "You," and does so many times. Similarly, the Holy Spirit is presented in the New Testament as God ("Ananias, why hath Satan tempted thy heart, that thou shouldst lie to the Holy Spirit? . . . Thou has not lied to men, but to God." Acts 5:3–4), and yet He is spoken of as someone Other than the Father and the Son when Jesus says, "And I will ask the Father, and he shall give you another Paraclete [that is, an Advocate, a Helper, a Consoler], that he may abide with you forever. . . . But the Paraclete, the Holy Spirit, whom the Father will send in my name, he will teach you all things" (John 14:16, 26).

Being close to the Hebraic culture in which Jesus lived, the early documents of the church do not mention the word *person* as such. Later on, particularly because of developments in the surrounding Hellenic culture, questions began to arise as to whether the emergent concept of person applied to God the Father, God the Son, and God the Holy Spirit. If we oversimplify a bit, we can say that the situation was as follows: People educated in a Greek-speaking culture and with some philosophical interests and acumen would approach Christians and say, "You talk about God the Father, God the Son, and God the Holy Spirit. You say each is God, the same, one God. Can you say whether each is or is not a Person, and if each is, whether they are all one Person or are separate Persons?" Doubtless, Christians were asking these same questions of themselves.

At this point, a new concept has been introduced into the discussion, the explicit concept of "Person," more or less recondite. And at this point, the church has to take thought to see whether, given what she had received from Jesus Christ, what was registered in the Scriptures and her tradition, the Three were Persons or not. After she had duly taken thought, there could be no mistaking the true state of affairs. An "I-You" relationship, such as the Scriptures register, is a personal relationship, and it involves more than one Person. Since Jesus speaks of Himself as I, of the Father as "You" (or "Thou," for the term is singular), and of the Holy Spirit as an additional Other who is addressed as an individual, there are obviously three Persons here. By the time of the so-called Athanasian Creed—probably the fourth century—we find explicit use of the term Person. In the Fifth Ecumenical Council, held at Constantinople in 553, we find definitions stating that there are three Hypostases, three Persons, in God.

One can see at this point the necessity which the Catholic Church insists upon for a living interpreter of divine revelation, which is the Catholic Church herself. Divine truth itself is more like a living person than an abstraction, such as we encounter in science. There has been a lot of talk about a Christianity which stays with the doctrines of the very early Church—the first seven ecumenical councils—but will accept no further developments in the understanding or enunciation of dogma. In the light of what we know today of the history of ideas, such a position appears quite untenable, for it supposes that one can retain truths in one's mind without developing them. This we now know is quite impossible. Men of subsequent ages always discern implications which earlier ages did not notice in a body of truths and discern them corporately as well as individually. Moreover, as the horizons of human knowledge expand, earlier truths become involved with knowledge of all sorts of things of which earlier man had not even dreamed, and unexpected questions arise, insistent questions which demand answers. These answers force the development of earlier knowledge, whether it be natural knowledge or revealed religion itself. In these circumstances, it does not suffice to have a rule or measure of belief which was set down in the distant past, however true it may be. For the believer's problem is not whether or not to deviate from earlier teaching. His problem is which way to go when he finds that *he has to develop the teaching further* than it was developed at the beginning. This problem of development is always with him. For God's revelation can never be compassed entirely in formulae, however accurate and true these may be. It is always more than what is explicitly said at any one period. It is, in Jesus' own words, a seed or a leaven which is destined to grow through human society until the end of time. As it grows, competing and even contradictory modes of possible growth are proposed. The Catholic Church understands herself, and her members understand her, as the organism in which growth of dogma takes place which remains true to the original divine revelation given by the Word of God. She is the concrete reality in which this revelation is embedded and from which dogmatic formulae are occasionally distilled as needed.

Undoubtedly, the major discovery of recent times which is occasioning the development of Catholic dogma and our theological understanding of this development is the discovery of evolution the evolution of the physical universe, the evolution of living organisms, the evolution of society, and the pattern of development as thought itself grows through the centuries. Evolution represents a new awareness, the injection of new concepts and a newly apprehended set of facts into our thinking. The discovery of evolution came about gradually, with some halting steps in the seventeenth century, some more confident ones in the eighteenth, and a decisive move forward with works such as Darwin's *On the Origin of Species* just over a hundred years ago. The discovery of evolution has raised further questions which can now be applied to the further understanding of God's revelation through Jesus Christ in His church. Many very exciting questions regarding God's plan of redemption have now to be worked out by theologians. Until we knew what we now know of the situation of our world in time and space, we were seeing divine revelation in rather pinched perspectives. Hitherto, although divine revelation was actually given in an evolving cosmos, and although God knew this fact, the men themselves receiving the revelation had not known that the world was evolving—or, for that matter, that it was revolving, either. Consequently, there were a great many aspects of divine revelation which the church had not thought about. To these she is applying herself now —slowly, for the issues are immensely complicated, but resolutely.

In speaking of revelation and the way in which the church makes it more and more explicit, I should mention finally what in Catholic teaching are the sources of revelation. These sources are defined by the church herself as Scripture and Tradition. A Catholic believes that both the Old Testament and the New Testament are the Word of God in the sense that these books are revelations from Almighty God. This much the church has said about revelation, and not much more: that these books are revealed in the sense that they have God as their author. This does not necessarily mean that God whispered in the various human writers' ears what to put in the books of the Bible. Parts of the Bible itself give us accounts of the writer's procedure which indicate otherwise. St. Luke tells how hard he had to labor to find out the facts which he puts into his Gospel. He had to ask about them.

The books of the Bible register not only God's revelation, but the individuality of those men and cultures involved in their composition. In these books are discernible the ordinary human processes of composition, the outlook of the age and culture in which each particular part of the Bible is composed, individual writers' peculiarities of style. Nevertheless, God uses the men who are writing these books. He uses them as His instruments, but without depriving them of free will, and He takes these words to Himself as His own. Believing as he does that the Bible is written by God in the sense that God was its principal author, a Catholic has of course a very reverential attitude toward Scripture.

But the Catholic also believes that God's revelation is present to us in Tradition as well as in the Bible. Perhaps the best way to conceive of Tradition in accordance with recent theological developments is to regard Tradition as simply the voice of the church speaking through the ages. There had been a tendency in earlier days to regard Tradition as somehow or other a kind of second volume of the Bible, a somehow invisible volume, which Catholics have and Protestants do not have. This, of course, is wrong. The precise fact about Tradition which differentiates it from the Scriptures is that it is *not* a second Bible. It is not of itself something written down, although it may at times be registered in writing—for instance, in acts of the Councils or decrees of the Holy See. It is certainly not medieval legends about Scriptural figures or saints.

It appears evident that the church has to have at least something like Tradition, whatever it may be called. You have to have something like Tradition to know what books are in the Bible and what to make of the ones which you decide are there. The Bible itself in its original form does not contain anything that tells you what all the books of the Bible are, not even a table of contents. There are—outside the books of the Bible—various lists of the books in the Bible, and these lists are not all the same, although it might be mentioned that lists in extant church documents of the fourth and fifth centuries are the same as that used by Catholics today. How do you know what books to accept and what not? One classical answer to this from people who are not Catholic is that you can tell a book which is part of the Bible from other books by the way it affects you. The trouble with this is that the same books will affect different people differently. And another trouble is that this attitude assumes that the Bible is basically a kind of private meditation book. When you look at the Bible, however, from the point of view of literary and cultural history, this is not what it is. The Psalms are songs to be sung aloud. Parts of the Bible are public genealogical records. Parts are military history. Parts are public, external law. Others are letters to individuals or to groups. And so on.

The Bible is a document, on the whole a kind of public document—it is something which, although it is God's word, reflects in a myriad of ways, first, various stages in Hebrew culture and then, in the New Testament, the life of the church at a very early stage of her development. It is certain that the church was in existence and performing her work of teaching before the Bible was completed.

In Catholic teaching, of course, Tradition is never opposed to the Bible. There is a kind of reciprocity between Tradition and Scripture. The present tendency in Catholic scholarship is to regard what is in Scripture and what is in Tradition as overlapping, and ultimately even as in some way coextensive, so that many theologians today will reject the formulation that revelation is contained "partly" in Scripture and "partly" in Tradition, maintaining rather that, while Tradition is needed to explain Scripture and while Scripture attests Tradition, the word of God is found somehow in its totality in both. The two complement one another not as two things which are separate, not as two different and separate volumes, but as two things which interpenetrate one another.

Having indicated the ways in which revelation becomes more and more explicit as the church moves through history and reflects on what God has given her in Jesus Christ in the beginning, I want to touch very briefly on two other effects which history has on the church. Or perhaps it would be better to say two other relations, two other historical aspects of the church. One of these is the Catholic Church's orientation toward the future, not toward the past. Although occasionally the way some Catholics talk may give one the impression that the church is oriented permanently toward the Middle Ages, in the depths of her being she is not. Medievalism is simply a phase which some people, particularly Americans, go through. The church herself does not preach that people should go back to the past. She does not preach that we should go back to the primal state before the fall of Adam. In her Holy Saturday liturgy the day before Easter, she even sings of Adam's sin as *felix culpa*—"O happy fault, which called for such and so great a Savior." The Saviour, Jesus Christ, leads us ahead into the world to come, not back to a world of primal innocence. The church looks to the future, where redemption will be finally completed. She moves to the future, but to the future seen somehow or other as what is last, final.

She needs to move forward through history and to move into the future to realize her potential and the potential of the

Incarnation itself. These are in actuality one and the same thing in the sense that the church is the Mystical Body of Christ, somehow or other in some mysterious way a kind of extension of his own human body. In the Epistle to the Colossians (1:24) we find St. Paul writing, "I now rejoice in my sufferings for you, and fill up those things that are wanting of the sufferings of Christ, in my flesh for His body which is the Church." The church in her movement through history and into the future is working out the salvation of mankind by filling up, in her members, in their individual sufferings, what is wanting of the sufferings of Christ. One must not impose on this a Pelagian interpretation. We are not really achieving anything here independently of Christ. God is using us, through His grace, in our suffering as in our achievement made possible through Him. Christ permits the members of His church to share in His suffering; He uses them to extend the merits of His own suffering to mankind now and in the future. The church then moves through history carrying Christ's life with her, because He is present in her as her Head.

The other point, and the last, which I would like to make concerning the relationship of history to the church is this: with the rest of the modern world, the church today is much more reflective about history, including her own history, than she has ever been before. The present-day mind is a historical mind, and the church, because she is living in the present day, has a historical mind too. She is present to our historical age with a reflectively, consciously historical mind of her own. This means that this kind of exposition which I have tried to present belongs to the twentieth century—it belongs to the here and now. It is an interpretation of Catholic dogma which runs back through the history of ages gone by, and which does so with today's own special emphasis on history.

THE CHURCH OF TODAY

One of the striking features of the Catholic Church today is her consciousness of present time, of the present age as "today." She has always felt the tension of time and eternity—not that she wants to get rid of either one, but in the sense that she sees them for what they are, different from one another. Nevertheless, in some ways this tension between time and eternity is more keenly realized now than formerly when men did not know the vast reaches of time through which our universe has evolved nor the importance of time in bringing the universe to its present condition—when men did not know as much cosmic and human history as we now know. The dialectic of time and eternity which has always been felt in the church is thus more keenly felt today because of our greater acquaintanceship with time. We know that today differs from earlier ages, and from the ages still ahead of us, much more drastically than earlier man could possibly have suspected.

What is it that divides today from yesterday when we speak of the church of today? One answer, the standard answer until fairly recent times, has been the Renaissance and Reformation. The sixteenth century has quite commonly been taken to be the watershed between premodern and modern times. But the perspectives which we have developed today suggest that the Renaissance, and by implication the Reformation, closed an age much more than it opened one. The Renaissance, as the historian Herbert Butterfield has said, was one of the most typically medieval things that the Middle Ages ever produced, the last in the series of revivals of classical antiquity. It appears from our present-day perspectives that the seventeenth-century beginnings of modern science offer a more feasible, more convenient, more serviceable point to take as the watershed between an earlier culture and our "today." Even Copernicus, who died in 1543, was largely medieval in his cast of mind, preoccupied with teleology in medieval fashion and even a bit animistic. Modern science of course has many medieval and Renaissance roots, but its effective development belongs rather to the age of Galileo, who died in 1642, of Descartes, who died in 1650, and of Newton, who did not die until 1727, although he did his significant work considerably earlier than that.

The relationship of the Roman Catholic Church to this "today" of the scientific—and, more recently, technological—age is quite complex. First of all, the entire world is not living in the scientific, technological age to the same degree. In a sense, the church is dealing with a great many ages simultaneously right now in the twentieth century. There are still cultures and states of mind where the work of Newton has barely penetrated and where the effects of the newer physics of Max Planck and Einstein have never quite made themselves felt. There are amalgams of old and new cultures with which the Catholic Church is faced—for instance, in Latin America, where there exist mixtures of pre-Columbian civilizations and European civilizations difficult for us, north of the Rio Grande, to understand. The church has to deal today with pastoral cultures, with cultures just emerging from the neolithic stage, and at the same time with highly industrialized technological civilizations. The Catholic Church has members, lay and clerical, all the way from the land of the Eskimo to the new republics of equatorial Africa, and from there to Manhattan Island, Fifth Avenue, and Broadway.

The church's sacraments and her foundation date from an age which was different from that of today. She is not a mere visitor in older civilizations any more than she is in technological society. She has lived and thrived, despite persecution, in the old and the new. The church arose from the teachings of Jesus Christ at a time when man found himself to be living within nature more than he finds himself in nature now. In the United States we exist in a technological civilization which even in the country situates us rather alongside nature as managers of nature. The church's liturgy, however, is shot through with an earlier, less managerial attitude toward the nonhuman world, a feeling for living things, for the trees, flowers, the seasons, the sun, moon, stars, as things which help us psychologically to relate ourselves to God. We find nature's symbolism in the church's sacraments, which she teaches were instituted at a certain time and place in human history by Jesus Christ: the sacrament of baptism, which is a washing, based upon the natural symbol of water; confirmation and the anointing of those seriously ill, where oil is used to symbolize strength; the Eucharist, where we find the simple naturalness of bread and wine as foodstuffs, and so on.

We have moved rather notably away from this feeling for nature and natural symbols today. The symbols of our mass media, while just as insistent, are of a different cut. But the movement away from nature symbolism was under way several hundred years ago, when the movement can be discerned in the Roman breviary of the Catholic Church. Here one notes that the hymns for saints' feasts which were written after the age of Renaissance humanism in the seventeenth century contrast quite markedly with the much earlier hymns in the breviary which are found on the ferial days—that is, which belong to the individual days of the week apart from the saints' feasts. These ferial hymns are cosmic in their imagery: highly conscious of the effect on man of dawn, noon, and evening, of the motionless stars, of the cock's crowing, of earth, water, air, fire, and light. By the seventeenth century straightforward interest in such things is largely gone, supplanted by rhetorically formalized commemoration of individual human experiences.

In our response, or lack of response, to earlier nature symbols, we cannot much help ourselves today. Even romanticism had lost the earlier feeling for these symbols. It talked a lot about nature, but it talked too much. The self-consciousness of nineteenth-century man's devotion to nature is evidence of the fact that to be close to nature the confirmed romantic has to resort to artificial dodges. Of course earlier nature symbolism has not really vanished into thin air. Psychologists such as Karl Jung, Ludwig Binswanger, and others point out that we have not got entirely away from such symbols, but that the old symbols have rather been covered and merged with more recent accretions, accretions which in some cases have even grown out of the earlier symbolism in the very process of separating from it and overlapping it. The new symbolism which is an accretion to the old and in many ways has really grown out of the old is the symbolism of our industrial technological society with its advertisements and slogans and its stepped-up hortatory techniques.

The church has lived through this whole symbolical change, the shift from the old to the new in our apprehension of symbols and our reaction to symbols. She belongs to both worlds here, the deep past caught permanently in the so-called subconscious of all men, not of Catholics alone, and the present technological world. The church is living through the shift as it is still going on today in some cultures just moving into the technological age. This, I think, is a thing to keep in mind in considering such burning issues at present as the separation of church and state. Separation of church and state can mean different things in different cultures, and you cannot import what was said about church and state in the Middle Ages directly into our American situation and say that it applies without reinterpretation. It may be relevant to consider what the church said about the state in the Middle Ages, but you cannot by any means transfer this immediately to the United States. Even the condition of church-state relationship in other countries today does not translate immediately into American terms because these other countries are often living in an entirely different stage of development from that in which we find ourselves here.

We cannot, obviously, in this brief treatment take up individually questions regarding the church today in all cultures. We are going to have to concentrate on one culture and since in the United States we know the church in a far advanced technological situation, it is here that we can chiefly focus in discussing the church and the modern technological age. We have ample justification for doing this because all civilizations are moving in the direction of technological society—although I think it is good for all of us as Americans to remind ourselves that their desire to develop technologically is by no means tantamount to a desire to become Americans. Others want to advance in their own way. Nevertheless, simply because we are in the forefront technologically, we are especially representative of our present era. In a real sense, although one which varies from culture to culture, today belongs to technology and technology belongs to today. In a very profound sense technology is today.

There are four titles or headings under which we can consider the relationship of the church to our technological world —or perhaps we could say under which we can consider her affinity for this world. We have already indicated her partial disinclination for it because of her ties with a past more rooted in nature. But her disinclination is probably no greater than that of men generally, all of whom in one way or another complain about and make fun of technological culture. Poking fun involves a release of hostility. We enjoy cartoons poking fun at technology. We make movies poking fun at it, such as the French movie *Mon Oncle*. We are quite obviously not entirely taken by technology, although we do respect it and live through it. Certainly the church respects it and lives through it. Neither Catholics nor those outside the church really want to get away from our present civilization back to an earlier one. We want to improve what we have.

The Catholic Church, however, has some special reasons for getting along rather well in technological society. The first one I should suggest is this: technological society is in great part a rational society. It is based on the conviction that things in this universe can be "figured out" because it is based on what we have learned to call science. The nuclear physicist proceeds in the conviction that his problems are on the whole soluble; that although he does not know the answer to a particular problem, there is an answer somewhere, and that, if he puts himself to his task devotedly enough, he will probably find it. This is a conviction which earlier man seldom, if ever, had. Even the ancient Greeks, whom we hold up as paragons of the scientific rational mind, were far less confident of the ultimate intelligibility of things than their later interpreters often seemed to think they were. There are lengthy studies on the irrational in Greek culture, such as Eric Robertson Dodd's book, *The Greeks and the Irrational*. In Sophocles' *Oedipus Rex* Oedipus says: "I was evil from my birth." This kind of statement seems to preclude total explanation. In the face of such an utterance, hope of explanation is dashed and hope of adequately accounting for tragedy in terms of the "tragic flaw" treated by Aristotle simply founders. You need no tragic flaw if you are evil from birth. This kind of thing suggests a world that you cannot really explain.

The source of the scientist's confidence in the explicability of everything he deals with, according to Alfred North Whitehead in *Science and the Modern World*, is a state of mind deriving from the Hebrew and Christian teaching about God. In this teaching, God is all-wise, and He is the creator of absolutely everything. Scripture scholars are still filling in important details in our understanding of the book of Genesis, but one thing is certain about the meaning of this book and has been certain from the beginning, namely, that Genesis is saying in its first chapters that the Lord God, Yahweh Elohim, made everything, absolutely everything that exists. He is not a local God, and He is not to be identified with the sun and the stars, because He made these too. Anything that can be named, besides Himself, God made. This Genesis certainly states. Since this is so, since God made everything that we deal with, and since He is absolutely wise, completely intelligent, there is always an explanation for everything, although perhaps the explanation may at times be hard to come upon.

It may take time for us to work out an explanation, but there is sure to be one there. This is the conviction, Whitehead points out, which seized the mind decisively in the Middle Ages and produced a typical product in scholastic philosophy. From Whitehead's point of view it appears that the rational approach of science has some kind of historical roots in the historical fact of the Christian faith. And I would submit that such roots establish a very close rapport between the technological world that we live in today and the Catholic mind. The rationality of science, you see, exists within a kind of overall faith in the explicability of things, a faith which cannot be accounted for scientifically. This faith is not the same as Christian faith, but it is something like it. Both in the church and in the scientific world, rationality exists within a context of faith. Rationality for the Catholic does not surround faith. On the contrary, faith surrounds rationality. But in the atmosphere of Catholic faith, rationality survives. The Vatican Council, following the Council of Trent, affirms first the insufficiency of reason with regard to the truths of faith, and secondly the relevance of reason to these truths. Reason has something to do with them. It can move toward them through what are known as the "preambles of faith." Moreover, the truths of faith themselves are not against reason, which they support, although they are, in the last analysis, beyond it. In a way somewhat similar, although not quite the same, the scientist professes a kind of natural faith that phenomena are rationally explainable. He cannot prove or explain this faith scientifically, and yet science is connected with such faith, for it is such faith which sparks and pushes through scientific endeavor.

In our American culture one phenomenon illustrates rather strikingly the accord between the Catholic Church and technology. In the United States today there are some 265 Catholic universities and colleges providing university-level training, with a total of 302,908 students as of 1959. It is striking that in a land of many universities and colleges, there is no other group anywhere near this size which is so thoroughly committed to a firm and identifiable religious faith and at the same time thoroughly committed to science. These universities and colleges have proved themselves perfectly viable in a thoroughly scientific world, carrying on the same kinds of basic research which are carried on in other universities and colleges, often with great difficulty, because they have difficulty financing themselves.

I must remind you here that these universities and colleges are church-affiliated but not church-supported. There is no common fund in the Catholic Church on which any parish, or any diocese, much less any university or college, can draw. From this point of view, the Catholic Church is the most decentralized organization you can possibly imagine. The support which Catholic universities receive from non-Catholic supporters, individuals and corporations, as well as the often high population of non-Catholic students in Catholic universities—in my own university, St. Louis University, one-fourth of the student body is not Catholic—can be credited largely to these universities' known commitment to science as to other forms of secular learning. The support which they freely receive from Catholics is based on this same commitment in relation to the universities' further commitment to the Catholic faith. Faith and scientific technology as well as humanism are here strikingly allied. Catholics like to criticize their educational system, but when they are doing so, they can always take heart from this tremendous record of achievement.

A second heading under which we can consider the relationship of the church to technology is this: technological society is a stage in an evolving universe in which the Catholic Church is historically embedded. Our present technological world is something to which the whole of human society has built up, and although it creates tensions in us by moving us a bit away from the world of nature, which used to be man's home, these tensions are natural in the sense that it is in the last analysis natural for man to move away from nature and to try to control it, to manage it. Technological society, then, is a stage in the evolution of the universe. The church herself is rooted in the evolving universe through her faith in a historical Incarnation. The Catholic Church makes much of the fact that the birth, life, death, and resurrection of Jesus Christ are historical realities comparable to other verifiable historical realities such as those in the lives of Cicero or Julius Caesar or Ptolemy or anyone else from history. And indeed, no one would seriously contest the historicity of Jesus of Nazareth any more. There was quite a bit of furor about this matter even among some serious scholars in the past century, but attacks on the historicity of Jesus Christ today are confined pretty much to the lunatic fringe.

The church feels herself rooted in the evolving universe because of the fact that she insists that she was founded in history. She does not belong outside history in the way in which the Greek mythologies do. If you asked an ancient Greek to tell you in what year Athena sprang forth from the head of Zeus, or in what year Dionysus was torn to pieces by the Bacchae, the ancient Greek would look at you as though you were out of your mind, because these things do not occur inside history. That is precisely the point of a myth of this sort: it is an extratemporal occurrence, a holiday from time. But Jesus Christ does come into history in this real historical universe. Here the very matter of this evolving universe becomes part of the physical body of Jesus, and is thus caught up into the scheme of human redemption. The technological age grows out of the patterns lodged in this very same material universe and marks the period when human intelligence, of itself spiritual, gains spectacular control over material forces. Attention to material things can be expressive, but of itself it is good, not evil. The operations of technology thus from a Catholic point of view are important in a special way because a Catholic is so certain, so profoundly sure that matter is not evil. There is a torque in human nature which seems to make us want to say, if we do not watch ourselves, that matter is evil. If you do say this, you can give a speciously plausible, superficial explanation for a great many things. But the church insists that matter is good, not evil. Matter has been sanctified by Christ and by His Mystical Body the church, this church which is physically apprehensible in her material members. The Catholic Church recalls the reminder in Genesis that God made everything in the material universe and "saw that it was good." She also recalls the first verse of the Epistle of St. John where the author speaks of the Word of Life Incarnate in tangible, material flesh: "That which was from the beginning . . . our hands have handled."

At this point, you can see the importance in the Catholic mind of devotion to Mary, the mother of Jesus, who the church, from the very earliest ages, said is the Mother of God, because Jesus her Son is God as well as man, one Person. Your mother furnishes you with what belongs to your human nature in furnishing your body, but she is the mother not merely of your nature but of *you*, a person. And Mary is the mother not merely of Jesus' human nature but of Jesus Himself, a Person who is not only man but also God. Thus in being the mother of Jesus, as Mary is quite properly and truly said to be the mother of a man, so she is also quite properly and truly said to be the Mother of God (although she is of course mother of only one of the three Persons in God, the Son or Word). The Catholic's devotion to Mary seals the fact that matter is not evil because Mary is honored the way she is for one principal reason, her motherhood: she gave Jesus His body, just as our mothers gave us our bodies; but the Person to whom she furnished His body was and is God. The church is grateful to her for this. She, of course, was given more spiritual graces than any other creature of God, including all the angels, who are spectacularly higher than man in the natural scheme of Creation. But she was given these graces because of a relationship founded on matter, for the reason that she was to be the Mother of God and give Jesus His body. Cardinal John Henry Newman points out very astutely that most heresies which start out by pulling away from Mary end up, or are likely to end up, by saying openly or obliquely that matter is an evil thing.

The third point under which we can consider the relationship of the church to technology is this: technological society faces consciously into the future. The future occupies a large part of the vision which technology has opened to us. In great part we have secured control of nature, and consequently, we want to know how we are to manage it in the ages to come. We plan today not only in units of years or in decades, but actually in centuries. Like technological society, the church too faces into the future and does so by the very nature of her being. The so-called "restoration" of all things in Christ, mentioned in documents of the church, does not refer to any return to the past. This is really a bringing of things to God under the headship of Christ, and it is called restoration not because there is any question of going back to the past, but because by Creation all things in a sense proceed from God, go out from Him, so in a sense they must ultimately return to Him as their fulfillment. And yet they return to Him in the future in a quite different condition from that in which they go out from Him. They go from Him by nature, naturally, by creation. They return through Jesus Christ. And this return is to be achieved in the future.

The church is becoming more and more conscious of her future orientation today precisely because of the fact that we live in a technological society, which draws attention to the future orientation of reality. When we say, however, that technology and the church both face into the future, we must remember that this facing into the future is not exactly the same for the two of them. Technology does not redeem us from our sins and past failings. It has obvious limits in its ability to bring contentment. The sometimes grim jokes we tell about machines show a fairly high awareness of technology's limitations and positive dangers, even among those devoted to technological development. But technology is certainly not necessarily evil. In fact, in itself it is good, because it represents a greater and greater control of the forces of matter by man's intellect. The intellect is spiritual, the intellect is a good of a very high order, and although technological knowledge is still natural knowledge, it is nevertheless something good in that by subjecting vast natural forces to man's intelligence, in a way it enlarges the field of operation for the spiritual in the totality of this universe in which we live. Consequently, technology in a sense even gives a greater range to the workings of grace itself. Grace cannot work on matter directly; it can only work on what is spiritual, on our souls. Consequently, if we enlarge the purchase which the spiritual has in the totality of our universe, we enlarge the area in which, in one way or another, the effects of grace can be felt. For this reason the Catholic, even when keenly aware of the limitations of technology, should see a greater and greater technological development as God's will and should favor such development—always, however, in conformity with God's law.

A fourth heading under which we can consider the relationship of the Catholic Church to technological civilization is that of mass culture. "Mass culture" is a somewhat emotive term and rather difficult to define, but we can take it here as meaning a culture in which there is a conscious orientation of thought, industrial activity, sports, entertainment, and other major forms of social activity toward the desires and behavior manifested by large numbers of persons taken as groups.

Technology and mass culture are intimately related, although which of them is cause and which effect is not easy to determine. With the scientific achievement which accompanies it, technology has produced the lowered mortality rate responsible for modern population densities and the means of communication, including rapid transportation, associated with the rise of mass languages—which are themselves very recent phenomena, if we mean by a mass language a vernacular native to hundreds of millions of persons. At the same time, the growth in population and in the mass languages has made technology possible. Whatever our present population problems may be, the sparse scattering of human beings in little pockets across the surface of the earth which has represented the state of affairs for almost all of man's time on the earth, beginning somewhere between 100,000 and 1,000,000 years ago, was a crippling disability. It made impossible any large-scale technological developments at all and, indeed, made impossible any highly developed civilizations until relatively recent millennia.

Technological civilization distresses many persons. The assembly-line techniques which we have perfected to deal with the masses of men have, it is charged, vulgarized most human responses to an intolerable degree. Fine, discriminatory responses to the better things in life, including religion, are disappearing. At this point, an indubitable alliance of the Catholic Church with technology appears, we are told by certain of the church's critics, but not an admirable alliance. She turns out to be in collusion with the vulgarizing forces. She is, and always has been, too willing to make common cause with low, unreflective, and even superstitious drives and practices. In the Middle Ages it was the craze for local saints and pilgrimages, and the mania for relics. Today it is novenas, pilgrimages on a still larger commercialized scale, an exaggerated interest in public religious spectacles, or a careless tolerance of an incredible amount of incredibly bad art, which any informed person with his wits about him cannot possibly associate with God, unless he is willing to debase God Himself.

The charge of vulgarity is, of course, not a new one for the Catholic Church. It has been leveled against her from the very beginning. In the second century of the Christian era, Origen's opponent Celsus, speaking in his treatise *The True Discourse*, of the people who make up the church as Christ's Mystical Body, asks the question, "Could the Body of God really be made of such coarse stuff as that?" We recall Goethe's reference, given with the Celsus quotation in Père Henri de Lubac, *The Splendour of the Church*, to "a narrow-minded mass, ready to cringe and be lorded over." The church knows this charge of being vulgar and, while she does not approve vulgarity and does encourage efforts to mitigate it—for bad art is evil, even if not directly a moral evil, and evil cannot be desired for itself—she knows nevertheless that she will always be vulnerable to it. She has to devote herself to a great many persons who are intellectually and emotionally and artistically badly disoriented, and she cannot—and probably does not know how to—restore their psychological and emotional integrity before looking to repentance and forgiveness of sins.

Although she includes among her members persons as truly discriminating, artistically and otherwise, as anyone has ever been, and although the Catholic faith is truly at ease only with good art and discerning social practices, the Catholic Church proposes a religion which is quite different from and superior to a religion restricted to sensitive souls who share with only a few their elite experience. The church, it is true, calls to high sanctity, a sanctity which relatively few of her members attain —although an impressive number do. The writings of her great mystics cannot be understood in their fullness by all, for many require a high degree of education and all require the disciplined life of Christian asceticism. And yet, for all this, there is no private Christianity.

There are no secrets into which one is inducted after a certain period in the church. The Catholic Church is not a fraternal lodge. The faith of a Trappist monk or the faith of the Pope himself is the same as that of the charwoman who may in her own mind have it confused a bit with superstitious or semisuperstitious observances. But what man can say that his life is free of all superstition? Our ability to recognize superstitions in others is perhaps at times like our ability to recognize faults in general. Sometimes those who see most faults in others are those who have more themselves. We might well be grateful that while the Catholic Church does not like superstition, which she considers a sin, she is still inclined, following the lead of her Founder, Jesus Christ, to put on all human actions, particularly irrational ones, the gentlest, most positive interpretation possible.

What gives our faith value is not mere freedom from superstition—although this is certainly a thing to be desired and to be worked for—but the fact that it is the faith of the church itself, that it is a thing shared with other members of the Mystical Body and made possible by God's grace given us with no merit whatsoever of our own through Jesus Christ. The faith of all Catholics is faith within the church, the position of Catholics as believing people is, "I take my stand in the church, which is the Mystical Body of Jesus Christ, who is God." Individual Catholics have no faith which they do not share, although they can as individuals be more or less devoted to their common faith. They have the faith of the community, which manifests itself exteriorly in more or less acceptable ways.

The Catholic concept of faith as something personal and interior to each individual and yet not private is perhaps on certain grounds more acceptable today than ever before. Depth psychology has advertised the fact that in a sense we have really no private thoughts nor even private imaginative creations. Thoughts and fantasies of seemingly the wildest sort are now seen as related to interpersonal communication, quite accessible to other persons and meaningful to them, particularly to those versed in depth psychology, or to phenomenologists familiar with the intersubjective aspects of human activity. A knowledge of intersubjectivity has made—or should have made—the idea of a gnosis, of a secret knowledge that saves, rather less plausible today than ever before. We have the opportunity today to know more acutely than ever before that what are really our own, what are truly private, are our decisions—they and nothing more. The decisions, deep within ourselves, the acts of our will which we alone know, acts of that faculty which Father Gerard Manley Hopkins, in his unfinished poem "On the Portrait of Two Beautiful Young People: A Brother and a Sister," refers to as

> The selfless self of self, most strange, most still,
> Fast furled and all foredrawn to No or Yes

—these are what we have as our own, what make us what we are.

The Catholic Church respects these interior acts of the will, values them above everything else, for out of such acts the web of each individual life is woven. But she knows that even these private acts, these utterly interior decisions, cannot come into being outside a social context—ultimately a context which includes all men. Even when approaching God, we must in some sense approach Him in common, with others of our kind, whom we experience not as a mass but as our brothers.

The rest, besides our decisions, our commitments, even the intellectual rest, is stuff common to all in the sense that it is accessible to all men and is a social as much as an individual creation. Man cannot refine himself out of contact with other men—in the last analysis, directly or indirectly, he must be in contact with *all* other men, today more than ever before. What the Catholic ultimately values is not withdrawal from other men but refinement of contacts between all men by grace and love through contact with Christ—who came to enter into contact with all men. His body itself was not made of refined matter, but of the same common matter as ours, old matter, billions of years old, properly aged to receive the soul and its self-consciousness. Christ does not isolate, but transforms. Matter, with all its imperfections, was rendered holy by being assumed to His person—but it remained matter, the principle of multiplicity and of limitation.

The church, too, the extension of Christ in time and space, does not isolate, but transforms. She is here on this earth among men on terms which men can understand, on the same terms on which they live—materially and spiritually, exteriorly and interiorly both, midway between the merely material and God, devoted to draw all things through the Person of Jesus Christ to the Father in the Holy Spirit.

Our Protestant Heritage

WILHELM PAUCK

Classical Protestantism

WHEN we speak of classical Protestantism, we really mean the Protestantism of the Reformation. Indeed, one should not use the term *classical* in connection with Protestantism, for there is no period of its history and no manifestation of its nature in any specific church-form that deserves to be called classical in the sense that it must be regarded as normative for all Protestantism.

Yet one thing emerged in the Reformation which has remained characteristic of Protestantism in all its variations of faith and practice. The *pulpit* was put into the *center* of the religious life. Roman Catholic Christianity lives by worship at the altar, or rather, by that which is enacted when the priest offers up the sacrifice of the altar. Judaism, in some sense or other, is centered in the lectern and what is taught from there. But Protestantism finds its inspiration in the words spoken from the pulpit. Protestantism is a preaching Christianity.

It is on this account that its life is characterized by the prominence of the *Bible*, which is God's word in the sense that one believes that God speaks from it; he who interprets God's word from the pulpit is, therefore, the spokesman of God. For God is understood to be a "speaking God"—*deus loquens*—as the reformers put it. He places himself in a relation with man through what he says. What is conveyed by the speaking of God is that which is embodied in the person of Christ. Jesus Christ is God's word or revelation, and on this account he is the Lord of the Bible. That is to say, the Bible must be understood as proclaiming what has become manifested in him. It, therefore, must be interpreted with a view toward him. It is God's word insofar as it is Christocentrically explained, for it is not just a series of instructions. It is a message of salvation, the "Gospel," good news. The Bible is the source of the Christian life. And for this reason it is authoritative. It is the norm of the Christian life to which everything that Christians exhibit must conform, because Protestant Christians, according to the teachings of the Reformers, live by what God speaks and discloses in the Bible as a message of salvation. Their faith is chiefly a soteriological one.

And here we come upon the second most distinctive feature of Protestantism. The message, which the Bible proclaims, is that man lives by *grace alone*, by the sheer divine promise which, from the human point of view, is ever insecure, in no way guaranteed to any man. This alone will save him—he is saved by grace alone and not by anything that he can point to as his own achievement. The contrast which runs through the entire preaching and teaching of the Reformation is that between grace and good works. In Roman Catholicism, good works were specific acts that made obvious the possibilities of man to obtain a certain religious or moral standard. They consisted chiefly of alms-giving; fasting; praying: some undertaking that would be of assistance to a fellow man; some self-denial, particularly expressed in asceticism, that would render obvious one's humiliation in the sight of God; and some form of prayer as a devotion directed toward the divine.

But in these good works, so it was believed, there was made manifest the ability of man in some way by his own efforts to render himself worthy of salvation. This the reformers rejected, passionately, radically, in order to put into the place of the piety of good works that of grace alone. One of the most telling slogans formulated by Martin Luther, the real originator of Protestantism, was: "Good works do not make a man good, but a good man does good works." That is to say, good actions which a man may be able to produce for himself in reliance on certain religious or moral possessions he may have, do not in the deepest sense make him good, because good works of some sort can also be performed by one who in his heart has not really embraced goodness; only one who is good in his whole inner being, that is to say, in relation to the *summum bonum*, the highest good, which at the same time is the origin of all good (Luther loved to call God the giver of all good) can regard himself or may be regarded as capable of performing good deeds.

And this now was the amazing teaching of the Protestant reformers which they transmitted to all who came after them: that a man becomes good only by receiving the divine promise of forgiveness. He becomes good only by experiencing or undergoing a transformation of what he naturally is. This transformation was seen to consist of repentance—a reconsideration of all motives of action—involving a readiness at every time and moment to start over again, making a new beginning. As far as life is directed toward a fulfillment of some sort, it is understood by the early Protestants as a life of progress. This was defined also by reference to the Law and the Gospel, understood as standing in a dialectical relationship with one another. The Law exhibits God's will to man and the Gospel shows him that, through the divine mercy expressed in forgiveness, and through it alone, man is capable of fulfilling the Law. The Law is holy and true and it can in no way be considered wrong. But he who knows the Law does thereby not also have the power of living up to it. The Law is merely a road sign and as such it is incapable of bestowing upon him who acknowledges it as right also the power of keeping it. Hence, the Gospel as the announcement that God alone and not man is the Saviour, is related to the Law as that power which enables one to fulfill it.

This religion was seen by the reformers as a life of *faith*. Everyone must believe for himself. Each is alone responsible for what he does before God; how he understands his own person and his destiny. The Protestant-Christian religiousness is personal through and through. Whether the divine message of salvation as exhibited in Christ and proclaimed through the Bible comes to life depends on how every individual responds to it. The Gospel as well as the Law is directed to individuals. And no one is able to take the place of another when the divine reality is disclosed to him. "You yourself must decide about it," said Luther. "*Your* neck is at stake," and your destiny is being formed. It is in this connection that we should become mindful of the fact that Reformation Protestantism was a religion of conscience—"conscience" being understood as that dimension of personal human existence at which an individual achieves selfhood in the deepest and strictest sense, as that level of being where a man assumes the most radical responsibility for his own person, aware that whatever life he has is his and his only, though he is not the master of it because he has merely received it. It is understandable that from here an individualistic religiousness necessarily had to develop—an individualistic religiousness which must be understood as a personal life but not necessarily as a way of living that one can describe as subjectivistic, being in all respects grounded and articulated in the subject alone. According to the teachings of reformers, the person who is brought into relation with God is in no way limited to himself.

Hence, from the personalism of faith, there results (as soon as the dynamics of this religion come to expression) a social religious life. When a person is related to God in his conscience he is also placed in a new connection with all his fellowmen. Every individual believer becomes a priest, and, as such, a mediator of God or of the divine life to others. This was the meaning of the remarkable teaching, first formulated by Luther and through him communicated to all early Protestants, namely, that of the *universal priesthood of believers*. This is an eminently social doctrine. It does not mean, as you can sometimes read, that every believer is to be his own priest. This is something that does not make much sense anyway. How can an individual be his own priest? Instead, the doctrine refers to the social responsibility which a believer must express.

In this connection one can also understand best a radical innovation which the Protestant Reformers introduced into Christendom, namely, a new view of grace. In Roman Catholicism, grace (as that power on which man depends in the last resort) was understood as a supernatural "something," a power of healing, a "medicine," as also certain ancient Christian teachers put it. According to the reformers, grace is the manifestation of God's friendship or mercy. It is not a supernatural power able to cure the mortal sickness of man, namely, that which, when he presents himself to God, must be interpreted as sin, unbelief, doing wrong. But grace is the disclosure of mercy which is a personal attitude making for friendship. The man of faith is one who has accepted God's promise of mercy, and in accepting it finds himself transformed in his inner being, his conscience, and thereby becomes one who himself is able to act as a giver of mercy to his fellow men, one who becomes useful to them, not because he is inspired by any sympathies for the other one, but because he sees in him a friend of God, who in the last resort must live by the same gift of unmerited grace.

And thus the Church, the community of those who together are the people of God, is interpreted as the *communio sanctorum* or the communion of believers. The church is a spiritual fellowship that is made up of all those who have listened to the promise of the divine word. It is a fellowship of hearers. Hence, it was possible for the Reformers to define the church as the *communio sanctorum* or the congregation of believers, as that people which comes into being when the word is rightly preached and heard.

Nothing is so characteristic of early Protestantism as the fact that whenever its spokesmen endeavored to define the church and its nature, they employed the following formula, or some version of it: where the word of God is rightly preached and heard, there is the church. One must understand that what is here meant is a spiritual kind of community, a relationship among men which is grounded in and derived from inner attitudes. Hence, the strange stress on the part of the Reformers upon the invisibility of the church. This does not mean, as certain Roman Catholics are inclined to think, that the church as an invisible fellowship is something ideal, as if it were a "Platonic city." But what it does mean is that before anything can become visible as the manifestation of the fellowship character of the church, there exists an invisible bond by which all believers (wherever they may be, regardless of time and space) find themselves related to one another.

This is the affirmation of the most remarkable humanitarianism. The Christian believer is understood to be one of an all-comprehensive fellowship of all men who, insofar as they are men, must live on the deepest level of their need by the grace of God alone. But this invisible spiritual source of the church must necessarily become visible—this inwardness must assume outwardness. The life of the church, therefore, as it assumes shape in the social life of men, must be inspired again and again by invisible sources. In this connection, I direct your attention to the fact that according to Luther, the source of a Christian's life must be understood to be *iustitia aliena*, a foreign righteousness, a fountain of goodness which is outside him, beyond his control, and which can become his possesion only insofar as it is *given* to him.

A man lives by sources that are not of his making. He lives by grace alone. He has an inwardness that he shapes in no way by his own powers, but which is merely a response to what is bestowed upon him from outside him. He is a servant of another than himself—in the last resort, of the giver of all good, God, who is in heaven and not on earth; who is eternal and not temporal; infinite, not finite; good and not merely one who strives after good; and so on.

But this life is not confined merely to the spiritual needs of the people who constitute the church as the people of God and the communion of believers. It is expressed in everything that fills human life. The Christian is a man of God not merely in those enterprises that are directed as forms of worship to God. He expresses his faith in whatever he finds he must do in terms of his busy-ness—his works, his daily labors. Faith and love, the two basic expressions of the Christian life, inspire whatever work a man has to perform as he makes his daily rounds. The labor of a man is seen as inspired by the motivations that are derived from faith. This is the early Protestant notion of *vocation.*

According to Scholastic teaching, the idea of vocation meant that which a man must do in response to God's demands. Hence, for medieval Roman Catholics the divine calling was fulfilled chiefly when a man chose to become a *religiosus* (a religious one)—that is to say, when he separated himself from the natural relationships of life, forsook the world, and entered a cloister and became a monk, who in fulfilling the vows tried to give the fullest possible expression to his devotion to God. The Reformers adopted the notion of vocation here expressed but they broadened it by affirming that it is possible for every man to follow the guidance of that to which he is directed by his faith, namely, the will of God, and live as a child of God in whatever comes to hand. So, for the early Protestants, there was nothing in the realm of human activity that could be regarded as exempt from the religious dimension: nothing is profane, everything is sacred. The realm of religion is not a special field of human endeavor, but it comprises all of human existence. All human life is hallowed and not only that life which has withdrawn itself from the ordinary, natural human relationships.

So then, in order to sum up the basic teachings of early Protestantism, they consisted of: (1) the interpretation of the Bible as God's word of salvation and (2) the belief that man is justified, made righteous, rendered acceptable in God's sight by grace alone, i.e., the promise of salvation given to him from without, to which therefore (3) he must reply in faith, trusting absolutely that what is promised to him is true; and from this there is derived (4) the awareness that under God all people are related in an invisible communion with one another, constituting a relationship which is invisible but must (5) manifest itself in deeds of love and service in that community—which is realized by whatever a man finds himself called upon to do in his daily work.

And now let us look at the practices of Old Protestantism, those ecclesiastical practices which, in the context of the whole civilization of the sixteenth century, brought to expression what this understanding of the Christian faith meant. Here we have to realize, in the first place, that the leaders of early Protestantism regarded themselves as "reformers." They did not think that, when they came into conflict with the authorities of the Roman Catholic Church, they were sectarians—people who cut themselves off from a common life in which they had shared. In thinking of themselves as reformers, they believed themselves to be spokesmen of true Christianity. They were convinced that, in Roman Catholicism, this true Christianity had become deformed. The deformation, they believed, consisted chiefly of certain additions that Roman Catholics had made to the Gospel, additions that were most prominently represented, on the one hand, by the priesthood and the whole order of the hierarchy, and on the other hand, by the sacraments—basically, the five sacraments which the Roman Church had added to baptism and the Lord's Supper.

In calling for a reformation, the early Protestants believed that they were of one mind with the Christians of the New Testament, indeed, the Christians of the ancient church. They insisted that they were in continuity with what had always prevailed in Christendom, liberating it, however, from the authoritarianism and the institutionalism of Roman Catholicism. It is on account of this that they found it possible to rely on the creeds of the ancient church in the belief that these creeds brought to an expression, not the Hellenization of Christianity and, as such, something that was added to the Gospel, but what the Gospel itself intended.

By identifying themselves with ancient Christendom, the Reformers absorbed the traditions of ancient classical civilization, just as Eastern Orthodox Christianity and Roman Catholicism had done. Thus they aligned themselves with the vast cultural tradition which had been in the background of Christianity from the beginning and which made Christianity the all-embracing cultural religion of the West. In undertaking the reformation of the church, over against Roman Catholicism, the early Protestants nevertheless maintained the sense of cultural mission which, for centuries, had drawn together into one unity of motivation specifically religious concerns of

Christianity and cultural interests and legacies of Greco-Roman origin.

When we speak of the churches which were formed during the Reformation, we refer to Lutheranism, Calvinism, Anglicanism, and certain sectarian groups which were labeled Anabaptists, because they interpreted the sacrament of baptism in a particular way, in denying infant baptism and advocating believer's baptism. It is important to underline the fact that there was a variety of churches in early Protestantism, because many people think incorrectly that the Reformation established but one form of the church.

The differences in the churches manifested themselves in several other directions but particularly in relation to the states. The majority of Reformation Protestants believed that a church could exist only in closest co-operation with the secular government, not in the sense that secular government should in any way assume a responsibility for the spiritual religious culture, i.e., for preaching or the administration of the sacraments, but in the sense that secular rulers had to assume a responsibility for the establishment of the true church because they had to care not only for the secular but also for the spiritual welfare of their subjects. Only the Anabaptists denied that the Christian life had to be realized through this co-operation of religion and politics. Instead, they depended on the separation of church and state. They insisted that the new churches that were to be built under the inspiration of the Reformation should not depend upon any assistance on the part of political rulers. They should be free churches. In this respect, the Anabaptists anticipated a later development in Christendom.

Also with respect to church polity (i.e., in connection with the organizational problem of the form of the church), there developed profound differences among the Protestants. Indeed, one can say that the variety of Protestant church life that came into being under the impact of this new understanding of Christianity, was caused by a difference in the basic conception of what the Christian life should be, as it assumed a concrete, socially organized form. For Luther everything had to be determined by the understanding of religion as trust—trust in the truthfulness of God. He felt that he could be liberal and generous wherever this trust was not hindered in any way. For the Calvinists all religious life was shaped by obedience—obedience to that which God had manifested in his disclosure of Himself in the Bible. Therefore the Calvinists derived from the Bible also a basic pattern of church organization. For the Anabaptists, the Christian life was interpreted as discipleship. They expected Christians as individuals and as members of the church to give evidence that they were followers of Christ, imitating Him and doing His will. Therefore, they tended toward a certain pietism. The Anglicans, finally, were motivated chiefly by a concern for the conservation of what had kept Christians together from the beginning. So they emphasized the spiritual continuity of all Christendom as manifested in episcopacy and the orders of the priesthood.

Liberal Protestantism

Liberal Protestantism is a part of that movement in modern western civilization which is identified by the name "liberalism" and which constitutes, in all fields of human endeavor, a reaction against authoritarianism in its several forms. Liberalism in Protestantism can therefore be properly understood only if one knows what it reacted against. It represents a protest against the forms which the Protestantism of the Reformation era had assumed. This was marked by a great variety, from the very beginning. At the end of the Reformation era there were in existence Lutheran, Calvinist, and Anglican churches, and there were "sectarians," represented by Anabaptists, Spiritualists, Anti-Trinitarians, and others like them. This variety of Reformation Protestantism was marked further by intolerance.

This intolerance had two chief causes. In the first place, each of the Protestant churches developed a body of teaching concerning which the belief was held that it agreed with the Bible and was therefore as sacrosanct as the divine revelation of God was deemed to be. Creeds, therefore, assumed almost the same importance as the Holy Book itself. Wherever such a conviction was held, it was expounded in opposition to all who differed in some way or form. In their creedalism all Protestant churches, therefore, practiced a theological exclusivism; what each taught in its own body of doctrine represented, in its estimation, the whole truth concerning Christianity.

But much more important was the fact that all the Protestant bodies, with the exception of some of the sects, especially the Anabaptists and certain of the Spiritualists, came to be shaped in national or territorial churches. And these churches were regarded as guaranteeing social and political unity. This meant that the rulers of the states, as well as the leaders of the churches, were convinced that religious uniformity was the true source of social and political unity. The organized churches thus became the protectors of that concord which one hoped would prevail in given states or societies. Here a remarkable development took place. Since the beginning of the Christian era, and most definitely since the time when Christianity opened itself to an alliance with the political orders, there was introduced into ecclesiastical life this remarkable principle: religious conformity, indeed, creedal and ecclesiastical uniformity of some sort, constitute the basis of social-political unity and peace. For centuries the political life among the European nations was marked by the fact that the political leaders everywhere looked to the churches as the resources of social order and peace.

The Protestant Reformers in fact were nonconformists. They were condemned, to be sure, by the highest ecclesiastical and political authorities, and they accepted for themselves this exclusion because they found their own interpretation of Christianity to be irreconcilable with that of the Roman Church. They believed it proper to speak in the name of what had always been true in Christianity. They regarded themselves as the advocates of true Catholicism, that is to say, of true Christian universalism. They considered themselves representatives of what had always been held among Christians. Nevertheless, over against Roman Catholicism and in terms of their own attitudes toward it, they were nonconformists. When they found themselves compelled to build their own churches and came to establish them in a context of variety, as I have shown, they gave to this nonconformism of theirs a very concrete expression. But now they proceeded to argue, with respect to these territorial, national ecclesiastical bodies which they called into being, that they had to be uniformitarian; in other words, that all who belonged to them within the confines of one church organization had to observe the same faith and the same religious-ecclesiastical practice in order to maintain social peace and control.

Thus it came about that the varieties of ecclesiastical politics, and in connection therewith the manifold Protestant creeds, came to be coupled with an active spirit of intolerance. The various Protestant churches (established as they were in individual nations or individual states), excluded themselves from each other. Thus the variety of faith which they exhibited was dogmatized. A kind of religious, ecclesiastical, theological authoritarianism came into being which, compared with the several forms which had prevailed earlier, was unyielding.

If one wants to understand how there developed a liberalism in Protestantism, one must take notice of still another feature in its early development. The Protestant Reformers could rightly claim to have rediscovered the Gospel. They had reached back to the sources of Christianity. They did this in connection with Biblicism. One can go so far as to say that, in the Reformation, the Bible came to new life. To be sure, in all ages Christians had cherished the Bible as the one ultimate source of Christianity. The Bible always had been *the* Christian book, but in the course of the development of the Church, all kinds of additions were made to it in the form of doctrines, liturgical teachings, moral laws, and a great many religious practices. The Reformers desired to separate the Bible from all these incrustations and additions. And, because they themselves fed their faith from the Bible, because they themselves were alive in the spirituality of the Bible, they largely succeeded. They reconstituted the Christian religion as a religion of salvation in which a man is dependent ultimately upon the gift of grace which God bestows upon him (grace being understood as forgiveness of sin), and in which he responds to this divine gift by the surrender of faith, trust, obedience, or discipleship.

But the power of the long-established religious doctrinal

traditions (of which the Reformers too were the heirs insofar as they came out of Roman Catholicism) was so strong that they found it impossible—though their basic religious understanding of Christianity could have led them to do so—to break with the doctrinal legacy. The dogmas that had been developed in antiquity in order that Christianity might be protected from too ready an intermingling with the other religions of the Roman empire, and the dogmas which the Church had communicated to the European nations when it introduced Christianity to them, were affirmed also by the Protestant Reformers; and so they blended their fresh understanding of the Christian Gospel in terms of the Bible with this old traditionalism. Indeed, their immediate successors found themselves compelled to adopt the intellectual forms and procedures which the schoolmen of medieval Roman Catholicism had produced in order to offer a theological explanation of Christianity.

And thus the faith that was carried in the teaching of the heirs of the Reformation was a strangely conservative something. It was, on the one hand (over against Roman Catholicism), a religious novelty; on the other hand, it was as traditionalist as Roman Catholicism itself was.

It is against this two-fold form of intolerance as it was expressed in authoritarian practices (by the exclusivistic state churches) and teachings (in connection with the Protestant creeds and doctrines) that liberalism gradually emerged. It arose partially out of the spirit of Christianity itself, because wherever Protestants practiced religious uniformity or conformity, dissenters arose who, in the name of the spirit of the Reformation and (in connection with this spirit) in the name of the Gospel itself, called for a liberation from the sanctions which those who tried to enforce uniformity imposed upon them. It is a remarkable historical fact that this spirit of dissent came to the fore especially in the context of the Anglican Church, which was theologically freer than the other bodies that had developed from the Reformation.

From early beginnings the Anglican Church had preserved certain traditions (episcopacy) and it also affirmed continuity with what had prevailed in Christianity throughout the ages. It regarded itself as embodying in its teaching and in its liturgy "a

Perennial Theology." Hence, the theological-devotional spirit of Anglicanism had never been as absolutistic and intolerant as that of other Protestant churches. But the Anglican Church had observed a very strict form of political-religious uniformitarianism. Indeed, the leaders of England, especially the Tudor Queen Elizabeth and the early Stuarts, had openly declared that religious uniformity was the surest guarantee of the national-political unity of England. And, indeed, one can say that during the sixteenth century and during the first part of the seventeenth century there had been engendered in England through Anglican conformity a high spirit of patriotism in relation to which Englishmen came to be assured of the special mission and destiny of their nation. So, in England religious uniformitarianism had served most directly the political end which had always inspired it.

The dissent which the Puritans advanced against this requirement of conformity was therefore at the same time religious and political. Hence the liberalism which came into being in connection with English Puritanism was a peculiar Protestant phenomenon, precisely because it was, on the one hand, a religious credo, and, on the other hand, a political choice. As this Puritanism spread in connection with the Cromwellian Revolution and came to be implanted in the mind of peoples everywhere, particularly those Englishmen who had chosen to emigrate to the coasts of North America, it released liberalizing forces which gradually nourished a concern for tolerance and religious freedom everywhere. However, one must know that what thus became a spiritual-intellectual movement was carried always by a minority. Moreover, one is confronted, of course, with the remarkable fact that when some of these Puritans, who for the sake of the freedom of the faith emigrated to distant lands, found themselves face to face with the task of establishing new political communities, they too took recourse to the practical principle of religious uniformity. In order to ensure unity and concord in their own society, they enforced religious conformity among their citizens and fellow men. This is a strong illustration of the power which this principle exercised over the minds of men.

Much more important was the fact that on account of these

forces of intolerance, the peoples of Europe and indeed of the Western world came to be involved in military conflicts—wars of religion. Hardly a European land was exempt from this catastrophe. Everywhere religious conflicts, rendered especially sharp on account of the exclusivism of intolerance, were carried out in military wars. The fighting that ensued, and the tremendous losses that were incurred everywhere, did not settle any religious problems. Gradually people came to understand that religious diversity, if it was coupled with the spirit of absolutism, led only to spiritual and physical misery. And so, by way of a reaction to the religious wars of early Protestant history, there developed a mood of fatigue which was coupled with doctrinal unconcern. People did not yet become skeptical concerning the truth of religion, concerning what they were compelled to believe; but they grew spiritually tired. And this meant practically that they ceased to co-operate with those who endeavored to maintain creedal forms of doctrinal uniformity or who tried to enforce requirements of ecclesiastical conformity.

Moreover, Protestant Orthodoxy, i.e., that teaching of right doctrine, which was characteristic especially of the Calvinists and the Lutherans, had identified religious faith with some kind of knowledge. But this knowledge, carried in doctrines and dogmatic teachings, was much too abstract to inspire religious devotion. Thus it came about that the whole doctrinal order of Orthodoxy was considered religiously faulty, because it did not engender a true elevation of mind. At the beginning of the eighteenth century there arose in all Protestant churches a movement which is labeled "Pietism," because its leaders called upon their followers to cultivate individual personal piety by way of a protest against the teachings of Orthodoxy. In the course of time there developed from this pietism a reaction against creedalism, and also an attitude which caused more and more people to identify true religion not with adherence to doctrines but with certain ways of life. To be sure, these ways of life were explained chiefly by reference to individual personal existence—what a person could accomplish under God for the salvation of his own soul. Pietism was no social movement, exercised no social public responsibility; it remained confined to the individual affairs of the human heart, but nevertheless it had the effect of weakening Orthodoxy and, together with it, the spirit of intolerance.

And then it happened gradually, but with ever greater frequency, that there spread among men a new spirit which, in the course of time, caused people to achieve a new understanding of themselves and their world. The movement which thus came into being was labeled by those who advocated it the Enlightenment, or, as the Germans called it, *Aufklaerung*. People learned to assume responsibility for their own lives, an intellectual responsibility for their own minds, relying upon the reason and the characteristic human capacity of reasonableness. They broke with the traditional authoritarianisms. And this happened in all fields, in politics and economics as well as in art, but especially in the realm of religion. Wherever, in connection with the intellectual disciplines that were now fashioned—in philosophy, mathematics, and especially the natural sciences, but gradually also in the field of history—the spirit of enlightenment deepened and expanded, men set themselves free from the conventional teachings, extricated themselves from the old dogmas and creeds, emancipated themselves from the requirements of religious and ecclesiastical conformity and uniformity.

Indeed, only now (in the course of the second part of the eighteenth century) it happened for the first time that Christian people consciously forsook the churches without publicly proclaiming that they had chosen to break with the traditional forms of the faith. They simply refused to participate in whatever the ecclesiastical institutions had come to require of them. The philosophers and thinkers who became the spokesmen of the new mind were not irreligious or un-Christian—but they were certainly not churchmen. Indeed, almost without exception they refused to identify themselves with the churches, in spiritual as well as in ecclesiastical practice. In this connection, one must think of Immanuel Kant as the most representative and influential spokesman of the Enlightenment. Kant spent all his life in Koenigsberg in East Prussia and was one of the most representative citizens of that community. He had a high sense of calling as a teacher and professor and as a scholar of science and philosophy. With greatest regularity he fulfilled all his duties as a member of the university. So Professor Kant (who until old age enjoyed good health) was always there when the university gathered for special occasions and particularly for the regular academic festivities. According to convention, academic celebrations in Koenigsberg were ended with a church service. It was customary for the professors and the students to march in procession from the university to the university church. The citizens always saw Professor Kant in his customary place in the procession. But as soon as the procession was about to enter the church, Professor Kant broke ranks and made his way to his own house, thus indicating that he would not make common cause with those who still felt it necessary to link scholarship with churchmanship.

Thus began the remarkable process (which is a characteristic phenomenon in modern Western civilization) by which many of the educated withdrew from active participation in the churches without necessarily severing thereby their links with Christianity. But insofar as they continued to be Christian, they did so in individualistic forms that satisfied their own personal religious needs. Thus it became now possible to advance a criticism of the Christian religion that was more basic than any protest that had been directed against it before. It was during the last decades of the eighteenth century that, for the first time in the history of Christendom, atheistic ideas were freely expressed. The requirements of religious uniformity, which had been imposed upon the people of the churches for so long a time, had proved so strong that the most basic antagonism against religion, namely sheer unbelief, never had a chance of gaining a following. But now at the end of the eighteenth century, this spirit of a fundamental hostility against religion itself was voiced for the first time. Atheism played a role in the French Revolution; it molded, shaped the spirit of this undertaking. Indeed, the two great bourgeois revolutions, the American Revolution and the French Revolution, embodied the principles of liberalism as they had been formulated up to that time. And insofar as these revolutions, and particularly that which brought forth the formation of the United States of America, were successful, they were a powerful inspiration to liberalism everywhere. Throughout the nineteenth century, liberals of various persuasions and active in many fields of human endeavor pointed to the declaration of human rights, which had been basic in these two revolutions and which had been given definitive form especially in the Constitution of the United States and its amendments.

Thus there gradually developed everywhere in Protestantism a freer churchmanship. But it was only by way of the consequence of the First World War, and of the several settlements of human affairs that were attempted at its end, that freedom of religion was politically and juristically guaranteed to the citizens of most European states. And although, everywhere in the world, there prevails today in some form the separation between church and state (so that finally the observance of the principle of the uniformity of religion as the source of political-social unity is undone) there still exists a co-ordination of the political order with the life of the churches in which many of the old traditions are embodied. The liberalism, which, with respect to Christianity, has assumed religious freedom, still has new fields to conquer.

It is against this background that one has to understand the rise of an intellectual movement in Protestantism which we call "liberal theology." It was the result of the rationalism of the Enlightenment insofar as it became a power in the Protestant churches. Because the churches succeeded, generally speaking, in maintaining the form they had assumed during the Reformation and fortified during the era of Orthodoxy, this liberal theology was able only slowly to make its way in organized religion. Even today the organized Protestant churches (especially in this country) are friendlier toward traditionalism (conservative theological teaching, and the doctrines of orthodoxy) than toward liberalism. Nevertheless, liberal theology is slowly gaining ground, and surely it will ultimately shape the outlook of men.

Now let me characterize the outstanding features of this liberal theology. It was given its earliest and maturest expression in the teachings of a professor of the University of Berlin, Friedrich Schleiermacher. He wrote a revolutionary theological book in 1799. He entitled it: *Speeches on Religion to Its*

Cultured Despisers. He addressed himself to those who had emancipated themselves from the ecclesiastical institutions and, in connection with this emancipation, had become despisers not only of the churches, but also of their teachings. Sympathizing with their criticisms, he endeavored to show them a way to a better understanding of religion, an understanding which would enable them to overcome not only conventional orthodoxies, but also their own doubts concerning religion and their own indolence with respect to the cultivation of its spirit.

In the course of time, Schleiermacher became a professor of theology, and he exercised the functions of this profession in connection with the duties of a regularly installed minister. He was the preacher of one of the churches in the center of Berlin. He did not identify himself with those who, because of their contempt for the religion of the churches, also broke with churchmanship. Throughout his career he was a faithful and active churchman, but precisely as such he proceeded in his theological teachings to formulate a new understanding of religion.

What he endeavored to do, one can express in the following way: He argued that in order to comprehend that whole realm which men call religion, one should not rely upon revelation —an act or event of God's self-disclosure, attested to in a special body of documents or books which, because they serve as the means of revelation, are themselves declared to be revelation. But one should rather depend upon an understanding of the nature of man's religious spirit. So Schleiermacher insisted that first of all one had to know the nature of religion. He assumed that any true definition of religion would clarify not only the mind of the living religions in general, but that of Christianity in particular. It was a revolutionary undertaking for Schleiermacher to seek to interpret Christianity not in terms of a divine revelation, but in terms of the religiousness of men; to see Christianity as one religion among others and to compare the several forms which the religious spirit had assumed among men in the course of the history of the race. He declared that religion represents a special province, a special potentiality of the human mind, namely, that by which man enters into a relationship with the universe. Indeed, he said, religion, expressing itself in many forms, is a sense and view of the universe. The Christian religion was defined by him in this formula: Christianity is a monotheistic religion of the teleological kind, in which the understanding of God and the world is determined by ends toward which everything appears to move—ends which must be understood as moral in nature. Christianity is a monotheistic religion of the teleological kind in which everything is related to Jesus of Nazareth insofar as he is man's Redeemer. As Schleiermacher saw it, Christ's inner life was determined by the fullest possible realization of religious dedication, and because of this He can be the Redeemer. Christians observe that special form of moral monotheism which distinguishes them, insofar as they are dependent upon Jesus of Nazareth as they let the impetus and influences that go out from His perfect God-consciousness shape their own religious self-consciousness.

By thus breaking with the conventional ways of theological thought, Schleiermacher made it possible to interpret religion in entirely new ways. He said that it is the theologian's task to describe the religious affections (this was the technical term he employed, meaning experiences, ideas, also practices) as they prevail in a given church at a given time and place. The theologian does not stand next to the philosopher proclaiming universal truths, but he stands next to the historian and the social leader, describing, analyzing, interpreting the religious practices and convictions as they prevail in a given group of believers. Functioning as an analyst and interpreter of the Christian religion as it prevailed in the churches he knew, Schleiermacher went on to develop an entirely new theological terminology. This terminology was inspired by modern philosophy, literature, and science, and particularly modern historiography.

Thus the beginnings were laid for theological procedures which, in the course of the nineteenth century, bore rich fruit. Christianity came now to be interpreted in terms of human values, on the basis of the best available scholarly and scientific methods of inquiry and examination. In the course of the nineteenth century, Christians, especially Protestants, thus obtained information about the development of their religion which was richer, wealthier, more fruitful than what earlier generations, even those of classical times, had owned.

The Genius of American Protestantism

In the following, I shall try to make an assessment of the present situation of American Protestantism and to indicate the direction which it may take in the immediate future. In other words, I shall describe the present situation of American Protestantism in the context of American civilization and in relation to the Protestant movement throughout the world.

First of all, something needs to be said about the genius of American Protestantism. The people of other lands, and especially the Protestants of Europe, have often tried to understand what sets American Protestantism apart from other Protestant churches in the world, and what it is that endows it with a character all its own. This difference has been noted especially in connection with the ecumenical movement and its several enterprises, during the last two decades. The Protestants of Europe observed that American Protestants seemed to be motivated by concerns that were not common to all Protestants. Some German interpreters tend to see the characteristic feature of American Protestantism in its Anglo-Saxon nature. But this certainly is a faulty characterization. Though English culture, chiefly through language and close historical influence, has indeed shaped American Protestantism, the Protestant churches of the United States are not Anglo-Saxon. They are much too cosmopolitan and varied to be linked to just one source. Others again, chiefly Continental Europeans, like to characterize American Protestantism as Calvinistic, or if not as Calvinistic, then as Puritan, as if its spirit had been developed exclusively by Calvinistic church groups. But this too is not true. In American life, Lutheranism and Anglicanism have always occupied a significant place next to Calvinism. And the free churches which are, as I shall show, the main representatives of American Protestantism really embody a special form of Christianity, though in some ways they are related to Calvinism.

What people have in mind when they describe American Protestantism as Anglo-Saxon or as Calvinistic is that in its nature something impresses them as dynamistic or activistic. These terms have been attached to American Protestantism not by its own spokesmen but by observers looking at it from the outside. And now it is indeed undeniable that, in comparison with other forms of Protestantism, particularly of the Old World, American Protestantism displays a peculiar dynamism. The traits of this can be readily identified and they manifest the peculiar genius of American Protestantism.

In all that I am about to say, I am taking for granted that the life of American Protestantism is marked by ways which are those of Protestantism generally. The Protestant churches of this country are related to classical Protestantism; and liberal Protestantism is also exhibited in it. Moreover, the various church groups that have emerged in Protestantism in connection with some issue or concern, often of a national or even local character, are represented in some of the groups that are part of American Protestantism. Nevertheless, one may, I think, generalize on the ways of American Protestants.

So then, in the first place, American Protestantism, whatever its form, is marked by the voluntary activity and cooperation of its members. No authoritarianism is constitutive of its life. Everything in it depends on voluntary participation on the part of individuals and groups. This voluntarism produces a kind of vitality which one can describe as activistic. It causes American churches to be determined largely by the concerns of the laity, so that American Protestantism is a lay movement. The interests which these people exhibit in their participation in church life are determined by the full variety of their several local, regional, and national interests. Hence, the voluntary nature of American church life has bestowed upon it a great range of activities.

Second, American Protestantism is congregationalist. This is to say that its life is concentrated in and springs from local congregations. Indeed, one of the most remarkable aspects of

American Protestant churches is that, regardless of their special heritage, polity, or organizational structure, they all concentrate their activities in the local congregations. Hence all American Protestant churches are in a very practical way congregationalist. Super- or transcongregational authorities, church presidents or bishops or synods, cannot shape the life of local congregations except by securing the voluntary cooperation of these local groups for their plans and purposes. Moreover, this congregationalism puts each local church in relation to its own environment and exposes it to the peculiar needs that its special situation presents. And thus it makes not only for a tremendous variety of enterprises but also for a great display of energy.

Third, American Protestantism is evangelistic. Each church looks to the unchurched, both here and abroad. At the time of the Revolution only 10 per cent of the people living in the American colonies were members of churches. In our own time church membership has grown, together with the general increase of population, so that today 60 per cent of the American people (if one can believe the statistics) are in some way or other identified with the churches through membership. What this means is that there have always been many who are unchurched, and their condition is the basis of all evangelistic activities. Everyone who is not of the church must be appealed to by the Christian message, and if possible he must be invited to become a church member. Out of consideration for those who may perhaps be induced to join the churches, there is produced in American Protestantism a peculiar kind of activism, namely, an aggressive and adaptable evangelism. This orientation to that which lies outside the churches has given to American Protestant life a strange dynamism.

Fourth, American Protestantism is denominationalistic. This entails consequences which come to expression in two strong features. In the first place, American Protestant Christianity is a pluralistic movement; that is to say, American Protestants are willing to recognize themselves as participants in an undertaking which in its very nature is pluralistic. Not long ago I participated in a symposium at the University of Notre Dame. The theme was "Catholicism in American Culture." A sociologist, a well-known Jesuit, offered a social-political interpretation of Roman Catholicism in this country. And he concluded by saying that no religious group could remain unaffected by the pluralism that is so characteristic of American civilization; indeed, that Protestantism had learned to come to terms with American cultural pluralism and was exhibiting a pluralism of its own. And he just raised the question whether also the Roman Church could adapt itself to American pluralism and admit into its own inner life certain pluralistic ways. This is a peculiarly American problem. But it is obvious that any spiritual movement that is pluralistic and permits the blossoming of various interests in its common life must release from itself a peculiar energy—a special form of vitality.

The second feature of denominationalism is that it exhibits a curious tension between tolerance and intolerance, and this is the source of considerable restlessness and aggressiveness. One can define denominationalism in the following manner: it is not only an ecclesiastical condition, namely, the maintenance of a variety of ecclesiastical forms, organizations, etc., but it is also a state of mind, and as such it is the peculiar relation of the members of any given denomination to themselves as a denomination and to other ecclesiastical groups. The denominations preserve and cling to special religious traditions, creeds (if they have any), liturgies, polities, moral codes, and so on, and they do this in a stubborn and even a self-satisfied way, as if no other forms of Christian faith or order existed or have the right to exist. Think, for example, of the behavior of some Lutherans, Unitarians, Presbyterians, or Episcopalians, to mention only these, who stick to their own particular traditions with a dogged determination. Have they ever taken the time to raise the question of whether there are other denominations and why they are there as other denominations? But—and this is the telling feature of denominationalism—while thus clinging to their own special religious positions, they grant to members of other denominations the right to hold and practice the same judgment concerning their beliefs, usages and conventions. Denominationalism is thus a curious combination of tolerance and intolerance. On the one hand, it reflects the exclusiveness that was characteristic of the churches when in the era prior to the establishment of religious freedom they had to conform to the requirement of religious uniformity. On the other hand, it exhibits the freedom of religious profession which was made possible when the modern state assumed a neutral attitude toward the religious faith of its members and citizens.

Under the auspices of denominationalism each church group is permitted to act as if there were no other churches in existence. But in so doing it concedes to the other churches, which do actually exist as its neighbors and rivals, the right to practice the same sort of isolationism. In other words, this attitude engenders a relativistic neutrality on the part of the denominations toward one another—a neutrality which makes it impossible for the members of any denomination to consider seriously the question whether the diversity of the churches is necessary to Christianity or not. As long as denominationalism maintains this combination of tolerance and intolerance, it kills a serious concern for the truth of Christianity, because it encourages neither self-criticism nor mutual criticism. This is the reason why denominationalism stifles theological vitality and why it fosters theological lethargy. Denominationalism as a state of mind displayed by churches and ecclesiastical groups makes for conservatism and the lethargic readiness of sustaining the status quo.

This brings me to the last and fifth characteristic of American Protestantism. It is on the whole nontheological and noncreedal. It represents, as some have said, an undogmatic Christianity. Creedal and theological interpretations of the Christian Gospel are not a major concern of American Protestants even if they belong to denominations which are traditionally creedal. Moreover, American Protestantism as a whole is most characteristically represented by those groups which exhibit the traits which I have just described, namely, these nontheological, noncreedal, even anticreedal ways. The groups which are most distinctly American are the Congregationalists, the Baptists, the Methodists, the Disciples, and the numerous evangelistic movements which have developed in more recent times. All these denominations—the Congregationalists, the Baptists, the Methodists and the Disciples—came to play their peculiar historical role on American soil. That is to say, they all came fully into a life of their own only when they were transplanted to this continent. The only truly indigenous American denomination is that of the Disciples of Christ, but the Baptists and the Methodists and also the Congregationalists have become powerful Christian movements only here in America and they grew to what they are today during the conquest of the frontier. So these denominations are the representative American Protestant churches. They have determined and still influence the life of all other denominations, though these preserve their own usages and traditions in a decisive way. But it is the Congregationalists, the Baptists, the Methodists, the Disciples and all the other groups that depend upon them or derive from them in some manner, who have made all American Protestants voluntary church members and influenced their ways of behavior so that they have become congregational, evangelical, denominational, noncreedal, and nontheological.

It is marvelous to observe, especially in view of their general indifference to creeds and doctrinal criteria, that American Protestants of the various denominations have succeeded in maintaining their identity. And they have done so by developing from within themselves a group life, a community spirit, a concern for fellowship, so that what the Christian religion inspires persons to look for as they shape their lives is carried in the common life of small local groups as well as larger regional ones. Indeed, because of these traits which are peculiar to American Protestantism and which set it apart from the churches of the Old World, American Protestantism has become, and still is, a social-religious movement.

In characterizing American Protestantism as a religious and also a social movement, we should not refrain from making the judgment that its influence is broad insofar as it penetrates all levels of cultural life, but that its impact is thin, insofar as it does not really determine the centers of decision by which the character of American civilization is being shaped. This is the conclusion at which one arrives on considering the implications of its nature as an activistic dynamism. It is always engaged in some action. Its members are always interested in making some conquest. But because they do not cultivate a definite sense of mission, largely by refusing to be theological in their outlook, they are unable decisively to form those centers of American life where the motivations of action are shaped.

As a religious-spiritual movement American Protestantism is characterized in the first place by a personalism which, to be sure, sets Protestants apart from Roman Catholic and Eastern Catholic Christians but which, in connection with the spirit of modern civilization, as manifested in the ways of Americans, tends among them to become a religious individualism and even a religious subjectivism. In other words, the emphasis upon the private nature of religion which is a feature of religious liberalism generally, but which marks the outlook of those who consciously participate in the making of American civilization, takes the form of individualism in religion, as if individual Protestants were able to determine, in reliance upon their own inner religious resources, not only what the nature of religion as a human possibility is, but also what the nature of Christianity is. This individualism, to be sure, is constantly held in check in the American Protestant groups by a strong concern for fellowship. Individual persons learn to depend upon others and adapt themselves to them, also in the spiritual concerns which they develop. Thus we may say that what characterizes American Protestantism as a spiritual movement is the manifestation of a social responsibility which is directed toward the moral character of civilization. In small and large fellowships American Protestants are always giving themselves to enterprises that are designed to improve the moral stature of civilization.

And thus it has happened that American Protestantism has assumed the character of a social-political movement. One may say that in its common life there is going on continuously a transition from spiritual to social-political interests. The spirituality of American Protestantism is an open, public one. It is identified with the major movements of American life, but certain tendencies are outstanding. In the first place, American Protestants tend to identify the democratic way of life with Protestant Christianity. In doing so, they point to the fact that some of the denominations which established themselves on American soil made, even in colonial times, a contribution to the making of that democratic order which finally assumed a political form through the American Constitution. Some Protestants even go so far as to say that American democracy is directly derived from certain left-wing groups that arose from the Reformation, and particularly from English Puritanism. It is undeniable that these Protestant groups made some contribution to the formation of American democracy, but American democracy as a whole is inspired by considerations that are not primarily religious or Christian. They are to be found in the movement of the Enlightenment. The so-called fathers of the American republic were not Protestants primarily (though, indeed, they were members of Protestant churches), but rationalists.

Nevertheless, American Protestants frequently consider themselves the spokesmen of American democracy. It is against this background that one must understand the remarkable fact that Protestant Christianity in its various denominational forms is often regarded as the faith of the leading American classes. Indeed, American Protestantism has become a middle-class movement in part in connection with its own understanding of itself, and in part through its active participation in American social-political life. The outlook of Protestants is determined largely by the interests characteristic of the middle class, and not necessarily by concerns that are identifiable as Christian. One can readily define this middle-class outlook of American Protestants especially by considering their relation to the social-political minority groups—to the Negroes, the Jews, the Roman Catholics. In the relations with all these, American Protestants experience certain tensions, some of them very strong. These tensions are determined by social-political considerations, not religious ones. And they are expressed in prejudices which are not chiefly religious but social-political and economic.

Consider, for instance, some of the judgments passed by Protestants with reference to these three groups in connection with the understanding of democracy. The Negroes emphasize the unifying, integrating tendencies of democracy—those forces in the common life which relate all men to one another regardless of differences. Because the Negroes, having been underprivileged for so long, hope to achieve status by identifying themselves with these unifying trends in democracy, they are being resisted by those with whom they must achieve equality if they are to succeed in achieving integration. Protestant churches find it exceedingly difficult in this respect to identify themselves with the hopes of Negroes. The Protestant churches' large-scale passive resistance to integration is an evidence of the fact that they are shaped in their life not by spiritual, specifically Christian motivations, but by social-political ones that are characteristic of the middle class.

In relation to the Jews other points are emphasized in a characteristic way. The Jews are unable to maintain the particular traditions they cherish except by stressing the particularistic, pluralistic tendencies which are also characteristic of democracy. On the one hand, it is an integrated, unified public order, embracing all members of society; on the other hand, it permits individual groups to remain among themselves and to stress their own peculiar ways. This paradoxical character of democracy is the secret of its great strength. Yet when the Jews insist on stressing the pluralistic possibilities of democracy which allow them to cultivate their own tradition, they are resented and accused of wanting to set themselves apart from the common life, and this judgment engenders powerful social prejudice. Insofar as it is cherished by Protestants it proves that they are shaped in their thinking not chiefly by spiritual considerations but by middle-class interests that reflect their way of identifying themselves with American democracy.

And in relation to the Roman Catholics, similar traits manifest themselves. Roman Catholicism is a priestly-sacramental form of Christianity and it does not allow the practice of religion except in relation to the priestly-sacramental church. So the priesthood is a spiritual necessity in Roman Catholicism. No Catholic can be a Christian apart from a priest. But this authoritarianism which, to be sure, sometimes expresses itself in social-political ways, is regarded by many American Protestants as politically authoritarian in its very nature, and, on this account, Roman Catholics are suspected of not being able to support the freedoms characteristic of democracy. This too is a prejudice which is inspired not by religious but by political, middle-class considerations.

In conclusion, a few words about some of the main problems which are in the center of contemporary American Protestant life. There is first of all the problem of the relation between religion and civilization—the problem of secularism. As I have suggested, modern civilization has become widely emancipated from religion—certainly from the churches. The churches which, once upon a time, were located in the very center of the common life have now been pushed to the fringes. This has made for a large-scale secularization. Many people, even those who nominally belong to churches and religious organizations, are no longer led in their thinking by religious motivations. Thus alternative gospels of salvation have come to appeal to people. In this country, the democratic spirit, nationalism, and scientific humanism have assumed the status of alternative gospels. Especially scientific humanism and nationalism appeal to many people as if they were endowed with a religious power, i.e., the possibility of bestowing salvation upon their followers. But it is a remarkable fact that none of these alternate gospels has so far succeeded in displacing Christianity.

In other parts of the world, especially in Europe, the situation of the churches is much more perilous than it is here. In most European countries the churches have become minority movements. But even there Christianity has not been displaced as the religion of the people of the West. There is no prospect in this country that Christianity will be undone. However, Christianity has been pushed into a position of defense. Hence, Protestants have come to insist that their peculiar religious resources must be freshly cultivated, and in this concern for the religious resources, certain judgments have been made. For instance, one has come to see the insufficiency of the conflict between fundamentalism and modernism, orthodoxy and liberalism, which has shaped the thinking of so many American Protestants for more than a generation. Fundamentalism denies the validity of the achievements of science and wraps up the essential truths of Christianity in obscurantism. Modernism, on the other hand, is inclined to sacrifice Christian insights insofar as its spokesmen try to prove that their thinking renders Christianity intellectually respectable. They treat religion as if the methods of science could be applied also to religion, as if moral progress could be determined by some kind of scientific outlook. But this is not so. Religion occupies a province of its own in individual life and in civilization. One cannot rightly make it subject to other interests and considerations.

Hence, American Protestants have been led to look to other sources for the renewal of their life. There is taking place some kind of a theological revival. Many American Protestants have come to conclude that noncreedalism and the neglect of theology reflect a weakness. And so we find ourselves confronted today with movements that bring to life a new Biblical theology. Moreover, the teachings of the Protestant Reformers and of certain theological spokesmen of modern Protestantism, Kierkegaard, for instance, find many followers. Others turn to liturgy and to devotional life and hope to derive therefrom a renewal of faith. Faced by secularism, many Protestants advocate a closing of ranks with all who are the spokesmen of religion. This makes for a wide religious co-operation also between Protestants and Roman Catholics, and Protestants and Jews. The same spirit has fostered interdenominationalism, and what is still more important, a concern for a world-wide unity of Christendom.

From these undertakings there may ultimately be brought forth some genuine renewal which may transform conventional American Protestantism and give it an entirely new character.

The Past and Future of Eschatological Thinking

ARTHUR A. COHEN

Characteristics of Eschatological Thinking

ESCHATOLOGY is the doctrine of "the last things." Simply construed, eschatology interprets that moment at which the phenomenal world—the world of time and space, nature and history—comes to an end. Violently construed, the *eschaton*, the ultimate moment, marks the destruction of terrestrial history and the advent of the reign of God.

At the same time, however, that we make mention of "last things" we should hasten to add that this rendering of the Greek term *eschaton* is already a definition which limits and interprets as it defines, for to speak of "last things"—however vague and imprecise and uncompromising this may seem—is already a *view* of eschatology. Implicit to our understanding of "last things" is a concentrated focus upon the end of the commonplace world with which our life is ordinarily preoccupied; moreover, this focus ignores the crucial fact in our Western understanding of eschatology that these last things are not last in the sense of being end-moments in a linear historical progression, but last because, through an action external to it (a juncture of the terrestrial and the extraterrestrial), an end-event occurs. It is more proper therefore to speak of eschatology as the doctrine of "the last event," for the word *event* suggests an action, not simply a state of being—an action, moreover, which is prefigured and anticipated throughout the course of history and has, therefore, special meaning for those who have awaited it.

What, then, are the characteristics of the eschatological event? (1) It is either one single event radically juxtaposed and unrelated to all previous historical events, or a culminating event, prefigured and formed by all previous historical events; (2) it is an event which occurs within the order of time and space, or else is an ultimate event which crystallizes at the same time that it annihilates time and space; (3) it is a "relational" event which is internally connected with everything historical; (4) it is an event which is "meaningful," for it interprets history for the historian (and here we consider every man a historian who reflects upon historical events with a view to self-understanding), or it is an event which, in more radical eschatological doctrine, explicates the meaning of all history, suggests that toward which history has been directed and for which purposes it has been intended; (5) and, last, whether the eschatological event occurs many times or is, as classic eschatologists thought, a single and irrevocable event, it is nevertheless a symbolic event which points *really* to that which transcends history and is its ground. It is symbolic for the simple reason that if it occurs many times, it becomes eschatological only for the believer who seeks within it the prefigurings of the consummation for which faith longs and if it is a single, cataclysmic event there is no judge who survives to estimate whether expectation and occurrence conform—whether such images as the reign of God, the judgment of history, the transfiguration of the saved, the resurrection of the dead indeed occur. Eschatology is thus mythological doctrine which undoubtedly beclouds and conceals a true symbolic assertion regarding man's locus in history, God's relation to history, and the community of man and God in the transformation of history.

These are the elements of eschatological doctrine—a view of man, the immersion of man in historical time and natural space, the seeking of man to locate himself beyond the flux and relativities of time and the static positioning of space, the conviction that as God confirms man's faith, He also authenticates the entelechy and goal of history. Eschatology is that doctrine, therefore, which unites man's trust in God with man's equally considerable passion to invest history with meaning. Narrowly conceived, there has been only one great age of eschatological thinking—the period of late Jewish prophetic and apocalyptic thought (from Deutero-Isaiah through the Book of Daniel and immediately thereafter) and early Christian apocalypticism reflected in the Gospels and the Pauline literature. Although subsequent revivals of eschatological thinking were to recur with man's reflections on historical disasters past and to come (St. Augustine, Martin Luther, and to a lesser extent in our own day), pure and unrationalized eschatology is a phenomenon of the Hebrew Bible, the Gospels, and the Epistles. All eschatological thinking, which follows this earliest and pristine period, is characterized by an effort to come to terms with the predicaments created by the image of man and history which it had projected, and the failure of God to confirm its expectation. All post-Scriptural eschatology is limited to a commentary upon the failure of Scriptural eschatology. This is a critical weakness of eschatological thinking which would seem to make all modern efforts at its renewal unavoidably barren and unproductive, for if the conditions of discourse are limited to a fixed and final historical event which is long since past, eschatological thinking is perforce restricted to the commentary and interpretation of a single, penultimate historical event. Eschatological thinking cannot, under such limitations, arise out of the present moment to confront the future with fresh insight unless the Bible is understood less as a finality than as an open and figural adumbration of the future.[1]

[1] This has the effect, if accomplished, of changing one's approach to the Bible from that of either a literal fideism or formal rationalism into

The unfortunate penalty which is paid for limiting historical eschatology to the short period which compasses the late books of the Hebrew Bible and the New Testament is that eschatology is essentially a special (however radical and specific) example of the metaphysics of history. As long as there is an effort to interpret the character and causality of history, there is an equally profound effort to define its meaning and purpose. The metaphysics of history (less a metaphysics of the historical event than a metaphysics of man, the creature who is preeminently historical) is prior to the emergence of eschatology, for the understanding of man's historicity precedes both in time and being the specific constructions of eschatology. The books of the Bible which announce and develop the providential course and development of the people of Israel take the historicity of man for granted. The convocation of the Hebrew people carries with it, beside all other commandments, the implicit and assumed "commandment" that the Hebrew understand himself as a creature of history—always liable to the temptations and possibilities of the historical moment, always open to the corrosive influence of the alien and the demanding corrective of God, always sensitized to the manner in which nature and history are interwoven by God to reward and chastise his activity. Hebrew thinking until the Babylonian exile was historical, although not eschatological. It always interpreted history—seeking out its origin and consequence—although its understanding of Providence was rooted in the finitude of life and the exigencies of its natural and political environment. The Hebrew view of history which prepared for and shaped the eschatology which would arise out of catastrophe was oriented to immanent fulfillment within history. But such was a metaphysics of history. However implicit and unexpressed, the Hebrew understanding of man was formed by categories which defined and interpreted the historicity of man. The Hebrew metaphysics of history raised questions which

---

the kind of approach which Bultmann, in one way, describes as the attitude of hermeneutics or which we have described as the way of "existential dogma" (cf. *The Natural and the Supernatural Jew: An Historical and Theological Introduction*, Pantheon, New York, 1962, Introduction).

would later become central to eschatology, for it wondered about the goal and destiny of its historical life. It matters little whether its understanding of history was as precisely formed by eschatological concerns as was the Apocalypse of Daniel or St. Paul's letter to the Romans; what matters is that any effort to define the meaning and goal of history (however much that meaning and goal may be understood to be rooted in the immanent movement of events) gives reality and significance to eschatological interpretations.

What differentiates eschatology from the philosophy of history (distinguished justifiably from the metaphysics of history), what permits it to share more in common with metaphysical speculation than with traditional rational and empirical philosophy, is that eschatology seeks not only the external form and observable causality of history, but also its internal spirit. Eschatology seeks to penetrate the shapes and constellations of historical events to the inner spirit which may be called their freedom. Freedom is at the heart of history—it matters little that man is a creature bound to his historical condition, that acting man is historical man, if the source of his action is not free. However much man may be linked to nature, however much he may be a highly sophisticated product of nature, when he acts he transcends his connection to nature, he exceeds his coterminal connection with his environment, he becomes historical and he becomes free.

A Short History of Eschatological Thinking

Modern eschatology, such as it is, is the bearer of two traditions—the tradition of classic eschatology, which is marked and stamped with failure, and the idea of history, as it developed following the disappointment of eschatological expectation.

The sense of history, however immanent and anchored in the thought of Biblical man, was not explicit as doctrine. History as a concept is not Biblical, but history as a reality suffuses the Bible. The Biblical historical sense prepared the way for the eschatological expectations of the late Hebrew tradition and its rabbinic legatees as well as for the early Christians. The eschatological sense was a special historical sense, a crystallization and condensation of the historical sense, a sharpening and focusing of the whole of history to a single point, a transformation of the psychological temper from awareness and exposure to all history as the bearer of hope to the anticipation of a single event which would eclipse all previous history and consummate it.

The oldest tracings of the sense of history do not appear as historical thinking, but as myth. Such myths are devised and transmitted to give coherence to what is not yet coherent, to structure and organize a universe for which no instruments of interpretation are available. The Babylonian cosmogonies, much like the myths of Sudanese tribesmen, or those of the peoples of New Guinea, or the aborigines of Australia, are means of coming to terms with the essential processes of nature, the mysterious fact of existence, and the psychological necessities which provoke men to the remarkably human effort to explain the fact of their own life. Such myths bear resemblance to history because they narrate events which connect man's own origins with supernatural personalities who lived, loved, died, and were reborn in them.

It is only when a people coheres into a nation, acquiring in addition to a divine lineage a lineage of historical events, that consciousness gives birth to historical memory. In the ancient world the myths of the Greeks or the narratives of the Assyrian kings center upon memorable events, important personages, heroic deeds—the recollection of these invest the routine of days with the emphatic underscoring of the poetic imagination. It is no longer mythological history; it is history so mixed with poetry that we properly describe it as epic. Epic does not have the purpose of simply providing a record of human acts, but rather of testifying to the grandeur of human origins.

In its earliest moments mythology may be polarized and contrasted with eschatology. Where the most ancient myths of man concern his origins and beginnings, eschatological mythologies concern his end—less the terror of death than the mystery of life agitates the most primitive level of the human psyche (it is for this reason that many primitive cultures cannot really believe, as Ernst Cassirer has noted, in the reality of death). Clearly, however, there can be no history if the only speculation is upon events that signalize the origin of man or on discrete and exemplary occurrences which reassure man of the importance of his beginnings. There can be historical thinking only when man becomes aware of his own finitude and of his own death, for death is every man's *eschaton.*

HISTORY ACCORDING TO HERODOTUS AND THUCYDIDES

Herodotus undertook to recount the history of the Greeks, as he observes, "lest the deeds of men should fade in the course of time, and the great and marvelous works which Greeks and Barbarians have performed should be without glory, and especially for what reason they carried on war against each other." The role of the historian at this early moment in Western civilization is to provide memory with the promptings and recollections of human achievement which enable it to supplement the instruction of the moralist with the evidence of history. And it could not be otherwise, for the Greek understood man to be embedded in nature, a sophistication and specialization of principles found in nature. Since man was a natural creature, his acts were to be investigated with the same degree of precision and with a view to the same degree of clarity as the investigation of any natural phenomenon. In such a view history could not be distinguished from nature, other than for the common observation that historical phenomena, being essentially transitory and subject to the caprice of memory, were less worthy objects of study. Since every practical science had as its end the education of virtue, the historical memory could be useful if it aided the formation of character. However, since history is an imprecise science, it is less serviceable even than poetry, for where poetry imitates discriminable human actions, distributing praise and blame according to merit, it is more difficult to determine the specifics of historical action and therefore more difficult to employ history in the instruction of man.

Since history was written in order that Herodotus might recollect the great and glorious works of man, the role of the gods was limited to their participation in the unfolding or inhibition of human purpose. The gods function in Herodotus as but secondary glosses upon otherwise palpably human activity; they are treated as so many agents, among other agents, of human activity. To be sure, they define the ever present background of fate to which both gods and mortals were liable, but they play a less significant role in the history of Herodotus than they earlier played in Greek popular religion and mythology. However, where Herodotus will permit the gods to chasten and correct, Thucydides succumbs to no such temptation. For him the action of history is wholly analogous to that of the cosmos; change is but the same reality appearing amid a new constellation of events—each element is the same, although the arrangement and patterning of history may vary.

The historiography of Herodotus and Thucydides is turned toward the past, not toward the future. The value of history consists in learning the lessons of the past in order that the past might be glorified in the memory of the living and imitated in the character and action of men. It is not concerned with informing man's attitude toward the future. The future could have little significance for a civilization which conceived the universe to be without beginning and end, whose understanding of freedom was inhibited by fate, whose orientation was to the imitation of the perfections of nature, and which believed that the practice of virtue could ensure the sufficient happiness of the wise.

HISTORY ACCORDING TO THE HEBREW BIBLE

A different, indeed radically different, sense of history informs the Scriptures of ancient Israel. The Bible commences with the assumption that a most privileged people is therefore the most likely to err. Where for the Greek, *hubris* is a defect of the individual, among the Hebrews the danger of excess and transgression is collectivized and ascribed to the entire people. Biblical history is recounted, therefore, not to improve the political counsels of its leaders or to sophisticate the moral judgments of its priests, but to instruct the whole nation. Even in the earlier Jahwist and Elohist histories of the Bible, history is narrated with some view of its unifying end—the integration of the nation in fulfillment of divine promise to the Patriarchs. In the later books of the Bible, the antiphon most characteristic of the Hebrew view of history becomes emphatic —divine instruction and human waywardness, divine warning and human transgression, man's disobedience and sin and God's justice and remission of sin, man's penance and God's forgiveness.

With the intrusion of the prophetic witness into the Biblical canon, the focus of error and forgiveness is as sharpened as it is broadened. No longer Israel, the single people—isolated and unconnected—but the people as a vehicle of world history comes under the dominion of God. Israel is transformed by even the most ardently nationalistic prophets into a viaticum of all history. The first glimmerings of paradigmatic history, inner history (as contrasted with the external flow of events) emerges. The connection and obligation of Israel to Assyria, Babylon, and Egypt, Phoenicia and the lands beyond the seas comes to the fore. It does not come to the center merely because Israel has had dealings with these nations, has conquered or been conquered by them; but rather because it begins to understand its place in history not as one in which terrestrial triumph or defeat really matters, but as one in which right and wrong action shift the divine balance to the side of justice or mercy.

The ancient Hebrew believed that what he did mattered to God and what God desired mattered to history. This interconnection was an authentic novelty. History ceased to be an analogue to nature and became a unity fashioned by rubrics of action and conduct whose origin could not be construed as historical. The God of Israel, unlike the gods of paganism, did not hover over nature, inserting himself into nature to sport with or discomfit the pretensions of man; God was immanent as a person addressing persons (and as such within nature) and transcendent as author, instructor, director, and counselor to history (and as such beyond nature).

The Hebrew view of history is not yet eschatology, but it already pre-empts the characteristic modes of any metaphysics of history. These modes are not stated as such because the Hebrew mind abhorred abstraction; but, in its insistence upon the interconnection and unity of historical events—both horizontally as they unfold from the creation and accompany the gathering and integration of the Hebrew peoples—and vertically—as God enters history to express its potency and possibility—a metaphysical view of history has been affirmed. It is a metaphysics which cannot, however, conceive of history as a simple whole. Since the understanding of history is complicated for the Hebrew by his incommensurability with God, he can speak of the wholeness of history synoptically and synthetically, but never completely: *synoptically* in that man, in his unaided finitude, can only distill meaning from memory and *synthetically* in that, with the revealed perspective of God, he is availed of the principles with which to clarify his apprehension of providence.

ESCHATOLOGY WITHOUT THE END: JEWISH APOCALYPTICISM

The idea of the *eschaton* enters man's reflections upon history at that moment at which he is prepared to accept the requirement of completion and perfection while acknowledging the retrogressive and sinful capacities of his nature. At such moments man shifts his focus from creation to salvation, from origin to end, from life to death. It is no wonder that for the Hebrew, death was utterly final and unmitigated as long as history was seen as a process which emerged, with creation, out of chaos. It is equally no wonder that the Hebrew view of history was dialectical, an alternation of divine demand and human response, essentially incomplete and uncompletable. The dimension of the eschatological entered Hebrew thought following the catastrophic Babylonian exile. The Babylonian exile registered two authoritative dissents from a simplistic dialectic: it affirmed that God not only could but would use *all* of history to bring his elected people to his service and, second, it introduced into the historic consciousness the awareness that history suffers from violent quakes and dislocations which anticipate and prefigure a consummate end. Henceforth not the interlocutions of the patriarchs with God or the judges and kings of Israel with God, but the whole people and all of history would be incorporated into the schema of providence.

Eschatology is, Rudolf Bultmann has suggested, the product of cosmic mythology historicized. It emerges as a result of man's transference of the periodicity of nature—the cycle of the seasons, the course of the heavens, the generation and destruction of natural life—to the sphere of history. If spring is born and dies amid the snow, if the sun rises and disappears, if the flower buds and decays, why is not human life, culture, society, indeed history, similarly patterned to be born and to die? The cyclical movement of time and nature, a view common to the Greek and Hellenistic world, was first rationalized in Greek science and historicized in late Jewish thinking. The Book of Daniel, for example, develops the idea of the four kingdoms to suggest the rise and degeneration of humanity. This notion of Daniel has its clear basis in Babylonian tradition according to which each era is ruled by an astral deity who is fashioned from a different metal (Daniel 2). With Daniel is born that most eschatological idea of the two kingdoms—the kingdom of history in which Israel vanquishes its enemies (the kingdom of terrestrial salvation) and the prior history of the world before the era of salvation commences, in which Israel is subject and on sufferance (the kingdom of evil). This dualism, later developed by Jewish Apocalypticism, is taken up by St. Paul, defined more radically again by Marcion and the gnostics, and restored in yet a different form by St. Augustine. But the Book of Daniel is not only an atypical document of late Judaism; it is also not yet an eschatology formed by insights and categories which came to make the eschatological sense of Christianity. Bultmann is therefore right in affirming that "in the Old Testament there is no eschatology in the true sense of a doctrine of the end of the world and a succeeding time of salvation." The question which one might ask is whether true eschatology need be Christian. Is the truth of eschatological doctrine its accommodation to established historical models (in which case Bultmann is surely correct) or its appropriateness to the condition of man and history? [2]

The dualism of the two kingdoms according to Daniel is, it

[2] If the latter, as we believe, it is really not possible to develop an eschatology unless one is also prepared to develope a doctrine of the interrelation of God, man, and history. Although we do not avoid this problem we have tried toward the end of this essay as well as in the closing chapter of our book, *The Natural and the Supernatural Jew* (*op. cit.*) to define some of the conditions of Jewish eschatology.

is well known, radicalized by Christian thought in its unexpurgated polarity of the God of salvation and the God of creation. Such a polarity is essentially alien to Judaism. The God of the Hebrew Bible does indeed judge and redeem, but it is judgment and redemption within history, not upon it. God always appears to act within the moment and never external to it. This, of course, creates enormous weakness of doctrine, for history is never conceived in Judaism to be closed or ended—as such, it is really impossible to speak of history other than synoptically or synthetically as we have suggested, but never completely. As long as the consummation of history is historical, there is no judgment beyond history other than the disclosures of revelation to history. This would seem to compromise Jewish messianism, indeed the Jewish doctrine of salvation, for the messiah comes to work in history and salvation is salvation of historical time. The messianic accession is never in Jewish thought (with the exception of works such as the Book of Daniel and not even truly there) an end of history. But this weakness—and it is a weakness which leads to incredible mythologizing of both the Jewish nation and the messianic age—is compensated for by an honest and convincing realism. Judaism must always explain to itself the defeats of history, and its explanation is always crudely dependent upon the assumption of divine punishment and exculpation. It does not, however, have to explain why history goes on even though the virtual "end of history" has come. Even though the eccentric German scholar, Hans Joachim Schoeps, believes this claim of strength to be a naïve argument against Pauline theology, it is a gravely serious one: according to Jewish lights there is no caesura in history which requires that an antihistorical dogma be set into the center of ongoing historical life.[3]

[3] "We do not perceive any caesura in history. We recognize in it no middle term, but only an end, the end of God's ways, and we believe that God does not interrupt his course. For us redemption is indissolubly one with the consummation of creation, with the establishment of the divine unity, no longer frustrated, suffering no contradiction, realized in the multiplicity of the world, one with the fulfilled sovereignty of God. We are unable to understand the idea of an anticipation of this consummation experience by one section of humanity, whose souls are already redeemed." Martin Buber, *Die Stunde und die Erkentnis*, Schocken Verlag, Berlin, 1936, pp. 153 f.

It is crucial to recognize that the nature and interpretation of history—enmeshed as it is in the fixities of space and the rush of time—are inseparable from the nature and understanding of eschatology. In its beginnings the doctrine of history was but an unconscious distillation from the doctrines of eschatology—the preprophetic and prophetic view of the covenanted relation of man and God and the anticipation of God's righteous rule through His anointed is eschatological teaching which reveals the Hebrew doctrine of history. At this moment, centuries and philosophies later, the recovery of the eschatological sense is brought about only through a rethinking of our understanding of history. Depending upon where one stands (whether one takes history as the stage upon which the intimacies of the divine-human encounter are played out or whether one takes history as the self-contained and self-interpreting whole for which all transcending exegesis is captious, false, and mythological) one has history with eschatology or history without eschatology. But whichever way one speaks of history one asks about its purpose and meaning (which is virtually to ask an eschatological question) and if one asks about the eschaton one is deeply and inextricably involved in history. It follows then that any doctrine of the end which severs the ending from the process which it ends (as did those paradoxes which juxtaposed the pure to the impure eons or the formalistic views which speak of the end as an act of supernature without connection with the nature which it consummates) is false. The beginning in creation and the end in salvation must unfold through history. It is with the matter of history that God must deal, for in creation he created the drama of history and in the eschaton he completes that drama—but between beginning and end the drama must be played.

Apocalyptic Judaism—a Judaism already heavily infiltrated by Iranian dualism and Hellenistic anxiety—expanded the idea of the two eons, the two kingdoms, and the two ages into an authentic eschatology. This apocalypticism, however, did not establish itself in the synagogue nor did it come to shape the basic emphases of the rabbinic mind other than by sharpening and accenting the alienation of apocalyptic movements from normative Judaism. According to apocalyptic eschatology—as it is found represented in IV Ezra, the Syriac Baruch, the Psalms of Solomon and such literature, the individual is spun out of the community to fend for his own salvation—and he fends well, for he is assured that when the final judgment comes he will be judged according to his own merit, that the community of the elect and sanctified will be ransomed from the fire, and that he will be among them. In such a view God no longer redeems the righteous community, raising up the individual to the perfection of his fellowship, but rather the individual in the age of apocalypse is splintered off from the community to work out his own salvation.

The ambiance of the first-century apocalyptic eschatology into which Jesus of Nazareth was born was not a single community of common mind and undivided attitude. Over and against the apocalyptists who feared death and despaired of redemption within history there were many tens of thousands of the House of Israel who were satisfied to give pleasure to God, to do His work, and leave the Day of the Lord to his own devising. This quiet Pharisaism, long unknown and still unknown, remains an enduring counterbalance to the common impression of a first-century world full of agitation, enthusiasm, and the sense of defeat.

EARLY CHRISTIANITY

In the New Testament, although the view of history defined by the Hebrew Bible is preserved, the apocalyptic view prevails. It is presently held, with reasonably unanimous agreement, that the reign of God which Jesus announced is the eschatological reign. The only question still open is whether Jesus believed that the reign of God was *shortly* to arrive or whether the advent of the *eschaton* was imminent or fulfilled in his own life, ministry, and death. There is little doubt but that Jesus believed that the attitude of others toward him was decisive—that is, that they were marked off or included in the imminent Kingdom by the position which they assumed toward him (Mark 2:18; Luke 10:18, 10:23 f.). But at the same time as Jesus saw his own generation to be "adulterous and sinful" (Mark 8:38) he affirmed that those elected by grace to believe in Him would be saved. Unlike the late prophets of

Israel, such as Isaiah and Deutero-Isaiah, he did not project the future of history beyond his own age to an age yet to come. His was, at least in the pristine sense of his teaching, the penultimate era which would be followed by the end, the resurrection of the dead, the salvation of his disciples, and divine judgment upon the unfaithful. The teaching of Jesus, however much it may be but a radicalization of prophetic tradition, is not to be understood—as Martin Buber has—as one of the suffering servants concealed in the unfathomable resource of divine instruction (to be hidden or revealed for the illumination of history), for Jesus, unlike the prophets, held out no hope to the future of man. His age, Jesus seems to affirm, was the consummating age and, if he be prophet, he is the last (and therefore truly no prophet, for there is no future to come).

In the rhythm of the narrative of the Gospels, Jesus ministers, is apprehended, tried, judged, crucified, and on the third day, according to the testimony of those who saw the empty tomb and were visited by him in posthumous revelation, he rose to glory to pass judgment upon man and the nations. It is here, upon this structure of quasihistorical recitation, that the problematic of Christian eschatology begins. For with Jesus came not the End, and after Jesus the End was still awaited, and beyond the end of waiting a new image was demanded which would justify the continuing demand of the End, while rationalizing its failure to occur.

The Christian community that was born between the death of Jesus and the elaboration of Pauline Christianity was not a continuation of the Jewish community. At the same time as Western investment in "the Judeo-Christian tradition" continues to accumulate, it should be noted that for the Jew there is not (rightly understood) such a tradition and for the Christian what is taken as Jewish is either a caricature of Judaism or a new construction of it. In neither alternative is there essential connection, although both communities survive the demands and exactions which each makes upon the other. The Christian community conceived itself for but a short time as bound by ties of lineage and genealogy to the community out of which it grew. Such ethnic connection evidently proved to be as hobbling to the new Church as it proved illusory and deceiving to the Jew. In seeing itself as a branch fashioned by God and grafted upon the stock of Israel, Paul expresses the exquisite irony and seriousness of Christianity's nexus with Judaism (Romans 11:23–24). The entire tradition of Israel is now to be read with the light that glows from the new eon, which illumines the shadowings and limnings of Christian possibility in the history of the Hebrews. The covenanted and elect community of Israel is sustained less by the cognition of its independent reality or as an eschatological countervalence than as a pious history full of allusion and animadversion to Christian promises.

Bultmann rightly describes the early Christian community as follows: "*The new people of God* has no real history, for it is the community of the end-time, an eschatological phenomenon."[4] With such a view it is no wonder that the ethical injunctions of Jesus and the moral teachings of the Gospels sustain the force of traditional Judaism, for in the between-time which separates the incarnation from the end, positive Judaism remains binding, while only preparatory fasts and abstinences are introduced to ready the believer for the consummation. The intervening ethic of the early Christian community is unoriginal (nor need it have been, given its eschatological preoccupation). Even Christian love is directionless, for it is not formed by specific tasks and obligations—it is a pure generality. And so it must be, for one cannot love and serve and work for a creation and a history which is shortly to be overwhelmed. In short, for early Christianity eschatology consumed history.

Jesus did not return. However Mark (13:30–37) and II Peter (3:4) move to interpret the delay, their gentle explanations fall leaden upon hearts that await the parousia in each instant. It is to this predicament of Christianity that the Pauline and Johannine answers are directed.

Since history up to the Incarnation and crucifixion is, according to Paul, a history of sin, there can be no natural unfolding and natural correction of history. History is not self-

[4] Rudolf Bultmann, *History and Eschatology*, The University Press, Edinburgh, 1957, p. 36.

regenerative. If it could restore itself, Paul reasons, it would have no need of incarnate grace nor could it accept and rationalize the grotesque death of its redeemer. History must end and its end must be brought about external to the processes of history. The goal of history is no longer within history but beyond it. God must end history to confirm Jesus as Christ. But this end, even though it cannot be founded upon historical events nor apprehended by a philosophy of history, is nevertheless given to history. God confers meaning upon history in the sense that he required the eon of sin that it might ache for the eon of grace. This bizarre—and to our view incomprehensible—Pauline dualism arises less from Pauline theology, strictly taken, than from Pauline anthropology. Jesus to be Christ does not necessitate the Pauline view of history, but rather the Pauline view of history necessitates Jesus as Christ. Paul's suspicion and contempt for the pretensions of man to fulfill the will of God requires that man be given over to sin that he might be ransomed by the grace which he believed to be in Jesus Christ. It is out of this Pauline polarity of the kingdom of the fallen Adam (ruled by the Law and condemned to sin) and the kingdom of Christ (ruled by a most unpolitical and impolitic grace) that the precious paradoxes of Christian faith arise.

The anthropology of Paul is possible only because he is deeply sensitive to the historicity of man. Man is a creation who acts and whose action before God defines him as either free or in bondage. If he imagines that he is ever liberated from his past subjection to sin, he is without grace; it is only when he recognizes that he can never relinquish his past, that he must make his peace with it and come to each new situation in order that he might become a new being before his future—without illusion and self-deception—that he achieves freedom and grace. Man's historical life is validated by faith. Thus, for Paul, history and grace become intertwined. The Pauline solution to the delay of the parousia of Christ is based upon man's historicity, upon man's having to satisfy the demands of renewal in the historical situation.

In the between-time which separates the believer coming to believe and the parousia what happens might be termed the routinization of eschatology (routine being understood as the renewed sense of continuous and unending historical life). History must now go on between the eschatological event past and the eschatological event anticipated. At the same time the believer must be sustained and comforted, assured and confirmed—and out of this human demand to support historical life in the between-time the sacramental system of Christianity emerges. The sacrament links the past and the future, taking both in one. But centuries elapsed and the enthusiasm which greeted Pauline expectation was institutionalized. The Church looked to its own history, became part of the world, wedded itself to the world in order to survive the world and, in the course of time, passed its eschatological enthusiasm through the wringers and dampers of historical vicissitude.

THE NEUTRALIZATION OF ESCHATOLOGY

St. Augustine's argument in *The City of God* provides the clue to the secularization of eschatology in the Age of Enlightenment. Augustine sets the drama of salvation on the stage of history—it is not God outside and beyond history, but God amid history who effects the achievement of its ends; moreover, history is now fashioned out of the human decision and the decisive event. The struggle between the terrestrial city and the city of God could be likened to the teleological view of history constructed by the ancients to provide the groundwork for a wholly secular view of history, for the struggle of the two cities could be reinterpreted—as it was—to mean that man had lost sight of virtue, fallen into ignorance and lust, but was freed from these by the rediscovery of reason and right conduct. This view, secularizing as it does the Augustinian view, is joined with a teleology which describes the tension of history as the struggle of the irrational forces in man and nature with science and rational understanding.

In the *Scienza Nuova* of Giambattista Vico the idea of a goal and consummation of history is eliminated. In its place the thesis of *course* and *recurrence* (*corso e ricorso*) comes to define the push and movement of history replacing the activity of divine intelligence. Indeed, Vico—pious son of the Church though he was—eliminates God from history. Having fulfilled the task of inseminating history with a natural light, Vico is able to relinquish history to unfold according to a natural, rational, internal logic.

Immanuel Kant, although preserving the idea of a teleology of history, considers its *telos* to be wholly immanent, to be the achievement of a rational and moral society within history. Pressing further along the same path, Hegel preserved the Christian understanding of history as an integral unity, but abandons any notion of Providence as being insufficiently rational. The divine plan which imparts unity to history is imposed by the Absolute Mind which passes, not through the neat cycles of Vico toward its end, but through the agonies of affirmation, denial, and synthetic reconciliation. History is a tension of events pressing toward unity and self-clarification. The goal of history is not in the remote future but in the process whereby history and absolute mind come to unity. The Christian moment in history is considered by Hegel to be absolute religion, because in Christ the unity of mind and history is prefigured.

The Hegelian metaphysical dialectic is transformed into dialectical materialism by Karl Marx. Marx retains the dialectical movement, but makes matter rather than mind its fundamental substance—matter here understood as those powers and forces in society and nature which are subject to an inexorable causation. Marx separates history from nature—a separation he could more effectively perform than could Hegel—for Marx sees the motives of historical events in the matter of socioeconomic life, not in the whole play of human forces which includes man's natural and biological life along with his social and intellectual life. All historical forms are seen by Marx as ideological masquerades which seek to perpetuate injustice and corruption. Only through their destruction by an undeluding materialism could a "Kingdom of God" without God be instituted. Historical materialism completes the secularization of eschatology.

The line which runs from Vico through Marx defines a secularization of eschatology through the devices of idealism—a running of the course from idealism to its antipode in materialism. There is, however, a countertrend of secularization which emerges from the doctrine of progress. Although, to be sure, an affirmation of progress is made by both Hegel and Marx, the notion of man's uninterrupted move toward a terrestrial utopia is more properly located in the Enlightenment of the eighteenth century in France. The faith in unlimited progress originated in a polemic against the Biblical understanding of Providence. Even before Voltaire sought to deliver the West from a Christian teleology of history, Fontenelle (1657–1757) had tried in his *Origin of Fables* to demonstrate the questionable foundations upon which the fantasies of Providence were founded.[5] Indeed, the tradition of humane reason—a Stoic tradition which is renewed in Erasmus and later in Montaigne, Montesquieu, Fontenelle and the notable enlighteners of the eighteenth century—had long insisted that much which religion imports into history reason might justifiably debunk. What begins as an insistence that reason be allowed to vacate the cobwebs of superstition ends with the insistence that reason replace Providence, that reason become its own lawmaker, its own Providence, and finally in Comte's temples of reason, its own divinity. Voltaire, Turgot, Condorcet, and later Comte and Saint Simon sustain a tradition in which the perfection of science and the accumulation of knowledge will enable man properly to assess his past, learn its lessons, and perfect his future. Although the idea of the unity of history is preserved, Providence is dispatched in favor of a secular version of the teleology of history, which consists in progress promoted by science; and eschatological perfection is secularized to mean the increasingly abundant comfort, security, and wisdom of mankind.

THE PRESENT CONDITION OF ESCHATOLOGICAL THINKING

History outlives its modes of exegesis and interpretation. Reason has not brought us to perfection nor has an immanent divinity (whether it be mind or the entelechy of society) realized the unity which it presumed. Views of history in which the goal is itself part of the historical process have not proved notably fruitful; nor have eschatological doctrines

[5] See Albert Salomon's discussion of Fontenelle in his book, *In Praise of Enlightenment*, Meridian Books, New York, 1963.

proved serviceable or meaningful. We are left, as we were before, with incomplete history. And yet in this particular aberrant age it has become ever more relevant to ask, to what end is history? May man acquire from history a meaning and instruction? Does history express a formal structure, a unity, a *telos?* Does history point itself to an end-moment or does God fashion, in His own good time, an end-moment to history? This is only to ask, is eschatological thinking relevant? Are the elaborate structures which apocalyptic Judaism and Pauline Christianity sharpened meaningful? Or are they but chimeric constructions which men project to allay despair, to transform and purge death of its finality, to render through devices of illusion and fantasy a meaningless concatenation of events meaningful and rich with purpose?

The only way to approach the answer to this question is to raise the fundamental question of man's nature. If man is a creature whose life is all temporal (a congerie of chemical and biological requirements which make him like to nature and a creature of action and will which make him wholly historical) then, indeed, his life does vanish and pass away, for there is nothing toward which he moves that is not of nature or of history. If such be the case, it may be said that history is transcended only in the memory of man, that the meaning of history lies only in the wisdom with which man learns to accept the decisions of history, that man—wholly defined by his historicity—transcends it only in the despairing self-awareness that this is all that he can expect, to know the fatality of the historical.

The despairing view of history or the Stoic contentment with the little that can be known does not mean that history is meaningless. It only means that the historian—and every man who asks questions of his own microcosm is a historian of the everyday—comes to his world with a viewpoint which is fashioned out of his own past, his own predilections and disposition, his own character and person. The subjective viewpoint of the historian—whether it be the simple man who wonders about his world or the scholar who investigates a very definite world—presupposes that he stands in an existential relation with the historical, that he be part of history and an acting creature within it. This view, beautifully stated by R. G. Collingwood, is that "to the historian, the activities whose history he is studying are not spectacles to be watched, but experiences to be lived through in his own mind; they are objective, or known to him, only because they are also subjective, or activities of his own." This does not mean that the historian is capricious, that he arbitrarily constructs the past—for the historian can never forget that he is in the present, that the historical event upon which he focuses is past and that he is the medium through whom the past is linked to the future. The historian enables the past to emerge from isolation and be bound to the future. And as the past is transmitted to the future, more of the past is illuminated, because more of the future unfolds the possibility concealed and hidden in the past. It may then be said that only when history is completed will history be known. It is no wonder that early speculation upon the nature of history projected its unity and completion from the point of view of its end.

It is proper at this juncture to distinguish between the end and the meaning of history: it may no longer be possible to speak of the end of history, except by resuscitating an archaic world view; however, we can speak of meaning in preapocalyptic terms, as the prophets did, without even placing before ourselves the image of the end. We may restore what early Christianity abolished—the sense that history unfolds through an agonizing dialectic of partial fulfillments and demonic distortions; that as creatures we are confined to the sufficient knowledge of our creatureliness; that any meaning which can be derived from history is realized by man entering the historical moment in search of meaning; and that—for those so blessed by the gift of faith—God reigns over all history. Man is thus finally and unavoidably that unique creature who seeks the meaning of his existence in history.

The problem of history and eschatology may be reconstructed by asserting a number of collateral propositions:

Historical thinking has for its proper subject matter the whole of human existence. This is not to say that natural events have no meaningful historical dimension (a natural event which affects the life of man is certainly historical insofar as it affects history, but not insofar as it is natural). At the same moment our definition eliminates from the field of history pure mythologies such as the prehistorical wars of the angels or God's conversations with Satan (except insofar as these mythologies have enabled man to comment and report symbolically upon his own historical condition).

In historical thinking the thinker not only seizes the object, but the object seizes him—they become intertwined and the thinker is himself involved in the object of thought. The thinker, in his involvement, seeks to pass beyond the dualism of subject and object; he seeks, not to prize or conquer history, but to become part of it and by living in and through it to understand it and himself the better. In this manner, when the thinker is also a believer he is placed in a different relation to history. There are certain events which are singled out from the very beginning—events which, though historical themselves, are paradigms of all other historical events. Such sacred events, the giving of the Torah on Sinai for the Jew or the Incarnation for the Christian, are contemporary events which enable the believer to come to every occasion prepared to discover something in routine history which carries a fulfillment or a reproach to the normative paradigm.

The purpose of historical thinking is that the thinker illumine his own existence and, more importantly, that since his existence is in time and itself historical, such thinking enables the thinker to decide for himself how he will live in the future. Historical thinking enables the existential decision. The relevance of this view to our view of sacred history is clear: the sacred event is no longer to be taken over whole as it is given. It is first to be freed of its own historical conditioning and disclosed in the nakedness of its teaching. It is then possible for the believing thinker to look to the Bible not as a univocal way—which is to deprive it of its historicity—but as a way for the future, as a possible way for the believing thinker himself. In this manner the Bible becomes transitive, pointing to the future existential decision in which at each moment it is met by the thinker in his own right time and in his own right historical moment. The Biblical event becomes a possible eschatological moment for each thinker. The thinker may negate its relevance, in which case what was opportunity for man becomes disobedience to God. Or the thinker may come to the Biblical event in an attitude of believing reluctance—that is, willingness to believe but a reluctance to authenticate the contemporaneity of the ancient event. Such a thinker will of necessity demythologize the event in order to reveal it (and it is a possibility that to *demythologize* the event is but to *remythologize* it, to divest it of irrelevant myth in order to invest it with relevant myth); he will seek to disclose its essential character in order to incorporate it into his own life. He will convert the closed historical event into the open Word of God. He will thus have transformed the historical into the eschatological, for no longer the causality of the historical (its sources and origins, which are the preoccupations of the scientist of history), but the end and direction of history shall have become his task.

A CLOSING WORD FOR THE JEWS

Judaism has never had to explain a failed eschatology. This is a questionable blessing, for had Judaism been triumphant in the West, its unfulfilled hopes, indeed the reverse, the trampling and despising of its hopes, would not have been as bitter. And yet Judaism has not had power in the West—which is only to say that it has never had the occasion of confusing power with justice or of confusing mercy with the charity of kings. It has continued unfailingly to await the day of the Lord and it has continued to invest that day with a meaning and a finality which is unrelentingly eschatological.

At the same time that Jewish eschatology is spared of past disappointment, its futurity is so absolute that it becomes somewhat vague and bare. The paradox to be sure is here: the Jewish believer must preserve its absolute futurity (to do otherwise is to run the risk of historicizing the *eschaton* as did Rabbi Akiba when he thought to proclaim the messiahship of the heroic Bar Kohkba), but he must also preserve its imminence (to do otherwise is to make his own salvation and that of all history into an abstraction—and salvation is never an abstraction to him who awaits salvation). The eschatological fulfillment which Christianity proclaims and the eschatological futurity which Judaism preserves both have defeating consequences: the former encourages the development of sacred mythologies in order to strengthen and preserve the memory of the past event whose repetition is awaited, while in the latter the forms and structures of past history—which is all that such a believer knows—are falsely eternalized and are gradually substituted for the event to come. In both cases differing mythologies complicate the awareness of the *eschaton:* in the former, mythologies which are drawn down from heaven complicate the image of historical time and in the latter, mythologies which are elicited from the history of man and nations are supernaturalized and compromise trust in the prerogatives of divine action.

The crucial task of the Jew is to keep the *eschaton* as empty of finality as possible while preserving the possibility that each moment might be final. As Martin Buber has observed: "There are no knots in the mighty cable of our Messianic belief, which fastened to a rock on Sinai, stretches to a still invisible peg anchored in the foundations of the world. In our view, redemption occurs forever, and none has yet occurred. Standing, bound and shackled, in the pillory of mankind, we demonstrate with the bloody body of our people the unredeemedness of the world. For us there is no cause of Jesus; only the cause of God exists for us." The sacred event to which the Jew, reflecting upon history, must turn is the event at Sinai, for in that event the nearness of God was forever made known and, notwithstanding His distance and however He be hidden, He is near at any moment that a man might go forth to hear Him again in his own life and in his own hour.

BIBLIOGRAPHY

This bibliography is less a comprehensive record of general sources than it is a personal acknowledgment of books which have shaped my own thinking. It is obvious that Berdyaev, Bultmann, Tillich, and Buber have had the most evident influence on my interpretation of eschatology, although without the Bible it is questionable whether they could have taught me what I have learned.

Althaus, Paul, "Eschatology," in *A Handbook of Christian Theology*, 1958.
Altizer, Thomas J. J., *Oriental Mysticism and Biblical Eschatology*, 1961.
Altmann, A., "Franz Rosenzweig on History," in *Between East and West*, 1958.
Baeck, Leo, *Judaism and Christianity*, 1958.
Buber, Martin, *Israel and the World*, 1948.
Buber, Martin, *Two Types of Faith*, 1951.
Bultmann, Rudolf, *History and Eschatology*, 1957.
Bultmann, Rudolf, *Jesus Christ and Mythology*, 1958.
Fackenheim, Emil L., *Metaphysics and Historicity*, 1961.
Macquarrie, John, *The Scope of Demythologizing*, 1960.
Mowinckel, S., *He That Cometh*, 1956.
Schoeps, H. J., *Paul*, 1961.
Tillich, Paul, "The Kingdom of God and History," in *The Kingdom of God and History*, 1938.
———, *The Interpretation of History*, 1936.
———, *Theology of Culture*, 1959.

PART TWO

The Religious Situation in America

REINHOLD NIEBUHR

My immediate task is to analyze the religious situation in our nation. To do this adequately, one is forced to examine not only its unique features but also the background of the religious situation in the whole of western European culture and the challenges which American religious communities must face in common with the whole of our civilization in a nuclear age.

The unique aspect of the religious situation in America consists in the degree of diversity and pluralism of our religious life. We are a nation composed of many Protestant sects and impressive Catholic and Jewish minorities. This pluralism in our nation is unique, however, in degree rather than in kind. All western European free societies are religiously pluralistic. Moreover, although European culture has been partially secularized since the rise of modern science in the seventeenth century, and although early European secularism confidently expected religious faith to atrophy through the years, the culture has given evidence of strong religious vitality running side by side with secular idealism. The latter has acted frequently as a purge within religious life, redeeming it from cultural obscurantism and involvement in traditional injustices.

If we inquire after the reasons for this persistent vitality of the religious life in a secular age, we can do no better than take our counsel from Blaise Pascal, himself no mean scientist, but a critic of the Cartesian rationalism, which seemed to make religious faith otiose. Pascal availed himself of a heretical form of Catholicism to become the father of modern "existentialism." He asserted that no rational or philosophical system could contain the incongruity of human existence. Pascal gives a vivid description of man's incongruity when he remarks: "What a prodigy, what a worm, what a monster, judge of all things, yet sink of iniquity and error." The incongruity of human existence which must be comprehended in what another existentialist thinker, Kierkegaard, termed "passionate subjectivity," and which cannot be easily fitted into a consistent scientific system, is derived from man's involvement in the natural and temporal process on the one hand, and the freedom of his spirit on the other: e.g., his capacity to "look before and after and pine for what is not," his ability to stand beyond and above the world and finally regard himself as an object in the world. It is this "double nature" of man which inspires religious faith, whether in a primitive or a sophisticated age. Religious faith grasps the nettle of this contradiction in the heart of human existence.

The second source of religious vitality is derived from the social character of human existence; from the fact that men cannot be themselves or fulfill themselves within themselves, but only in an affectionate and responsible relation to their fellows. It is this fact, rather than the fiat of any scripture, which makes the law of love the basic law for man. The law is not of purely religious origin, and indeed it is not necessary to be religious to ascertain its validity. Only profound religious frames of meaning, however, can help man to a complete understanding of the self-contradiction in which he is involved by reason of his law. He desires to keep the law; yet he violates it and has an uneasy conscience. St. Paul defines the contradiction in these terms: "I delight in the law of God [the law of love] after the inward man; but there is a law in my members [the law of self-regard] which wars against the law which is in my mind." The experience of the majesty of the self in its moral impulses and the misery of the self in its sense of guilt, the sense derived from the self-betrayal of the self in seeking fulfillment within itself and sometimes at the expense of the neighbor, can be and has been the source of an experience which makes the traditions and the symbolic dimensions of Biblical religion relevant to every age. This is true because only in a religious dimension of experience can the self feel both the responsibility for the neighbor, the sovereign freedom of affirming the other beyond the self, and the "misery" of a guilty conscience for its betrayal of this categorical imperative. To refer to Pascal again, the philosophers assure us of our dignity and tempt us to pride; or remind us of our misery and drive us to despair. "Where but in the simplicity of the Gospel can both pride and despair be conquered?"

"The simplicity of the Gospel" means the affirmation of the basic paradox of human existence: the fact, namely, that man is both a child of God and a sinner, that the same majestic freedom which enables man to be creative also gives him the capacity, and perhaps the inclination, to do evil, which means, usually, perversely to make himself the center of every value scheme. There is a mystery about the human capacity for good and the human inclination to evil which has been explicated in Biblical faith but obscured in even the profoundest philosophies.

Whether or not these causes are the sole reasons for the vitality of religion in a secular age, or whether or not we should include the perennial apprehension of the meaning and mystery of the world as well as the mystery and meaning of human existence, we know that religious life in both its individual and collective dimensions has not suffered the decline which seventeenth- and eighteenth-century critics prophesied and expected. This refutation of expectations has taken place despite the heavy weight of cultural obscurantism which traditional religions carried with them.

This is the situation of religious life in Western civilization. The American scene adds some particular elements to the general situation. The most conspicuous element is the greater degree of religious diversity and pluralism in America as contrasted with the general pluralism of western Europe, created by the Renaissance and Reformation, and the rise of free governments. The greater degree of pluralism in America was evident even in the colonial period, when the colonies were settled by refugees from every form of political and religious absolutism, and when one colony, at least, Roger Williams' Rhode Island, was formed as a protest against the Calvinist theocracy which had developed in New England.

This pluralism was accentuated by the Bill of Rights in the Constitution of the new nation, particularly the First Amendment, which prohibited the governmental establishment or suppression of any religion. The essentially secular government, defined by the First Amendment, proved a boon to all religious communities. They were freed to develop their own vitalities without aid or hostility from the state.

The successive waves of migration which peopled the empty western territories and filled the growing industries of the expanding nation after the Civil War increased this pluralism to an even greater degree. Among the specific effects of the migrations, particularly from Ireland, the Slavic and East European nations and Italy, were the increase of the Catholic and Jewish minorities, the proliferation of Protestant sects through the immigrant church, and the triumph of the radical sects. These radical sects—in the European framework these "gathered" sects are not churches—conquered the frontier by the vigor of their evangelism and the mobility of their lay preachers and became the most successful "churches" of the nation.

In Europe, the churches had been in organic relation to their culture, and were frequently state establishments. The "sects," on the other hand, were minority groups of pietists and perfectionists. These immigrant churches on the one hand, and the sectarian churches on the other, gave a unique flavor to American religious life.

In America the immigrant church became disestablished, and was forced to rely on lay activity and responsibility. Moreover, it became a social center for its immigrant group. In short, it resembled the "sect" of Europe. On the other hand the "sect," flourished on the frontier, became almost as inclusive as the traditional church. But it preserved its emphasis on lay activity and responsibility. These two types of religious communities, so unlike in Europe and so similar in America, accounted both for the pluralism of American Protestantism and for the degree of lay loyalty to the religious communities.

This loyalty marks the difference between the religious indifference of European culture and the alleged religiousness of the American culture. Religious piety and devoutness in America may not be as definitely formed and informed by the great religious traditions as in Europe. It may degenerate to religiosity and sentimentality. But its one virtue is that the religious congregations now offer a haven of integral community for the imperiled persons of an increasingly urban and technical civilization whose technical togetherness hardly furnishes these people the kind of organic and integral community which is the vital environment of personality.

This virtue of offering the human person a haven of integral community in an increasingly technical civilization is unfortunately, however, not enough to enable the American church to respond to the moral and political challenges of our era, to the analysis of which we must now address ourselves. These challenges may be sketchily defined as consisting of two domestic issues and one issue of foreign policy.

One of the two dominant domestic issues is the giving to Negro citizens a full participation in the national community which has been denied them ever since the Civil War settled the problem of the unity of the nation but failed to solve the problem of fully emancipating the Negro. The Negro had been "emancipated" from the institution of slavery, but suffered from many disabilities, legal, cultural, and customary, and was reduced to the status of second-class citizenship. The recent decision of the Supreme Court, outlawing segregated schools, has brought this challenge into sharp focus.

The second domestic problem, facing both the nation and the religious communities of the nation, takes the form of finding instruments of justice to apply and implement the "love Commandment," a person's responsibility for his fellowman, in the increasingly intricate relations of a technical society.

The challenge is to make contemporary application of a moral imperative which all three religious traditions rooted in Biblical faith regard as basic.

Unfortunately, the very virtues of the various Protestant sects were sources of weakness in meeting these two dominant issues. The congregational community, so intimate and integral, tended to degenerate into a white middle-class conventicle "chumminess" which obscured the universal scope of the love Commandment. It tempted the Protestant Church to become a chief instrument of the "white man's arrogance" and to make the Sunday church hour "the most segregated hour in the nation."

Moreover, the perfectionist orientation of the sectarian churches tended to obscure the dimension of collective evils such as slavery and race prejudice. Therefore, even before we were forced to face contemporary issues of racial justice, the perfectionist churches, confronted with the issue of slavery, hid their evasion of the issue by turning their old evangelicalism into a frantic legalism, by sabbatarianism, by a prurient sex ethic, by any assurance, in short, which might delude the uneasy conscience of the Christian that he was fulfilling all of the "divine commandments."

In facing the second dominant issue of contemporary American civilization, the resources of the Protestant churches were hardly more adequate. The "individualism" of Protestantism, its emphasis on self-reliance, initiative, and on the "Protestant" virtues of "honesty, frugality and diligence," did not equip it for dealing with problems of social justice in modern industry, where men might be poor not because they were lazy, but because they lacked the social power to set themselves against the social and economic power of the "owners" of an ever more centralized industrial process. The problem was not eased by the fact that most of the beneficiaries of the injustices of nineteenth-century industrialism were the older immigration strains of Protestant owners, while most of the victims were the later immigrants, probably more Catholic and Jewish than Protestant. These latter groups were the "hewers of wood and drawers of water" in our new industries.

The "Social Gospel" movement in the Protestant churches

had indeed rescued the churches from that curious combination of Calvinist and Social Darwinist individualism, in which the "laws of nature" of Social Darwinism were baptized by the Calvinists as "Laws of God." The Social Gospel was informed partly by Calvinist theocratic impulses, partly by sectarian radicalism, some of it dating from the Cromwellian period, and partly by Comtean optimism. It was probably too optimistic and perfectionist to come to terms with the hard realities of power and interest in the economic and political realm; but it did arouse the sleeping conscience of Protestantism. It was therefore creative in adjusting the religious conscience to the problems of justice in an industrial age and culture. It was, however, too sentimental, and too obtuse to the perennial intransigence of the human heart, to come to terms with all the problems of justice. Its mild combination of socialism and pacifism was hardly tough enough for the problems which could be solved only by raising organized labor to become an equal power with organized management in the modern equilibrium of power of the current "welfare state."

Fortunately, the two minority religious groups, the Jews and Catholics, furnished insights for these modern problems in which Protestants were deficient. Both minority groups had some wisdom drawn from the experience of the workers in industry. They also had a more adequate scheme of value, or system of ethics, for the collective relations of men.

The Jews were the inheritors of the prophetic tradition of the Old Testament. That tradition made justice, rather than perfect love, the final norm of human conduct. Perfect or self-sacrificing love is indeed the final pinnacle of morality for the individual life, in the sense that both a mother's love and a martyr's sacrifice are universally acknowledged to be the final norm. But in collective relations we must be content with the norm of justice, with the disposition to "give each man his due." This remains true even though no one has ever invented a calculus or criterion for measuring what each man's due is. Democratic societies have merely regarded liberty and equality as the guiding principles of justice, without sharing the illusions of the eighteenth century that each of these principles was a simple possibility.

The Catholic version of the Christian faith is admittedly a more social version than that of Protestantism. It had incorporated Stoic and Aristotelian conceptions of "natural law" into a system of moral norms. These "laws" were taken from a metaphysical interpretation of historical reality, and were therefore too inflexible to come to terms with all historical contingencies. Catholicism's stubborn prohibition of contraception in a neo-Malthusian age in which population pressures threaten to negate the slow climb from poverty of the "undeveloped" countries, is a case in point. But whatever the defects of these classical norms of justice, they had and have the merit of never leaving the church in doubt about the social substance of human existence.

The tendency to incorporate the social predispositions of medieval feudalism into its system of "natural law" has made it impossible for Catholicism to extricate itself from a feudal culture, whether in Spain or Latin America. But if modern forces have extricated the church, it is able to transfer the insights gained from the organic collectivism of feudalism to the technical collectivism of modern industrial society. Not only in the United States, where the church has a particular interest in protecting its working-class members from the crises of modern industrialism, but in the whole of western Europe, the Catholic church, particularly since the Papal encyclicals beginning with Leo XIII's Rerum Novarum have defined the social teachings of modern Catholicism, has been a creative force in modern industrial communities. It has never lost the industrial workers after the manner of Protestantism. In our nation the industrial experts of the National Catholic Welfare Conference have the prestige which is accorded expert knowledge, and they have played a creative role in the adjustment of labor disputes.

The final problem which challenges the nation and with it all religious communities which have a mission to guide the conscience of men, is not domestic but international. It is the problem of the "nuclear dilemma" which the nuclear age has forced upon us. The nuclear dilemma may best be defined as the moral dilemma created by the fact that the uneasy peace we have in the "cold war" with the world wide Communist movement is maintained by a "balance of terror" or by the equal capacity of both sides to destroy the adversary, should he be tempted to initiate the dread nuclear global war. This capacity for retaliation in the event of an attack means that a nation and a democratic culture which has never fully looked into the depths of the moral ambiguity of the political order is now forced to choose between capitulation to a shrewd and vigorous adversary, or be covered with the proleptic guilt of engaging in a conflict of such destructive power that the future of mankind, and certainly of civilization itself, may well be in doubt.

Thus the moral ambiguity of the political realm, derived from the fact that justice and order cannot be established without the use of power, a proposition which neither the secular nor the religious portions of our culture were prepared to grant as man's ineluctable fate, has been suddenly raised to the *n*th degree. To complicate the dilemma still further, our own nation, which had youthful messianic visions and a sense of mission, to bestow freedom and justice on all mankind, has become destined to be a great power of imperial dimensions, the only non-Communist nation with the economic resources to sustain the non-Communist side of the "balance of terror."

The strong strain of perfectionist moralism in both the nation and in the churches of the nation would prompt us to give an unequivocally moral answer to the dilemma. But individual pacifism spelled out into public policy would mean unilateral disarmament. That policy contradicts the impulse to responsibility, which has always balanced the impulse to moral purity in classical Christianity and prevented perfectionism from being more than a minority movement in either the Christian or Jewish religious communities. The tremendous power of our nation, with the inevitable weight of concomitant responsibilities in the whole world, has naturally strengthened the impulse toward responsibility. Therefore the temptation to an irresponsible isolationism, for either moral or nationalistic reasons, has become a thing of the past. We are "committed" to defend our whole civilization and what we call, somewhat pretentiously, "the Free World."

The temptation of both the nation and its religious communities now assails from the opposite side. It assails the adversary as the embodiment of evil, as the protagonist of "atheistic materialism" or "despotism" and to embark on "Christian anti-Communist crusades" which obscure the common predicament in which we are involved with our adversary by reason of the nuclear dilemma, and the common responsibility we both have for avoiding a nuclear catastrophe.

Fortunately, the National Catholic Welfare Council and the National Council of Churches have both warned against this kind of anti-Communist extremism. But the problem of preserving a tension between the "vertical" and "horizontal" dimensions of this moral problem, between the "vertical" sense of universal inclusiveness, which transcends present enmities and emphasizes a common humanity and a common responsibility, and the "horizontal" sense of responsibility for the preservation of a democratic civilization, is always with us. It is, in fact, a perpetual tension in all problems of the political community, which has been also raised to the *n*th degree by the cold war and the nuclear dilemma.

Fortunately, our nation has a national hero, Abraham Lincoln, who, more than any Western statesman, preserved the balance between political and moral rigor in opposing a social evil. Lincoln also had a religious reservation, which prevented the self-righteous fury and the consequent vindictive fury in which the abolitionist idealist lost himself. Lincoln, in preserving this balance, was morally and religiously superior to such religious-minded statesmen as Oliver Cromwell, William Gladstone, and Woodrow Wilson. All these, despite their virtues, tended to identify their political cause with the sanctities of their religious commitment. Lincoln alone made a distinction between the moral dimension in which it was necessary to condemn slavery, and the religious dimension in which it became obvious that in God's sight "no man living is justified."

Lincoln was no pacifist. He was, in fact, the responsible leader of a nation imperiled by the secession of the slave states. He believed that slavery was wrong, and that religious justifications of the evil were particularly odious. "It may seem strange," he said, "that men should ask the assistance of a just God in wringing their bread from the sweat of other men's brows," but then he added immediately, "Let us judge not that we be not judged." It was by the power of this religious reservation that he could say, "With malice toward none, with charity for all, with firmness in the right as God gives us to see the right, let us strive to do the work we are in." Had Lincoln lived, this spirit would surely have saved the nation from the vindictive fury of Reconstruction days, which did more harm than all the bloodletting of the sanguinary Civil War.

The task of religious communities in a nation which has the double responsibility of preserving the precious values of a free society on the one hand, and of avoiding a nuclear catastrophe on the other hand, is to nurture a religious life in these two dimensions, and to help the nation to be rigorous in its acceptance of the awful responsibilities for the non-Communist world; and at the same time to be imaginative in building bridges across the terrible ideological chasm which divides the world, in the hope that it may yet be "one world" and not the shambles of a nuclear catastrophe.

No greater moral and religious challenge has ever confronted any of the great nations of history. It is great enough to prompt us to "separate the precious from the vile," the wheat from the chaff, in our religious life, and to justify the religious life of a nation as a leaven, which is intended to "leaven the whole lump."

Church-State Relations: Our Constitutional Heritage

HARRY W. JONES

Religious Liberty: Constitutional Text and Judicial Exegesis

LAWYERS rush in where angels fear to tread. They have to, because a certain rashness is inseparable from a vocation that takes disputes, and the settlement of disputes, as its special province. The preceding chapters have dealt mainly with theology. Why, at this stage, bring in the ugly and disputatious old duckling from the law school, with his constitutional texts, his thorny Supreme Court cases, and his emphasis not on interfaith harmony but on political and religious controversy? The answer, and a sufficient one, is that no one can fully understand and appraise the place of religion in American society without taking serious account of a certain legal, specifically constitutional, ingredient in that society.

The often atonal chorus of American religious pluralism is made up of many voices: Protestantism in its varied forms, the tradition of Roman Catholicism, the three versions of Judaism, and the continuing heritage, sometimes secular and sometimes not so secular, of humanism. Indeed, as the Great Authority has said: "In my Father's house are many mansions; if it were not so, I would have told you." But whatever relations may exist somewhere and hereafter among the residents of these many mansions, they are not always good and cordial neighbors on earth. The history of religious conflict furnishes striking illustrations of the evil that good men can do:

> The centuries immediately before and contemporaneous with the colonization of America had been filled with turmoil, civil strife and persecutions. . . . Catholics had persecuted Protestants, Protestants had persecuted Catholics, Protestant sects had persecuted other Protestant sects, Catholics of one shade of belief had persecuted Catholics of another shade of belief, and all of these had from time to time persecuted Jews.[1]

It is a rare prophet who will fight to secure for others the freedom that he asserts for his own religious revelation. "Deep-seated preferences can not be argued about," Justice Holmes once sadly concluded; men are ensnared when they regard "what has been familiar and accepted by them and their neighbors as something that must be accepted by all men everywhere."[2] Problems of accommodation are uniquely difficult when faiths come into competition. Over the course of history, influential groups have worked and often fought to secure political arrangements advantageous to their religious view of things: legal restrictions on the liberty of dissenters, as in Anglican Virginia and Puritan New England, the use of governmental powers, including the power of the purse, in support of church activities, even full-fledged "establishment" of a denomination as an exclusive or preferred state church.

We forget sometimes that "established" churches are not phenomena of a remote past and that they exist today in many lands and forms: the confessional church relationship existing by concordat in Italy, Spain and Austria, the "establishment" of the Church of England, the national churches of Sweden and Norway, the civil jurisdiction of the rabbinical courts in

[1] Black, J., in Everson v. Board of Education, 330 U.S. 1 (1947).
[2] *Collected Legal Papers,* p. 312 (1920).

Israel, the declaration of the Muslim faith expressed in the constitution of Pakistan, and, within recent months, the promulgation of Buddhism as the official national faith in Burma. No such official confessional relationship is sought, even as a remote aspiration, by churchmen of any American denomination, but our several religious traditions are, in a sense, competitors for the allegiance of the uncommitted, and, when men or groups are competitors, disputes are certain to arise, and the task becomes one for law. For it is law's unique role in a democratic society to accomplish a resolution, at least a tolerable accommodation, of the conflicting interests and opposed demands that are inevitable in any dynamic community.

"Democracy," as once defined by Judge Learned Hand, "is a political contrivance by which the group conflicts inevitable in all society should find a relatively harmless outlet in the give and take of legislative compromise." [3] The religion clauses of the Constitution of the United States are designed to provide a framework and structure within which problems of church-state relations may be worked out rationally and with the least possible bitterness. Certain conceivable solutions of the problem of religious diversity are ruled out by the constitutional text. Whatever the "legislative compromise" may be, it must not approach a federal or state "establishment of religion," and it must not have the effect of impairing anyone's "free exercise" of his religion. But these outer limits on permissible political adjustment of asserted religious demands are very broadly expressed. The words of the Constitution provide, at most, the standard and long-range objective which must be respected in deciding the specific controversies that arise from time to time in American church-state relations. The task of application, of constitutional exegesis, is ultimately the responsibility of the courts. This essay is not a four-part exercise in constitutional history, for we seek not the remembrance of things past but understanding and guidance for problems present and future.

THE CONSTITUTIONAL TEXTS

The original Constitution, as agreed on in Philadelphia and submitted to the thirteen states for ratification in 1787, con-

[3] Hand, *The Spirit of Liberty*, p. 204 (1952).

tained but one religion-related clause. This provision, of which a great deal was heard during the 1960 presidential campaign, appears as the last clause of Article VI and reads as follows:

> But no religious Test shall ever be required as a Qualification to any Office or public Trust under the United States.

The immediate impact of the clause is clear enough; it would be unconstitutional for Congress to enact legislation to the effect that elective or appointive federal office, or federal employment, shall not be open to Baptists or to Roman Catholics or to Jews or to Mohammedans or, for that matter, to persons of no religion at all. Any act of Congress restricting federal candidacy or employment on religious grounds is void and unenforceable. That is as far as the letter of the clause extends.

It is arguable by analogy that it is against the spirit of the "no religious Test" provision for individual voters or voting groups to take the position that they will in no circumstances cast their ballots for a candidate of whose religious affiliation, or lack of religious affiliation, they disapprove. I am inclined to agree with this reading of the clause, provided that it is not taken out of context and interpreted as making it improper to consider religious conviction, or lack of it, as *a* consideration to be taken into account along with other aspects of the candidate's social perspective and world view. I suspect, however, that a good many people who would regard it as violative of the spirit of "no religious Test" for a Protestant to vote against a Roman Catholic on exclusively religious grounds—or for a Roman Catholic to vote against a Protestant or a Jew on such grounds exclusively—would think it quite proper for Protestants, Catholics and Jews alike to vote against a candidate of explicitly agnostic views, whatever his other merits might be. The suggested distinction is clearly untenable; "no religious Test" applies as fully to the unreligious candidate as to the candidate of specific religious identification.

In the fall of 1960 it was my own view, as a Protestant who happened to be a supporter of Senator Kennedy, that those who opposed the Senator solely because he was a Roman Catholic —or who supported him for that reason only—were acting in a way inconsistent with the spirit of the "no religious Test" clause, but that those who gave weight to the Senator's religious affiliation as one of the considerations, and an important one, that might affect his conduct in the Presidency were acting properly and responsibly. Any other view can only proceed from a belief, for which neither theological literature nor constitutional law gives the slightest support, that religious values and religious convictions are irrelevant to issues of domestic policy and world affairs.

It will be noted that the "no religious Test" clause applies expressly only to federal office, that is, to "any Office or public Trust under the United States," and does not in its terms apply to state or municipal candidacies or employments. Indeed, religious qualifications for state and municipal offices existed in the thirteen original states at the time the Constitution was ratified and continued on the books for many years thereafter. A curious old case, *Hale v. Everett*,[4] decided by the Supreme Court of New Hampshire in 1868, reveals that the New Hampshire state constitution provided even then that no one was eligible to be elected governor, or to the State Senate or House of Representatives, "unless he shall be of the Protestant religion." Such restrictions proceeded, of course from anti-Catholic motivation—indeed, the dissenting judge in *Hale v. Everett* insisted that "practical construction shows that the Protestant test is an anti-Catholic test and nothing else" and "does not disable for unbelief any non-Catholic"—and they have virtually disappeared from state law. In any event, the joint operation of the "no establishment" clause of the First Amendment and the equal-protection and due-process clauses of the Fourteenth Amendment would, as we shall see, invalidate any such state restriction if enacted or continued today.

Any doubts that may have been entertained on the point have now been removed by the Supreme Court's decision, in June of 1961, in *Torcaso v. Watkins*.[5] In that case, the appellant, Torcaso, was a philosophical atheist, who had qualified for appointment as a notary public in the State of Maryland. Maryland has a long and admirable history of religious toleration, and Article 37 of the Declaration of Rights of the Maryland Constitution provides that:

[4] 53 N.H. 9.
[5] 367 U.S. 488.

No religious test ought ever to be required as a qualification for any office of profit or trust in this State, other than a declaration of belief in the existence of God.

Paradoxically, this originally tolerant provision operated against the twentieth-century dissenter, for Mr. Torcaso was a total nonbeliever and could not conscientiously declare his belief in God's existence. He was refused his commission as a notary public, and he sought relief in the Maryland courts. The highest court of Maryland ruled that the provision in its Declaration of Rights clearly required an affirmation of belief in God as a qualification for public office and that Mr. Torcaso had properly been refused his commission. Torcaso promptly appealed, successfully, as it resulted, to the Supreme Court of the United States.

It is worth noting, for future reference, that the *Torcaso* case raises a general issue of major significance in interpretation of the religion clauses of the Constitution; that is, does the Constitution merely prohibit the preferential treatment of one religious denomination over another, or does it go so far as to prohibit discriminatory treatment as between religious activities, on the one hand, and nonreligious activities on the other, between religionists, of all and any faiths, and persons who have no religious belief at all? To state the issue rather more bluntly, does the Constitution guarantee not only full freedom *of* religion but also an effective freedom *from* religion? The *Torcaso* decision suggests the broader interpretation, since the Supreme Court held—and, for once, without dissent—that the Maryland provision amounted to a religious test for public office, unconstitutionally invaded the appellant's freedom of belief—in this case freedom from religion—and could not be enforced against him. The court carefully refrained from any holding that Article VI of the Constitution applies as such to state or local office as well as to federal office, but the effect of its decision is clear beyond question. No religious test, not even a nonsectarian theistic test, may constitutionally be imposed in the United States, whether for federal, state, or municipal employment.

The controlling texts on church-state relations are found, however, not in the Constitution as originally framed and ratified, but in the First Amendment. A word is in order, first, about the circumstances which led to the statement of these religious theses in the Bill of Rights and about the men who insisted on their inclusion and ratification. What was their sense of the historical occasion, and what were the purposes they sought to achieve?

It is bad history to sentimentalize the religious views of the founding fathers of American constitutionalism. The conventional portrayal of them as men of homogeneous religious conviction, uniform in simple, unquestioning piety, is false to them and to the currents of religious and philosophical opinion at the end of the eighteenth century. Actually, the delegates who assembled in Philadelphia in 1787, and the men who participated in the drafting of the Bill of Rights two years later, were, by and large, sophisticated intellectuals, considerably more sophisticated than any group of American politicians since, and far from homogeneous in their religious views.

Some were Episcopalians, but estranged from the Anglican Church because of that church's ambiguous position during the period immediately before the American Revolution. Those from New England were chiefly Congregationalists, of one variety or another, and some of their ministers had gone into battle with them. Many of the delegates were religious only as Jefferson was, with a most remote and unardent deism. All of them knew the history of religious conflict. They feared both national power in matters of religion and clerical interference in matters of politics. They were concerned about the possibility that the new national authority to which they were giving life might, conceivably, establish a monolithic national church or impose restrictions on the right of the individual citizen to profess the religion of his own personal conviction or, for that matter, to profess no religion at all. The Constitution itself was insufficiently explicit, many of these men thought, in barring federal power in matters of religion. Before the First Congress was well under way, they succeeded in their insistence that these limitations be spelled out, so that all might read, at the head of the ten great Amendments that are the ark of American constitutional liberty.

It is no historical accident that the two religion-related guarantees of the Bill of Rights are stated as the very first provisions of that historic document. The First Amendment begins: "*Congress shall make no law respecting an establishment of religion or prohibiting the free exercise thereof.*" (The words are italicized here, because widespread paraphrases, incautious or willful, of the text of the First Amendment have contributed immeasurably to confusion and bitterness in public discussion of contemporary church-state issues.) All the other guarantees of American liberty—freedom of speech and of the press, due process of law, procedural safeguards in court proceedings—appear later. The draftsmen of the Bill of Rights, working in the perspective of a history known to them all, put first things first.

I have spoken of *two* religious guarantees in the First Amendment, and they are two, although brought together in a single sentence. The first: "Congress shall make no law respecting an establishment of religion." The second: "[Congress shall make no law] prohibiting the free exercise thereof," that is, the free exercise of religion. The first will be referred to throughout as the "no establishment" clause, the second as the "free-exercise" clause.

The two clauses, in a sense, serve a broad common objective, one often paraphrased, though inexactly, in terms of a "wall of separation between church and state," which are Jefferson's words, not the Constitution's. Each clause, however, has its separate independent vitality for American constitutional law. At times the provinces may overlap. Thus, for example, sectarian religious instruction as an integral part of a public school program is subject to challenge both as a forbidden "establishment" of religion and as an interference with the "free exercise" of religion by dissenting students and their parents. But at other times the provinces are quite separate. If Congress were to enact a statute flatly underwriting 50 per cent of the construction and teaching costs of church-connected schools, that would hardly be an interference with anyone's free exercise of his religion, but it would almost certainly be characterized as a forbidden "establishment" of religion, since *establishment*, at the time the Bill of Rights was proposed and ratified, clearly meant financial support as well as other forms of state sponsorship of church programs.

It is important, then, that the twofold nature of the First Amendment's religious prohibition be clearly discerned; important, too, that care be taken not to paraphrase the constitutional texts too freely. The first clause does not say merely that Congress shall not create a state church; it says that Congress shall make no law respecting an establishment of *religion.* The second clause does not declare simply that Congress shall respect the individual conscience in matters of inner religious faith; it guarantees the free *exercise* of religion against government restraint.

It is unavoidable now that account be taken of a difficult point in American constitutional law, one that seems to have escaped the attention of many authors who write with assurance on church-state problems. Close readers will have observed that the First Amendment speaks only in terms of what *Congress*, the federal government, may not do by way of religious establishment or restriction of religious liberty. "Congress shall make no law . . ."—so the First Amendment begins. Does it follow, then, that each of the fifty states may, if its own legislature so chooses, enact legislation "respecting an establishment of religion or prohibiting the free exercise thereof"? If the states are so free, how do we account for the fact that almost every leading church-state decision has involved the constitutionality not of federal legislation but of state or municipal action? How could it even have been argued, successfully in *McCollum v. Board of Education* [6] and unsuccessfully in *Zorach v. Clauson* [7] that the respective Illinois and New York religious-instruction programs amounted to the unconstitutional "establishment of religion"? *Congress* had passed no law requiring or authorizing these state programs. Where, then, was the asserted violation of the First Amendment?

The explanation is that the First Amendment must be read together with the Fourteenth Amendment and specifically with the latter's due-process clause. The Fourteenth Amend-

[6] 333 U.S. 203 (1948).
[7] 343 U.S. 306 (1952).

ment provides, in pertinent part: ". . . nor shall any State deprive any person of life, liberty, or property without due process of law." In *Cantwell v. Connecticut*,[8] a 1940 Jehovah's Witness controversy, the Supreme Court of the United States held explicitly that the religious freedoms guaranteed against the federal government by the First Amendment are aspects of the "liberty" guaranteed against state action by the Fourteenth Amendment. The following words, from Justice Roberts' opinion for the Court in *Cantwell*, provide the rationale:

> The fundamental concept of liberty embodied in that [the Fourteenth] Amendment embraces the liberties guaranteed by the First Amendment. The First Amendment declares that Congress shall make no law respecting an establishment of religion or prohibiting the free exercise thereof. The Fourteenth Amendment has rendered the legislatures of the states as incompetent as Congress to enact such laws.

In short, and oversimplifying only slightly, the states were free until 1868 to enact legislation "respecting an establishment of religion or prohibiting the free exercise thereof." But since 1868, when the Fourteenth Amendment became a part of the Constitution, the First Amendment must be understood as if it read:

> *Neither* Congress *nor any state legislature* shall make any law respecting an establishment of religion or prohibiting the free exercise thereof.

The liberty guaranteed against state interference by the Fourteenth Amendment now includes and incorporates the religious guarantees of the First Amendment. The *Cantwell* decision, seen in this perspective, is perhaps the most important case ever decided in American church-state relations. It is arguable, and indeed argued by such authorities as Professor Mark Howe, that the "no establishment" clause should be applied less severely against state action than against federal action—as, for example, in the matter of the constitutionality of financial aid to parochial schools—but it is universally agreed that the religious guarantees of the First Amendment are not exhausted

[8] 310 U.S. 296.

by their effect on federal legislation but apply fully in principle to action taken under state legislative authority as well.

JUDICIAL EXEGESIS

The religious and other civil liberties spelled out in the American Bill of Rights differ, in a crucial respect, from the liberties recited in most other political constitutions. They are not only stated in words; they are judicially enforced. We Americans are often misled by the literary resemblance of other constitutions to our own. The constitution of the U.S.S.R., for example, contains an impressive catalogue, far more detailed than our own Bill of Rights, of the civil privileges, including freedom of religious belief, assured to all Soviet citizens. Sentimental liberals take profound comfort from the circumstance that the constitutions of certain of the new "emerging" nations —the constitution of Ghana is, or was, the one most often publicly admired—recite all the traditional civil liberties, and many new ones, as inviolable freedoms of the individual. The trouble is that these recitals are usually but pious admonitions; the constitutions involved state that the individual is not to be deprived of his civil liberties, but if government power holders decide to impair these liberties, there is nothing that the individual can do about it. There is no effective remedy.

It is the first axiom of constitutional government that declarations of rights are meaningless, or can be made so, if there are no remedies to enforce them. That remedy is provided in American constitutionalism by the power of the courts, the ordinary courts, to review the constitutionality of legislative and executive action and, if it violates constitutional principle, declare it void and ineffective. This is not a complete umbrella of protection; there is at least one very important area in which judicial review is unavailable to challenge legislation thought to be violative of the First Amendment. But, by and large, American religious and civil liberty is enforceable liberty, and that makes all the difference.

In the three sections which follow this introductory one, my principal references will be to cases, actual decisions of the Supreme Court of the United States and other courts. This stress on what might be called the "original sources" is not for want of an available secondary literature. Copious citations might have been made to treatises on constitutional law and to books and learned articles by many commentators on the legal aspects of church-state relations: John Bennett, Mark Howe, Wilber Katz, Paul Kauper, Philip Kurland, Leo Pfeffer and a number of others. I believe, however, that a focus on the cases themselves will be more rewarding on this occasion than a review of the critical literature could be. Indeed, if I had my way about it, I would conscript my readers as law students *pro tempore* and compel them to read through the factual and doctrinal intricacies of the lengthy Supreme Court opinions in at least a dozen major litigated controversies. No one begins to understand the constitutional ingredient in American church-state relations until he has closely examined a fair sampling of the actual decisions in point. Conceivably these would be operative as an aperitif and whet a few appetites for case reading.

"General propositions do not decide concrete cases." These are the words of Oliver Wendell Holmes, Jr., as great a constitutional judge as we have had. Abstractions, general principles, are superbly deluding in their apparent clarity and simplicity. Consider the constitutional principles on which these discussions center. "No law respecting an establishment of religion." Everybody agrees with that, so long as it remains a general principle. "The free exercise of religion." Who could object to that? But when we move from the tranquil universe of abstraction to the confused and shifting one of empirical fact, consensus tends to disappear, and controversy takes over. The point at hand is, I think, best stated in a passage, not from the lawyers but from a great contemporary theologian, Martin Buber:

> Of course there are all sorts of similarities in different situations; one can construct types of situations, one can always find to what section the particular code belongs, and draw what is appropriate from the hoard of established maxims and habits, apply the appropriate maxim, bring into operation the appropriate habit. But what is untypical in the particular situation remains unnoticed and unanswered. . . . Every living situation has, like a new-born

child, a new face, that has never been before and will never come again. . . . It demands a reaction which cannot be prepared beforehand.[9]

So it is in church-state relations, as controversies come to the courts to be decided. Judicial decision in these and other constitutional cases is not simply the logical application of preexisting principles; it is purposeful, pragmatic, and inescapably creative. For, in the words of another great judge, Justice Cardozo:

It is when the colors do not match, when the references in the index fail, when there is no decisive precedent, that the serious business of the judge begins.[10]

Constitutional decision-making is not an exercise in history or in formal logic; it is a tough enterprise in responsible problem-solving. The task is as old as philosophy: the application of universal principles to the endless and infinitely varied concrete instances that occur in the real world. Of course there are many conceivable situations for which the constitutional text would supply a clear and single answer. If the next session of Congress were to pass an act creating an American National Church, headed by a Secretary of Religion in the President's cabinet, that would unquestionably be a "law respecting an establishment of religion," and the act would not be worth the paper on which it was enrolled. Or if Congress or some state legislature should enact a statute requiring a license—or a loyalty oath—from priests, ministers, and rabbis, that would clearly be unconstitutional as a "law prohibiting the free exercise" of religion. One is reminded of an off-the-record pronouncement by a late and greatly admired Justice of the Supreme Court: "I can think of a thousand hypothetical cases that we could dispose of simply by reference to the words of the Constitution. But, doggone it, our Court never seems to get a case like that to decide."

The hard cases, the ones that come to high courts for adjudication, are not so cut and dried. They are borderline cases, arguable controversies, problems of judgment and choice on

[9] *Between Man and Man*, pp. 113–114 (Beacon ed., 1955).
[10] *The Nature of the Judicial Process*, p. 21 (1921).

which reasonable men can disagree and reasonable Justices of the Supreme Court of the United States divide five to four, or six to three, or in some other ratio. How happy the Court must have been with the *Torcaso* case, on which the nine brethren had the opportunity, rare in church-state matters, to proclaim their result in harmony and unanimity! With the Court so often divided—five to four on bus transportation to parochial schools, six to three on released time after having once been eight to one the other way, six to three again on Sunday closing for Kosher butchers—who will have the hardihood and intellectual recklessness to offer dogmatic absolute answers for today's problems of church-state relations? To suggest the range and complexity of contemporary church-state issues, I offer four problems, each taken from an actual controversy that arose somewhere in the United States during the past two years.

1. THE CASE OF THE REGENTS' PRAYER

Acting pursuant to a "recommendation" of its State Board of Regents, a local board of education has directed that daily sessions at the public schools within its district be opened by class recitation of the following prayer:

> Almighty God, we acknowledge our dependence upon Thee, and we beg Thy blessings upon us, our parents, our teachers and our country.

Certain parents in the community object to this ceremony and, at their instance, suit is brought in the courts challenging the opening prayer as an unconstitutional "establishment of religion" and possible impairment of the religious liberty of dissenting children. The highest court of the state, by a five-to-two decision,[11] upholds the morning prayer as "non-compulsory," since students may be excused from the exercise on request of their parents, and "non-sectarian," and the complainants prosecute their further appeal to the Supreme Court of the United States. *Decision?* Does the morning prayer exercise violate the First Amendment to the Constitution of the

[11] Engel v. Vitale, 10 N.Y. 2d 174 (Court of Appeals of New York, 1961).

United States? The case was argued before the Supreme Court on April 3, 1962, and I suggest that the decision be watched for as another instance of the Supreme Court's continuing task as interpreter and patrolman of the religion-related clauses of the First Amendment.

2. RIBICOFF RIDES AGAIN

In late November of 1961, Abraham Ribicoff, Secretary of Health, Education and Welfare, announced that the Administration, during the next Congressional session, would introduce a bill entitled "The Health Professions Educational Assistance Act of 1961," by which, under a matching-funds arrangement, $600,000,000 would be expended, over the next ten years, for medical and dental school buildings. Two thirds of the cost of the new school construction would be paid by federal funds, and the government would also pay half the cost of expanding present medical school facilities. The federal funds, said the Secretary, would be available both to public, that is, state university medical schools and to medical schools associated with private universities. It happens that many private universities have one form or another of church connection. Suppose, as the bill clearly contemplates, a church-connected private university applies for federal financial assistance for the expansion of its medical school. Is it unconstitutional, under the First Amendment, to permit that university to share in the $600,000,000 fund? More precisely, would it be an "establishment of religion," in the constitutional sense of the term, to make federal funds available for the construction of medical school facilities—or other facilities—at a church-connected private university? Does constitutional principle require that the Administration's proposal be amended to make church-connected universities, and them alone, ineligible for federal grants to their medical schools? The issue, as many will observe at once, is closely related to the church-state question raised by Proposal No. 6, submitted to the voters of New York State on November 7, 1961 and rejected by a close vote.

3. DARBY VERSUS JOAN

Joan, a girl brought up as a Unitarian, marries Darby, a devout Orthodox Jew. Before they are married, Joan signs a written contract by which she formally agrees that any children born of the marriage will be brought up in the Orthodox faith. Ten years later, Darby and Joan find life together intolerable, and they repair to the divorce court. They have two children, a boy of eight and a girl of six, and Joan, of course, is awarded custody of the children. Shortly thereafter, Joan returns to her Unitarian faith and transfers the children to a Unitarian Sunday school. Darby, concerned for his children's religious welfare, applies to the court for an order enforcing the antenuptial agreement that the children are to be raised in the Orthodox faith. The court, after argument, orders Joan, under penalty of contempt of court, to resume the children's Orthodox religious training. Joan appeals to a higher court, asserting that the privilege to control the religious upbringing of her children is an aspect of her "free exercise of religion" and that the court's order enforcing the antenuptial agreement is state action unconstitutionally impairing her, and the children's, religious liberty. *Decision?* At this writing, the general issue, in one form or another, is before the courts in at least ten states.

4. THE CASE OF THE NONTHEISTIC CONSCIENTIOUS OBJECTOR

During the First World War and until 1940, the Selective Service Act authorized draft boards to grant exemption from combat service to any conscientious objector who could prove his membership in a "well recognized religious sect whose existing creed or principles forbid its members to participate in war in any form." Thus, as the law then stood, a Quaker conscientious objector might secure the exemption but not a Methodist or a Roman Catholic or a Reform Jew, however profound his individual religious objection to war, since Methodism, Roman Catholicism and Reform Judaism have no "existing creed" *forbidding* their members to participate in war.

This sectarian preference was strongly criticized in the years between the World Wars, and in 1940 the draft law was changed so as to authorize exemption from combat service for anyone, whatever his denomination, who "by reason of religious training and belief, is conscientiously opposed to participation in war in any form." "Religious training and belief," so the statute continues, "means an individual's belief in relation to a Supreme Being involving duties superior to those arising from any human action." In short, as the law now stands, the objector no longer has to prove that his church forbids his participation in war and will be excused from combat service upon proof that his conscientious objection stems from his individual "religious training and belief." But if his conscientious objection is nontheistic, merely a "social belief," even one that proceeds from "devotion to a high moral philosophy," off to combat service he goes, or, if not there, to jail.

The constitutional issues posed by this fourth of my test problems are, perhaps, subtler and more involved than those raised by my first three. Is the Selective Service Act constitutional in its present, amended form? That depends on one's interpretation of the thrust and purpose of the First Amendment. If the First Amendment is read as doing no more than to forbid preferential treatment of one religious sect or denomination over another—that is, as permitting nonpreferential encouragement to religion generally—the statute appears to be constitutional. If we follow a more austere interpretation and regard the First Amendment as forbidding the preference of religious ideas and activities over other, nonreligious ideas and activities, the selective-service statute clearly falls. As amended, it is surely "nonsectarian," for any kind of "religious training and belief" is enough to justify exemption from combat duty. But our problem forces us to deeper analysis: Is a preference of religion-based opposition to war over philosophically-based opposition to war consistent with a constitutional prohibition which speaks, as we have seen, not in terms of the establishment of a national church but in terms of "an establishment of *religion*"?

The four problems just stated are but illustrative of dozens that might have been given. The definition of constitutional principle becomes an incomparably harder task when one gets down to cases, as judges must always do. As I have written in another place: [12]

In any account of the judicial process, there is a substantial incidence of cases that can be decided, and justified with all traditional common law proprieties, either way. Whatever the incidence may be—a fifth, a fourth, a third—it is indisputable that the work of the judge involves the inescapability of choice and so of responsibility for externally uncontrolled decisions. . . . In realist perspective, choice, decision, and responsibility for decision are central elements for a philosophy of law.

The process of judicial review, in church-state cases as in others, involves incomparably more than an attempt by a court to discover what the founding fathers "meant" by the words they used in 1787 or 1789. Could they have forseen, even in the remotest of outline, the vast growth of America or the dynamics of American religious pluralism? It has already been noted, and the point is crucially important, that the draftsmen of the Bill of Rights could not possibly have considered the effect of the First Amendment as a limit on *state*, as distinguished from federal, action. It was not until 1868 that the First Amendment became applicable to the states at all. Yet most of the Supreme Court cases to which the latter part of this chapter will call attention are cases in which it is state action that is challenged as violative of the First Amendment. To consider constitutional law as if it were a mere attempted reconstruction of the intention of the founding fathers is about as helpful as the old query: "If I had had an uncle, would he have liked prunes?" Nowhere is this more true than in the constitutional law of church-state relations. It is the task of the Supreme Court in this area to keep the historic purpose of the First Amendment a living influence in contemporary society. That, as we shall see, takes more than a little doing!

[12] "Law and Morality in the Perspective of Legal Realism," 61 Columbia Law Review 709 (1961).

The "Free Exercise" of Religion

"No law . . . prohibiting the free exercise" of religion. Let us be careful not to paraphrase the words of the First Amendment. The draftsmen of the Bill of Rights knew what they meant and knew how to say what they meant. The First Amendment is more than a guarantee of freedom, immunity from state coercion and control, in matters of individual conscience and belief. The words are brisker and more muscular; the free *exercise* of religion is what is guaranteed. Manifestly, the exercise of one's religion is more than a privilege to retire into a small room or private chapel and meditate alone on sacred things. Religiously authoritarian countries like Colombia and Saudi Arabia are likely to concede that much to the individual religious conscience, so long as it remains solitary. "Free exercise" of religion goes much further and includes freedom to worship publicly in community, freedom to proclaim a faith—to advocate and evangelize—and freedom to bring religious criteria to bear in social criticism, on controversial social and political questions as well as on abstract moral issues.

The reach of "free exercise" is well enough suggested by three leading cases in the Supreme Court's church-state literature: *Pierce v. Society of Sisters*,[13] *West Virginia Board of Education v. Barnette*,[14] and *Cantwell v. Connecticut*.[15] The *Pierce* case, which held unconstitutional an Oregon statute requiring all children of school age to attend the state's public schools, was decided in 1925, a full fifteen years before the Supreme Court stated explicitly that the two great religious guarantees of the First Amendment are incorporated in the "liberty" secured against state action by the Fourteenth. The rhetoric of the *Pierce* opinion is therefore rather different from that in the cases since *Cantwell v. Connecticut*, but it is clear beyond doubt that the present-day significance of the *Pierce* decision is that one's choice to have his children educated in

[13] 268 U.S. 510 (1925).
[14] 319 U.S. 624 (1943).
[15] 310 U.S. 296 (1940).

church-related schools is an aspect of his "free exercise of religion" and so beyond interference by state legislation designed to compel universal attendance at public schools. Prevailing Roman Catholic opinion has sometimes been critical of more recent Supreme Court decisions in the area of church-state relations; let it not be forgotten that *Pierce v. Society of Sisters* invalidated a state statute warmly supported by local public opinion at the time of its enactment and was, in a real sense, the Magna Carta of the American parochial-schools movement.

I think that the *Pierce* decision was right and the local desire for monopolistic public schools misguided, but it is only fair to take note that the judicial protection of religious liberties has worked, on balance, to aid the Roman Catholic Church immeasurably in its excellent institutional adjustment to the conditions of American religious diversity. The judicious John Courtney Murray concurs with this appraisal in his recent book, *We Hold These Truths: Catholic Reflections on the American Proposition*":

> The point is that the goodness of the First Amendment as constitutional law is manifested not only by political but also by religious experience. By and large (for no historical record is without blots) it has been good for religion, for Catholicism, to have had simply the right of freedom.[16]

And he continues, characteristically:

> The American Catholic . . . takes the highest ground available in this matter of the relations between religion and government when he asserts that his commitment to the religion clauses of the Constitution is a moral commitment to them as articles of peace in a pluralistic society.[17]

We move to another area of guaranteed religious liberty. The flag-salute cases of the early 1940's saw a dissenting group's "free exercise of religion" in collision with the prevailing patriotic conformism of the years just before Pearl Harbor. Many states and communities enacted statutes and regulations requiring all school children to salute the flag of the United States and, in public ceremonies, repeat the familiar pledge of

[16] Murray, *We Hold These Truths: Catholic Reflections on the American Proposition*, p. 76 (1960).

[17] *Ibid.*, p. 78.

allegiance. Quite a few children, most but not all of them from families belonging to the Jehovah's Witnesses, refused to participate in the ceremony, on grounds reminiscent of the old Quaker objection to oath-taking. The children were excluded from school—presumably as Security Risks (Junior Grade)—and they or their parents challenged the constitutionality of compulsory flag saluting as an impairment of the free exercise of their religion. In the 1940 *Gobitis* case [18] the Supreme Court decided, Justice Stone alone dissenting, that the requirement was legitimate and not unreasonable and that children refusing to take part in the ceremony, even on sincere religious grounds, might be excluded from school.

After no great lapse of time, the issue came back to the federal courts in a factually indistinguishable case, *West Virginia Board of Education v. Barnette*. The result? One of the quickest judicial changes of heart in American constitutional history. In an unexpected show of disapproval and defiance, three lower federal court judges simply refused to follow a Supreme Court decision so profoundly inconsistent with their deeply felt convictions concerning the free exercise of religion.[19] Their action was virtually unprecedented, an outright refusal by a lower federal court to follow a direct precedent of the highest court of the land. And yet, when *Barnette* reached the Supreme Court in 1943, the rebels were vindicated, and the 1940 *Gobitis* precedent overruled by a vote of 6 to 3.[20] Chief Justice Stone's solitary dissent of 1940 became the measure of constitutional "free exercise" in 1943.

Nonconformists always provide the test cases in the judicial protection of civil liberties, and this is as true in church-state relations as in matters of secular free speech and free press. It is the extremist sects, most notably the Jehovah's Witnesses,

[18] Minersville School District (Pa.) v. Gobitis, 310 U.S. 586.

[19] Barnette v. West Virginia State Board of Education, 47 F. Supp. 251 (D.C.W.D. Va., 1942). A few weeks before this District Court decision was handed down, three of the Supreme Court justices (Black, Douglas, and Murphy) who had been with the majority in the *Gobitis* case had declared that they now believed the *Gobitis* case to have been wrongly decided. Jones v. City of Opelika, 316 U.S. 584 (1942).

[20] West Virginia State Board of Education v. Barnette, 319 U.S. 624 (1943).

that have forced the issues on "free exercise" and so brought about the consistent constitutional decisions of the Supreme Court which make it clear beyond question that the constitutionally protected free exercise of religion includes the right to evangelize, to seek converts on the highways and byways, even by means which—to the more sedate of us—amount to making a nuisance of oneself.

Cantwell v. Connecticut,[21] to which earlier reference has been made, indicates how loose the state's rein must be on the exercise of religious conviction. The case itself involved the exercise of religious zeal in its most exasperating form. I quote from the Supreme Court's opinion:

> The record played by Cantwell embodies a general attack on all organized religious systems as instruments of Satan and injurious to man; it then singles out the Roman Catholic Church for strictures couched in terms which naturally would offend not only persons of that persuasion, but all others who respect the honestly held religious faith of their fellows. The hearers were in fact highly offended. One of them said that he felt like hitting Cantwell and the other that he was tempted to throw Cantwell off the street.

It is evident enough from this quotation that Cantwell was no gentle St. Francis and that he was not likely to make a convert of the author of the opinion, Mr. Justice Roberts, or of any of his Supreme Court colleagues. Nevertheless the Supreme Court held, without dissent, that Cantwell's abrasive evangelistic efforts were within the protected zone of "free exercise of religion" and hence could not subject him to prosecution for breach of the peace.

Someone has wisely said that "one man's freedom is always some other man's pain in the neck." This is true not only of the free exercise of religion but of the exercise of all civil liberties. When a Communist sympathizer exercises his constitutional privilege of free speech, it annoys the American Legion. When Martin Luther King exercises his right of free speech, the Citizens Councils are angered and upset. The utterances of Führer Rockwell and his American Nazi party are profoundly disturbing to the Jewish community. Certain elements of the

[21] 310 U.S. 296 (1940).

American radical right exercise their right of free press in a manner that exasperates me almost beyond endurance. Each of us, when irritated by utterance distasteful to him, wishes that the speaker or the writer or the self-proclaimed prophet would shut up and go away. But I think we know, at least in the back of our minds, that constitutional liberty is in danger whenever the power of the state is invoked to shut the speaker up, or punish him for what he has said, or chase him away.

In civil liberties adjudication, the showdown case is always one in which the pronouncements or publications sought to be restrained are annoying and obnoxious to other groups, usually to majority feeling in the community. No one nowadays attempts to restrain the free exercise of religion by Presbyterians, Reform Jews, Roman Catholics, Unitarians, Lutherans or other respectable and established denominations, just as no one attempts nowadays to put limits on the freedom of speech of the Chamber of Commerce or the AFL-CIO, muzzle the free-press expressions of *The Christian Science Monitor* or *The New York Times*, or censor the publications of the Book-of-the-Month Club. It is the nuts, or those so regarded by the rest of us, on whom government restraint and censorship are brought to bear. When they resolutely defend their constitutional liberties, the nuts are surrogates for the freedom of us all.

The typical leading case, in church-state relations as elsewhere in the area of civil liberties, centers on a conflict of interests. The court must decide between competing claims: on the one hand, an individual or group claim to the unrestrained exercise of religious conviction; on the other hand, the claim of a majority or other influential group to be let alone and kept free from annoyance. By and large, the decisions in point have resolved this conflict of interests by giving greater weight to the claim for liberty of religious expression than to the claim of the larger group not to be bothered, annoyed, or even vilified. That, in a sense, is the significance of the *Cantwell* decision and of the many later cases that could be cited to the same effect.

Is this giving undue preference to the claim—even if it be an eccentric and exasperating claim—of freedom in the exercise of religious convictions? Why should the likes of the

Cantwells be permitted to annoy peaceable, God-fearing members of other religious faiths? Before you answer that one from the hip, I urge you to think of Church history through the ages. In imperial Rome, the first Christians were thought of as a disturbing, unpatriotic group of eccentrics; even Marcus Aurelius would have called them crackpots had the term been in Latin circulation. We recall with pain that a sweet-faced Quaker lady was hanged three centuries ago on Boston Common. Lutherans, Methodists, Baptists were all thought of as eccentric splinter groups at the time of their beginnings; indeed, Patrick Henry first came into public prominence through his spirited defense of Baptist preachers criminally charged, in Virginia, for the offense of preaching the Gospel without a license. In many states of the United States, Roman Catholics were regarded as foreigners, a deviationist and potentially subversive minority, by the overwhelming Protestant majority of a few generations ago. Prejudice against Jewish religious observances persisted even longer. More than one Midwestern town has had an ordinance forbidding the erection of a synagogue within the city limits, and as late as July 13, 1961, a community of Hasidic Jews had to go to the New York Supreme Court to compel the Rockland County township of Ramapo to issue a certificate permitting the community's incorporation as a village. The moral of this is clear enough. If there is any area of human aspiration in which no man, and certainly no state functionary, can safely be granted the power to censor—to determine what doctrines are "true" and what activities permissible and reasonable—it is the area characterized in the First Amendment as "the free exercise of religion."

This is not to say that constitutional liberty in matters of religion is unlimited or absolute. Religious liberty is more nearly absolute, I think, than any other of the civil liberties, but even here limits have been imposed and, from time to time, upheld by the Supreme Court. If I wake up in the middle of tonight and believe—even sincerely believe—that God has called me to heal the sick and, in the course of that vocation, to perform surgical operations, it is lawful to deny me a license to practice medicine, however urgent my conviction that medical practice is the only effective "exercise" of my religion. Similarly, a state or community may constitutionally require smallpox vaccination of school children, even though vaccination is abhorrent to the religious principles of certain children and their parents. A father convinced on religious grounds that his children should go to work at age ten and not fritter their time away on schooling cannot use the First Amendment to deny the constitutionality of child labor and compulsory education laws. Municipal ordinances forbidding certain practices of Holiness snake-handling sects have been sustained against contentions that snake-handling is a sincerely held religious tenet and so a form of the free exercise of religion.

The historic precedent—a rather hard one to explain in terms of general principle, by the way—is the prohibition of plural marriage, as by the enforcement of bigamy laws against certain Mormon sects to whom plural marriage was a matter of religious obligation.[22] As always in constitutional law, a line must be drawn somewhere, and the line bounding permissible state interference with religious practices is not an easy one to formulate. This much can be said, to account for the court decisions to date:

Principle No. 1: Conduct, even though proceeding from sincere religious motivation, may be restrained by the state if reasonably deemed to be dangerous to the public health or safety. This ground, public health and safety, accounts for such restrictions as were involved in our medical licensing, compulsory vaccination, and snake-handling illustrations.

Principle No. 2: Conduct, even though proceeding from sincere religious motivation, may be restrained if the legislature reasonably considers it to be seriously injurious to public morals or gravely offensive to prevailing community moral standards. This is, perhaps, an acceptable generalized statement of the result in the Mormon polygamy cases and of the doctrine applicable in our child labor and compulsory education examples.

[22] Reynolds v. United States, 98 U.S. (1878) was the first case in which the Supreme Court held that a federal polygamy statute could constitutionally be applied to a Mormon.

The situations covered by the two principles just given are, of course, the exceptional and unusual ones. In the exercise of religion, freedom is the general rule and allowable state restraint the exception. As to all forms of religious expression beyond the relatively narrow area of conduct demonstrably dangerous to public health, safety, and morals, the governing principle is this third, permissive one:

Principle No. 3: It is not enough to justify state restraint that the religious expression or conduct be considered absurd by majority public opinion or even that it be offensive or annoying to the majority, or to other groups, in the community. If there is no demonstrable threat to public health, safety, or morals, the exercise of religious conviction is outside the sphere of lawful public regulation.

These are the principles, and, at first glance, they seem clear enough. But we should be mindful of our earlier warning that general principles do not always afford clear direction for the settlement of concrete human controversies. To illustrate the difficulties involved in determining the specific application of the "free exercise" clause, let us consider a specific case, one that compels us to think our problem through and, in a sense, put our convictions on the line. It is a good problem case for present purposes, because it appears open-and-shut on first examination and then, as one reflects on it, is exposed as a problem for which there is no easy solution—indeed, insofar as I have ever been able to see, no really satisfying solution at all.

Suppose that a self-styled prophet advertises, as did the defendants in the 1943 Supreme Court case of *United States v. Ballard*,[23] that he is a kind of reincarnation of St. Germain—also, by the way, of George Washington—that Jesus Christ had appeared to him on a street corner, shaken his hand warmly, and designated him to be the founder and divine messenger of a new theology called "I Am." Suppose that our prophet advertises further that he can spiritually heal afflicted persons and that anyone purchasing "I Am" membership and literature from his cult will be assured of material and spiritual benefits in this world and in the hereafter. As one might guess, Prophet

[23] 322 U.S. 78.

Ballard and his affiliated saints advertised from a Los Angeles address.

Now, as the saying goes, we make a federal case out of it. A skeptical United States Attorney proceeds to have our prophet indicted for use of the mails to defraud, and our prophet rests his defense on the constitutional ground that the prosecution is an interference with his and his followers' free exercise of religion. "Nonsense!" one is tempted to reply. But is it nonsense? The case sounds easy enough, but, examined in depth, it becomes a constitutional lawyer's headache.

Consider the difficulties. The defendant, at his criminal trial, will repeat his advertised claims: he is the sole authorized messenger of a new, exclusive religious revelation. Shall the jury be instructed that it may convict the self-styled prophet, and send him to meditate in jail, if his claims are untrue, that is, if the jury concludes, after hearing the evidence, that the defendant is not St. Germain, that he has not shaken hands with Jesus, and that "I Am" theology is balderdash? Look out! Could we tolerate for a moment a principle that the free exercise of religion means only the free exercise of "true" religion, and that judges and juries are empowered to decide whose religious faiths are true and whose are untrue? That is the discredited medieval notion that "error has no rights," and it would undermine the whole institution of religious toleration. Would we have an ordinary jury, or any group in our society, empowered to pass judgment on the objective truth of the religious beliefs of, say, Dr. Billy Graham, Bishop Fulton Sheen, or Rabbi Abraham Heschel? I recall fundamentalist juries in the American Midwest who would at once convict Harry Emerson Fosdick and probably send Reinhold Niebuhr to the chair. So, whatever else, it is certainly not enough to prove against the Great I Am that his claims are not "true" to the satisfaction of his jury.

Shall we say, then, that the free exercise of religion extends only to religious affirmations that are made sincerely, that is, to religious claims that the speaker makes in subjectively honest belief of their truth? That, at first, appears as the reasonable and workable compromise: the constitutional guarantee of the free exercise of religion extends even to "untrue" views if the spokesman honestly holds them, but not to untrue views fraudulently and dishonestly espoused. The trial court so ruled in the *Ballard* prosecution itself. But how are we to prove, how is a jury or a judge to ascertain, the inner subjective state of mind of the prophet in the dock?

Our reluctant but unavoidable conclusion is that it would be fully as bad, in practice, to use the test of "honest belief" as to use that of objective "truth." If a jury or a judge is already prepared to decide that some novel and curious religious revelation is provably and objectively nonsense, would the same jury or judge have any difficulty in going one short step further and deciding that no one, including the self-proclaimed "messenger," could possibly have an honest belief that such nonsense is true? We were appalled a moment ago by the suggestion that clergymen might be summoned before a state tribunal to defend the objective truth of their respective religious witnesses. Is it not equally unthinkable that a clergyman be called before a state tribunal to defend the subjective honesty of his belief in the religious doctrines he expounds? I think I know Protestant ministers who have lingering intellectual difficulties with the idea of the virgin birth, Catholic priests who have their intellectual doubts about the dogma of the bodily assumption of Mary, rabbis who are troubled intellectually and ethically by the drama of Abraham and Isaac. Shall we have civil tribunals examining clergymen, even offbeat ones, as to the sincerity of their inner religious convictions?

The inevitable answer is that the possibility of fraudulent imposition on the unduly credulous is simply a part of the price we have to pay for meaningful religious liberty. This, I think, is an entirely proper weighing of the interests involved. I have never seen the issue better stated than in the late Justice Jackson's dissenting opinion in the *Ballard* case itself:

> The chief wrong which false prophets do to their following is not financial. . . . The real harm is on the mental and spiritual plane; it is not the money the victims part with half so much as the mental and spiritual poison they get. But that is precisely the thing the Constitution put beyond the reach of the prosecutor, for the price of freedom of religion or speech or of the press is that we must put up with, and even pay for, a good deal of rubbish.

Prosecutions of this character could easily degenerate into religious persecution. I do not doubt that religious leaders may be convicted of fraud for making false representations on matters other than faith or experience. As for example, if one represents that funds are being used to construct a church when in fact they are being used for personal purposes. But that is not this case, which reaches into wholly dangerous ground. When does less than full belief in a professional credo become actionable fraud if one is soliciting gifts or legacies? Such inquiries may discomfort orthodox as well as unconventional religious teachers for even the most regular of them are sometimes accused of taking their orthodoxy with a grain of salt.

I would dismiss this indictment and have done with this business of judicially examining other people's faiths.[24]

If Justice Jackson is right, and I profoundly believe that he is, it means that the law is without power, in many instances, to take effective action against the St. Ballard Germains and the Father Divines. It means, as Justice Jackson saw fully as clearly as anyone else, that fraud can and will be practiced under the cover of constitutionally protected religious liberty. But there is simply no way to take action against the fraudulent practices without setting a precedent entirely out of tone with the whole fabric of American religious liberty. When we get down to the hard cases, we are forced, however unwillingly, to the conclusion that the free exercise of religion means and must mean both "true" religion and "untrue" religion, must include the extravagances of the false prophet as well as the witness of the genuinely inspired.

The best test of truth, for constitutional purposes if for no other, is the power of an idea to get itself accepted. Holmes said this many years ago, and it is a formulation worth keeping in mind. We may choose the "truth," as God gives us to see the truth, but government and the officials of government must not be empowered to pass on questions concerning the truth or sincerity of religious professions. In a genuinely free society, the forum of choice is in the intellect and conscience of the individual, not in the jurisdiction of a judge, jury, postmaster, or licensing official. The American prophet, however venal or misguided, is not without freedom in his own country.

[24] United States v. Ballard, 322 U.S. 78, at p. 92 (1943).

The First Amendment and the Schools

Unequivocal answers to today's problems cannot be found in the constitutional history of more than 170 years ago. Some awareness of the historical situation in 1789 is needed, however, if the "no establishment" clause of the First Amendment is to be read in proper context. The draftsmen of the Bill of Rights could have written, very simply: "Congress shall make no law establishing a church." They did not say that. They wrote instead: "Congress shall make no law respecting an establishment of religion."

Why this more technical form of words? I suggest that the several Congressmen from several states who participated in the formulation of the First Amendment used the words they chose, "respecting an establishment of religion," because there were at least three ideas they wanted to express. Manifestly, they wanted to rule out every possibility that Congress might establish an official United States Church, like the Church of England or the Catholic Church of pre-Revolutionary France. Further, it would seem, they wanted to bar Federal financial support to any church or group of churches, or even to religion in general. "Establishment," in late eighteenth century usage, meant financial support as well as full-fledged confessional relationship; the "established churches" that existed in the American colonies before, and for that matter after, the Revolution were "established" only in the sense that they received support from public taxation. It will be noted, too, that the First Amendment speaks not of the establishment of a church but of an establishment of "religion." If these words are given their plain meaning, they rule out not only preferential financial assistance to a single church but also nonpreferential assistance to all churches, that is, to "religion."

But there is a third point. The First Amendment's precise terms, "*respecting* an establishment of religion," suggest that its framers wanted to keep the national government out of the picture altogether. Besides making it clear that Congress could not establish a national church or aid churches generally, they wanted also to be sure that Congress would not have the power to interfere with any of the state-wide religious establishments that existed in the states when the Bill of Rights was proposed for ratification.

One finds, as a matter of history, that there were established churches in some of the original thirteen states at the time the First Amendment was ratified, "established" churches in the sense that their ministers derived support from public revenues. The Congregational churches enjoyed this special status in 1789 in Massachusetts and New Hampshire. The special privileges of the Episcopal Church were on the way out in Virginia, but it was still an "established" church in the historical meaning of the term. A case can be made that the words of the First Amendment should be read as embodying a historical compromise. The Virginians, as we know from the correspondence of Jefferson and Madison, were passionately opposed to any kind of public financial assistance to religious endeavor. By contrast, a belief survived in New England that state governments should give affirmative support to religion, that is, support to the specific "truths," New Englanders would have said, of Protestant Christianity. New England schools did this for many decades after 1789. They were "public" schools in the sense that they were open to all and supported by tax revenues, but Protestant Christianity was taught to all students, and the birch rod was often applied to Roman Catholic children who expressed reluctance about the learning. How were the First Amendment's words, "no law respecting an establishment of religion," understood by those who proposed the amendment and voted for its ratification? This seems the probable answer: Congress shall not itself establish a religion, and Congress shall be equally powerless to interfere with existing state arrangements in matters of religion. It is not until adoption of the Fourteenth Amendment in 1868—indeed, not until the explicit application of that amendment to the states in *Cantwell v. Connecticut*—that there is anything in the Constitution of the United States bearing on state religious "establishments."

Since ratification of the Fourteenth Amendment, the principle against establishment applies against the states as well as against the federal government. This does not mean, however, that practice from state to state will be 100% uniform in matters of church-state relations. All the states must measure up to the minimum standards of church-state separation fixed by the First Amendment as interpreted by the Supreme Court of the United States, but a state constitution may impose far more severe restrictions on what that particular state government may do in such matters as indirect financial assistance to church-related schools. For example, it does not, I think, violate the federal constitution if a state furnishes free standard textbooks to parochial-school students—that is not, as we shall see, a violation of the "no establishment" clause of the First Amendment—but such a furnishing of free books to parochial-school students is forbidden by more explicit *state* constitutional provisions in many states. Indeed, on November 14, 1961, the Supreme Court of Oregon held, six to one, that a twenty-year-old Oregon statute authorizing public school districts to provide free textbooks to parochial schools was invalid under an explicit provision of the Oregon state constitution forbidding the expenditure of money by state authorities for the benefit of any religious institution. Similarly, Article XI, Section 4 of the Constitution of the State of New York is far more explicit than the First Amendment in its prohibition of the direct or indirect use of state funds in aid of church-related institutions. In short, to say that a state statute is permissible under the First Amendment to the Constitution of the United States is not to say that that statute satisfies what may be the stricter requirements of the local state constitution. It is quite possible that a state program in the general area of school aid may satisfy the minimum standards of the federal constitution and yet fail to meet some more severe standard of the local state constitution. But state constitutional law would be another and very long story, and our analysis here must be limited to the nationally applicable First Amendment.

How, then, does the "no establishment" clause of the First Amendment apply in matters of education? As to this, a frequently bitter controversy has been going on in the courts and, even more importantly, in Congress and the state legislatures, for over twenty years. There are two aspects of the problem:

(1) the constitutionality of religious education and religion-related observances in the public schools; and (2) the constitutionality of federal or state aid to church-connected schools. Since the governing considerations are quite different ones, the issues will be considered separately.

RELIGIOUS EDUCATION IN THE PUBLIC SCHOOLS

There are many thoughtful people—my long-time colleague, Bishop James A. Pike is one—who are dedicated to the American proposition of church-state separation and yet concerned that the systematic exclusion of all religious insights from public school curricula may give students an incomplete, wholly secular world view. Their position is about this: it is all right that the public schools be neutral in religious matters, but an exclusively secular education is not neutral but anti-religious in its impact and influence. Other critics of the public schools, far less sophisticated in their analysis, are simply unhappy about the low intellectual standards at American Sunday schools and are eager to have some positive religious content included as a part of public school instruction.

One expression of this concern appears in the released-time programs now in force in many states and municipalities. "Released time" operates by setting aside a certain time in the school day, or school week, during which public school students attend religious classes taught by clergymen of the child's, or rather the parents', selection. The arrangement might be that on Fridays from ten to eleven o'clock in the morning Methodist children attend special Methodist classes, Roman Catholic children special Catholic classes, and others accordingly. Or, as in certain roughly ecumenical programs in smaller communities, all children, like all Gaul, may be divided into three parts and assigned, respectively, to Protestant, Catholic, and Jewish religious classes. A difference should be noted, in passing, between "released time" and so-called "dismissed time." The latter arrangement is one by which classes are dismissed an hour or two earlier in the day, to permit those children who choose to attend religious classes after school is over. Under "released time," typically, the child's attendance is required, either at religious classes of his or his parents' choice or at some school activity, usually the school library study hall.

Ardent believers in a distinct separation of functions between church and state were at once appalled by what they considered the inescapably divisive effects of released-time programs on a public school community. Over the years, the public school has been the great instrument of the American melting pot. Is it good policy, the critics of released time asked, to have children thinking of themselves as members of exclusive groups? Is there not danger that the children of secularist parents, electing no denominational class at all, will be the butts of scorn and ridicule from their peers? Is not released time the kind of thing against which the "no establishment" clause was originally directed?

McCollum v. Board of Education,[25] the first released-time case, came to the Supreme Court in 1948. The constitutional challenger, Mrs. Vashti McCollum, was the freethinking mother of a child affected by the released-time program in force in the public schools at Champaign, Illinois. Her objection was vindicated and her challenge successful. By the unusually decisive vote of eight justices to one, the Supreme Court held that the "no establishment" clause of the First Amendment, as made applicable to the states by the Fourteenth, prohibits the "commingling of sectarian with secular instruction in the public schools" and so requires that the Illinois released-time program be ruled unconstitutional.

A storm of protest, chiefly but by no means entirely from churchmen, at once descended on the Supreme Court. The criticisms, or many of them, were almost as violent as those more recently leveled at the Court by white Southerners for the Court's decision in the great school-segregation case, *Brown v. Board of Education.*[26] "Shall the States be powerless to combat athiesm and ungodliness?" "Has the community no right to the free exercise of its religious conviction?" "Is the Supreme Court to be the new national school board?" The foregoing are but samples of the adverse comment on the *McCollum* decision from church quarters and in the popular press.

Four years later, released time was back in the Supreme

[25] 333 U.S. 203 (1948).
[26] 347 U.S. 483 (1954).

Court, the case *Zorach v. Clauson*[27] from the State of New York. I was teaching a seminar in Church-State Relations at that time, and my students asked me how I thought the Supreme Court would decide the *Zorach* appeal. I freely confess that I guessed wrong; it seemed to me that the Court's reasoning in *McCollum* clearly compelled a prediction that the New York released-time program would also be held unconstitutional. It comforts me that others guessed wrong, too, including one of America's greatest judges, Stanley Fuld of the Court of Appeals of New York. Judge Fuld, too, had considered the *McCollum* precedent controlling against the constitutionality of the New York program when *Zorach v. Clauson* was before his court.[28]

Zorach v. Clauson may have been indistinguishable to me, and, I venture to say, to most other scholars in the church-state area, but six of the nine Supreme Court justices found a distinction. The *McCollum* decision, said the Court, invalidated an Illinois program whereby public school students were released for religious classes conducted *on* the school premises. But the New York program challenged by Mrs. Zorach provides that the religious classes shall be held *off* the school premises. Of such fine lines is constitutional law, at times, composed.

The stated distinction—on school grounds or off school grounds—was, by the way, entirely unacceptable to the very justices who had written the opinions in the *McCollum* case. They rose in protest, Justice Black particularly, to insist that the constitutional vice held fatal in *McCollum* had not been the use of school premises for religious instruction but the use of compulsory school attendance laws to insure attendance at religious classes, and that the New York program was fully as objectionable in this crucial matter as the program already held unconstitutional in Illinois. But *Zorach v. Clauson* is the controlling decision, and released time is thus adjudged consistent with the "no establishment" clause, provided, one might say, that a little of the time released is consumed transporting

[27] 343 U.S. 306 (1952).
[28] Zorach v. Clauson, 303 N.Y. 161 (1951).

the children from the school grounds to some other location and back again.

I find the factual distinction—off school premises or on school premises—quite unconvincing. What had happened between the *McCollum* decision in 1948 and the *Zorach* decision in 1952? We can, at least, look at the box score. Eight justices had joined in the *McCollum* holding against Illinois released time. Two of these eight had left the Supreme Court, and their successors were apparently more favorable to an element of religious instruction in public education. Of the remaining six justices, three seem to have had long second thoughts about the *McCollum* decision. This leaves only three of the original eight still faithful to the separationist mood of the *McCollum* judgment, Justices Black, Frankfurter, and Jackson. Thus can a majority of eight become a minority of three, and within four years. Is it irreverent to say of the Black, Frankfurter, Jackson trio: "The boys stood on the burning deck, whence all but them had fled"?

This detailed account of the personnel shifts on the Supreme Court between *McCollum* and *Zorach* has been undertaken in an effort to communicate something of a "feel" for the realities that characterize and influence the constitutional law of church-state relations. Three important hypotheses are suggested. It is evident, first, that the constitutional issues involved are often close ones on which men of equal intelligence and good will can come to exactly opposite conclusions. Second, it is manifest that Court decisions do not establish immutable principles of church-state relations; an earlier case can be overruled or distinguished away if the same Court years later, even four years later, now thinks that it was wrongly decided. Our third hypothesis: that even Supreme Court justices may—just conceivably—be influenced unconsciously in their future deliberations by public opinion sharply critical of a past decision. The mood of Justice Douglas' opinion for the Court in *Zorach v. Clauson* differs strikingly from the mood and tone of the *McCollum* opinion in which Justice Douglas himself had joined. "We are a religious people," says Justice Douglas—in words doomed to be quoted wildly out of context by persons opposed to the whole idea of church-state separation—and Mr. Jefferson's "wall of separation" is breached a little more.

However he may strive for objectivity, a writer on church-state relations should not conceal his own political and religious convictions. Church-state separation, as a constitutional standard and goal, is not necessarily a secularist position. It can also be held, as I believe I hold it, as a matter of religious conviction. Will my biases show too much if I confess that I find the Court's *Zorach* opinion profoundly unconvincing and prefer infinitely the grand old Presbyterian Memorial of June 12, 1776,[29] when deeply religious men had this to say:

> Neither can it be made to appear that the gospel needs any such civil aid; [we] rather conceive that when our blessed Savior declares his kingdom is not of this world, he renounces all dependence upon State power, and . . . [we] are persuaded that if mankind were left in the quiet possession of their inalienable religious privileges, Christianity . . . would flourish in the greatest purity by its own native excellence, and under the all dispensing providence of God.

I think of these words every time I see some misguided effort to make the civil state a kind of promoter of religious truth. In illustration, one thinks of the almost blasphemous "commercial," "In God We Trust," put—of all inappropriate places in the world—on our *coins*, as if the meaning of the parable of the tribute money had wholly escaped the American Christian consciousness. "Establishment" is a dubious privilege that subjects religious leadership to officious state interference and can, at worst, make established religion an instrument of state policy. Our ancestors knew this from experience. We, I suggest, are in danger of forgetting it.

PUBLIC FINANCIAL AID TO CHURCH-CONNECTED SCHOOLS

Is the First Amendment's prohibition against "an establishment of religion" a bar to financial assistance, from state or federal funds, to church-connected schools? This is by far the most hotly disputed constitutional issue in contemporary church-state relations. Roman Catholic parochial schools are by no means the only church-related educational institutions

[29] Howe, *Cases on Church and State in the United States*, p. 5 (1952).

in the United States. Many colleges and universities have Protestant church connections of long standing, and Lutherans, Orthodox Jews, Episcopalians, and other denominations are expanding their sponsorship of private elementary and secondary schools. But the Catholic parochial schools are very much larger, in number of schools and of students, than all the rest combined, and current controversies tend to center on the Catholic elementary and secondary school system.

Let us be sure to consider this question fairly and on its merits; it is not a problem to be brushed off lightly or dismissed by deduction from some fancied absolute principle. There is no question but that the parochial and other church-connected schools are in a situation of grave financial crisis, one that endangers their survival. Vast increases in the school-age population, mounting educational costs, and the effects of relative inflation and high upper-income tax rates on private educational endowments and contributions are among the factors contributing to this financial crisis. It is equally manifest that public school expenditures would have to be far higher than they are, if financial difficulties compelled an abandonment of the parochial school system or a severe cutback in the number of students now being educated in the parochial schools and their Protestant and Jewish equivalents. The situation is but an aspect, although a very important one, of a general financial problem that threatens the future of private education, even in the colleges and universities, throughout the United States.

Inevitably and increasingly, churchmen and others concerned about the future of the church-connected schools are asking that some part of total public educational expenditures be allocated, directly or indirectly, to reduce existing financial pressures on the churches for support of their schools. The issue figured briefly during the 1960 presidential election. Presidential candidate Kennedy, at his Houston meeting with the Protestant ministers, expressed himself clearly against assistance from public revenues to church-connected schools. Mr. Lodge made one off-the-cuff pronouncement the other way, but Mr. Nixon did not endorse his running mate's proposal, and the issue disappeared from the campaign. It reappeared, however, as soon as the Kennedy administration brought forth its proposal for federal aid to education, a proposal strictly limited, for stated constitutional reasons, to the public schools alone.

The leading Supreme Court decision in point is *Everson v. Board of Education,*[30] decided in 1947, in which the Court held, five to four, that the "no establishment" clause of the First (and Fourteenth) Amendments was not violated by a New Jersey statute authorizing local school districts to reimburse the parents of parochial and other private school children, equally with the parents of public school children, for the costs of bus transportation to and from school. This was the first case in which the Supreme Court had ever squarely considered the effect of the "no establishment" clause as a constitutional limitation on state legislative power, and Justice Black's opinion for the Court, and the dissenting opinions of Justices Jackson and Rutledge, are long and sharply written. Justice Rutledge's carefully documented dissent was the most detailed historical study of the "no establishment" clause written by anyone up to that time. Since the majority prevails however close the margin, in Supreme Court litigation as in presidential elections, our analysis will concentrate on the prevailing, Black, opinion.

Justice Black is at least a relative "purist" on church-state separation, as one will recall from the vigor of his dissent in the New York released-time case, *Zorach v. Clauson.* His *Everson* opinion is written with great care and caution; its tone, essentially, is "this far you can go, but no farther." Jefferson, even Madison, would have found no fault with the last paragraph of the opinion:

> The First Amendment has erected a wall between church and state. That wall must be kept high and impregnable. We could not approve the slightest breach.

Even so measured, however, the New Jersey statute passes the test for five of the nine justices. In the words of the opinion itself:

> The State contributes no money to the schools. It does not support them. Its legislation, as applied, does no more than provide a general program to help parents get their children, regardless of

[30] 330 U.S. 1.

their religion, safely and expeditiously to and from accredited schools.

In short, as a matter of federal constitutional law—although local state constitutional provisions may require a different result in particular states—bus transportation for parochial school students does not breach the "high and impregnable wall" of church-state separation.

In most quarters, the five-to-four *Everson* decision has been taken as fixing the outer limit of permissible public aid to church-connected schools. How is that outer limit to be expressed, more generally, in words? For years after *Everson*, at least until last year, scholars, legislators and lower-court judges, in quest of a general standard, turned most often to the rhetoric of an older case, the 1930 decision in *Cochran v. Board of Education*,[31] in which the Supreme Court, without dissent, rejected a constitutional challenge of Louisiana legislation providing for the distribution of free standard textbooks to children in church-connected, as well as public, schools. Of course, *Cochran* would have been a closer case—indeed, would almost certainly not have been a unanimous decision—if it had come to the Supreme Court ten or more years later, that is, after the explicit decision in *Cantwell v. Connecticut* that the religious clauses of the First Amendment are incorporated into the "liberty" guaranteed against state action by the Fourteenth. The taxpayers who challenged Louisiana's free schoolbook program did so only on the ground that the distribution of free books to private and parochial school students was the use of state power for a nonpublic purpose. They did not argue, nor could they have been expected to foresee the possible post-*Cantwell* argument, that the furnishing of free books to students in church-connected schools is unconstitutional as a state law "respecting an establishment of religion." But it is the consensus among most constitutional lawyers, and I am in full agreement on the point, that the 1930 *Cochran* decision is still a reliable statement of constitutional law and that a state may furnish free books to parochial school students—assuming, of course, that they are the same books as are given free to

[31] 281 U.S. 370.

public school students—just as it may make bus transportation available, on an equal basis, to students in public and church-connected schools alike.

The existing constitutional dividing line is usually stated in about these terms: although public funds cannot be given to the church-connected schools, the furnishing of such auxiliary services as bus transportation, free books, free school lunches, public health facilities, and the like operates not for the benefit of the churches and their schools but for the benefit of the students; the state's aid is not to the schools but to the students who attend them. Whatever its logic, this so-called "pupil benefit" theory became a kind of working compromise, acceptable to most of the lawmakers in Congress and the state legislatures and, until very recently, to most of the spokesmen for Protestant, Catholic, and Jewish church opinion. A few church-school advocates have always rejected the "pupil benefit" theory as insufficient and urged outright support of church schools from public revenues. At the other end of the spectrum, some proponents of "absolute separation"—the P.O.A.U., for example—assail the "pupil benefit" theory as illogical, arguing that programs for free bus transportation, free books and the like are really for the benefit of the churches and their schools, since, if the state did not underwrite the costs, the church schools would have to do it themselves.

It is my own judgment, based on some experience with the practical legislative problem since the federal aid-to-education bill of 1949, that the "pupil benefit" theory, reasonably applied, is a workable compromise interpretation of the First Amendment and no threat to the integrity of American constitutional church-state relationships. Direct, outright grants to churches or church schools for building, maintenance and teachers' salaries are foreclosed as beyond a fair construction of the "pupil benefit" theory, and it is still my guess—although the "pupil benefit" theory is under increasing attack from both sides and showing signs of wear and tear—that financial aid from public funds to the church-connected schools will be provided, within the foreseeable future, only in the indirect forms that can be squared with the "pupil benefit" formula.

Thus far, of course, our discussion has been directed almost entirely to direct or indirect financial aid to church schools or their students from state or local funds. The idea of federal aid to education, even to public education, is still in its infancy, although we have an old precedent in the land grants made by the federal government to state universities many years ago, and a more recent precedent in the scholarship aid given to veterans after World War II by the G.I. Bill of Rights. Now, however, it seems almost certain—or did until the last session of Congress—that massive federal grants will soon be made to the states for educational purposes. The question arises whether any share of this federal aid will be available, directly or indirectly, to assist the hard-pressed church-related schools.

Judicial enforcement of the First Amendment, as of other constitutional limitations, is incomplete in one very important respect. Our point here is, in a sense, a technical, lawyer's point, but no appraisal of the constitutional ingredient in American church-state relations is realistic or useful unless the point is understood and kept in mind. Federal spending power, unlike most other federal legislative powers, is not subject to judicial review by the Supreme Court or any other court. A citizen can always challenge the lawfulness of an expenditure of state funds, by the kind of "taxpayer's suit" brought in the *Everson* and *Cochran* cases, but it has been settled for many years that no individual taxpayer has standing to sue to challenge the constitutionality of a federal expenditure.[32] As the theory goes, the federal budget is so vast that no individual taxpayer can show that his tax bill would be appreciably reduced if the challenged expenditure were eliminated.

Perhaps an extreme case is best to make the technical point. If the federal Congress were to vote an outright grant of $10,000,000 a year to every American church denomination, or even to certain preferred denominations, that would clearly be unconstitutional as a flagrant violation of the "no establishment" clause, but there would appear to be no way to get that grant into court for a judicial declaration of its unconstitutionality. Congress, of course, will do nothing of the sort. The members of Congress share the responsibility of the members

[32] Frothingham v. Mellon, 262 U.S. 447 (1923).

of the Supreme Court in matters of constitutionality and take the same oath to support the Constitution. But if Congress did make the grant—or, more likely, if it passed a financial-aid statute closer to the borderline of permissible assistance, as, for example, a statute underwriting the full cost of scientific and foreign-language instruction in the church-connected schools—the courts, it would seem, could not pass on the constitutionality of that expenditure of funds. Congress, in this sense, is the final constitutional court on questions of federal expenditure unless, and even this is disputed by a few constitutional lawyers, Congress includes an express provision in its appropriation act explicitly making the constitutionality of the expenditure reviewable in court at the suit of an interested party.

One sees, then, the special significance that attaches to constitutional arguments made whenever a proposal for federal aid to education is before the Congress of the United States. People are often surprised to hear that a major bill for federal aid to education passed the Senate of the United States thirteen years ago, in 1949, by an overwhelming vote. That bill, sponsored by the late Senator Robert Taft, died in the House of Representatives, not because the members of the House objected to federal aid to education in principle, but because the controlling members of the House committee in charge of the bill could not arrive at a tolerable compromise on the issue whether any of the federal funds might be so allocated as to benefit church-connected schools or their students.[33] In the last session of Congress, it was demonstrated again that impassioned disagreements on issues of church-state policy can be disastrous to educational and other social welfare proposals. The Kennedy administration's aid-to-education bill would have authorized vast grants to the states to help meet school construction costs and teachers' salaries. These are forms of assistance which it would seem at the present state of constitutional law cannot validly be extended to church-connected schools, and the administration's bill was strictly limited to public school construction and public school salaries. Spokesmen for the parochial schools demanded at once that some

[33] This now ancient history is recorded in Jones, "Federal Aid to Education: Constitutional Overtones," 36 Am. Bar Assn. Journal 68 (1950).

compensating provision be made in the bill to reduce financial pressures on the church-related schools and suggested several forms—long term low-interest loans, grants for scientific equipment and science instruction, tuition tax deductions for parents of parochial school children, etc.—in which, they contended, "indirect" assistance might be furnished without infringing the First Amendment.

As in 1949, compromise could not be reached. The bishops of the Roman Catholic Church expressed themselves in firm opposition to any federal aid-to-education bill which does not make some provision for parochial schools and their students, and the administration's bold plan for aid to education fizzled out and died in the closing days of the Congressional session. The bishops, since November of 1961, have twice renewed their warning that they will oppose any federal aid-to-education bill that is without provision for the parochial schools. Their constitutional theory, stated oversimply as limited space requires, is that the religious liberty of the First Amendment imports a claim by church-school students, too, to some share of the benefits resulting from public educational expenditures. Church-state separationists reply that no such benefits can be extended without violating the First Amendment's prohibition of any "establishment of religion."

Those concerned about the future of American education and American church-state relations have, as one great and immediate task, the fair and constitutional accommodation of these conflicting perspectives toward the First Amendment. There are those on both sides of the current controversy who are inclined to sneer at this as the way of compromise. Before one speaks too condescendingly of compromise, however, he might give heed again to Judge Hand's judicious reminder that democracy itself is "a political contrivance by which the group conflicts inevitable in all society should find a relatively harmless outlet in the give and take of legislative compromise." [34]

The accommodation necessary to overcome today's aid-to-education stalemate must be, and I believe can be, worked out within the bounds set for us by the First Amendment. The Roman Catholic bishops, as I understand their position, are not

[34] *The Spirit of Liberty*, p. 204 (1952).

demanding an outright public subsidy of church-connected schools. But others are beginning to ask just that, and I suggest only that these advocates consider, as not one of them has yet considered, the full implications of their position. It seems to be taken for granted in these appeals that outright 100 per cent subsidy of church-related schools would mean that there would be, at most, four different school systems in any pluralistic community: the public schools, Catholic schools, Jewish schools, and Protestant schools, all, of course, paid for from public revenues. This is not a happy prospect, to my way of thinking, but American education could, I suppose, live with it. But it is unthinkable, in the light of American constitutional principle, that the state or federal government could withhold its subsidy, once generally offered, from any denomination that decided to establish its own separate school system.

Once a separate school system could be operated at public expense by any denomination that wanted it, a fantastic Balkanization of American education would become possible. To be sure, only one Roman Catholic parochial school system would have to be supported in each community. But would Reform Jewish parents be willing to have their children educated at an Orthodox yeshiva? And what of the diversity within Protestantism? There could never be one for-all-the-Protestants school, nor would American constitutional principle permit governmental choice or preference among applying denominations. We would have, I suggest, publicly supported schools for, at least, Seventh Day Adventists, Jehovah's Witnesses, Episcopalians, Southern Baptists, and many more. Even the Lutherans, who have so far resolutely rejected public financial aid for their schools, might find it impossible to reject such funds if public monies were flowing to every other denomination.

In suggesting this problem of the Balkanization of elementary and secondary education, I am not saying, of course, that church-state financial separation is to be justified only on such practical grounds. But I have never thought that constitutional principle is made less attractive by the circumstance that the application of principle makes good common sense in an endlessly complex practical situation.

Never on Sunday: Church-State Issues in the Supreme Court, October Term, 1960

On May 29, 1961, after almost six months of collegial reflection, the Supreme Court of the United States announced its decisions in four cases challenging state Sunday closing laws as unconstitutional under the "no establishment" and "free exercise" clauses of the First Amendment. The challenged statutes were from three states, Maryland, Massachusetts, and Pennsylvania, but the 1961 test cases have a far wider significance, since the statutes called into question are fairly typical of the Sunday closing laws now on the books in forty-nine of our fifty states, Alaska alone excluded. These "never on Sunday" cases are the most recent church-state decisions we have had from the Supreme Court, and they are good ones to use for inventory, synthesis, and prediction of things to come.

In two of the four cases, *Gallagher v. Crown Kosher Market* [35] and *Braunfeld v. Brown*,[36] the constitutionality of compulsory Sunday closing was challenged on behalf of persons of the Orthodox Jewish faith, who, it was conceded, were obliged in religious conscience to keep Saturday rather than Sunday as a day of rest. Thus, in *Gallagher* and in *Braunfeld*, the contestants had a double-barreled First Amendment argument: first, that state-enforced Sunday closing is a kind of "establishment" of the Christian religion; and, second, that compulsory Sunday closing, by leaving the Orthodox storekeeper no alternative but to operate his store only five days a week, unconstitutionally impairs the "free exercise" of his religion. In the other two cases, *McGowan v. Maryland* [37] and the quaintly named *Two Guys from Harrison-Allentown v. McGinley*,[38] the challengers were not Orthodox Jews, were not under religious obligation to keep a day other than Sunday as a day of

[35] 366 U.S. 617.
[36] 366 U.S. 599.
[37] 366 U.S. 420.
[38] 366 U.S. 582.

rest, and so were in a position to raise only the single argument that state action to enforce the Christian day of rest is unconstitutional as a "law respecting an establishment of religion."

The several opinions in the four cases take up 110 pages in the *Supreme Court Reporter*. Many constitutional issues were presented; specifically, the Sunday closing statutes before the Court were attacked not only on First Amendment grounds but also as unconstitutionally vague and discriminatory under the due process and equal protection clauses of the Fourteenth Amendment. As to this, any reasonably detached observer will concede that existing Sunday closing laws, throughout the United States, are a crazy-quilt construction of legislative concessions to special interests. Typically, one may shop on Sunday for potato salad but not for potatoes, for bathing suits and sun-tan lotion but not for needles and thread, for cut flowers but not for cauliflower, for a new car but not for a bicycle or a baby carriage. But space compels us to limit our consideration to the explicitly church-state issues involved in the "never on Sunday" cases, and we cannot pause to examine the theory on which the Supreme Court rejected the appellants' uncertainty and equal protection arguments. What, then, is the substance of the contention that compulsory Sunday closing laws violate the "no establishment" and "free exercise" clauses of the First Amendment? What is the theory on which the Supreme Court, by a vote of eight to one on the "no establishment" point and six to three on the "free exercise" issue, sustains the constitutionality of enforced Sunday closing?

The Supreme Court nowadays is often criticized as unduly "activist" in disposition, that is, as being too willing to pass on politically controversial matters and too ready to impose its views of public policy on the rest of the national community. Whatever there may be to this criticism—and I, candidly, do not think that there is much to it—the Court was certainly not over-eager to pass on the thorny constitutional issues raised by state-enforced Sunday closing. As far back as 1896, and again in 1900, the Court had upheld the constitutionality of Sunday closing laws, from Georgia and Minnesota respectively, and in 1908 a challenge of the Sunday closing law of the State of Washington was dismissed on the plaintiff challenger's own motion. No other efforts were made to secure Supreme Court review of the validity of Sunday closing until after 1940, when the decision in *Cantwell v. Connecticut* declared explicitly that the "no establishment" and "free exercise" clauses of the First Amendment were applicable to state action as well as to Federal action, and so suggested to many people that the Supreme Court might decide the constitutional issue of compulsory Sunday closing differently if faced with the problem again.

Between 1950 and 1960, nine different attempts were made to secure Supreme Court review of state court decisions sustaining the constitutionality of local "never on Sunday" statutes. In each instance, the Supreme Court refused the sought review, with the cryptic notation, "appeal dismissed for want of a substantial federal question." But the constitutional issue could not be put off forever. In 1960, faced with the four cases now under discussion, the Supreme Court conceded, in effect, that a substantial Federal question was presented by compulsory Sunday closing and set the four cases for argument on the merits. Whatever else might be said of this incident in constitutional history, there is hardly ground to charge the Supreme Court with undue "activism" in the matter. If so, Mr. Wilkens Micawber was the greatest activist of all time.

The four cases—*McGowan* from Maryland, *Crown Kosher* from Massachusetts, and *Two Guys* and *Braunfeld* from Pennsylvania—were argued together on December 8, 1960. The best evidence of the seriousness of the Court's reflection on the issues involved is that the decisions did not come down until almost six months later, on May 29, 1961. So it had been a pretty substantial constitutional question, after all and all along! Indeed, on the "free exercise" issue, three of the nine justices dissented from the holding of the Court, and two of the other six found it necessary to express their agreement with the result in a separate concurring opinion.

We turn first to the line of reasoning by which the Court, Justice Douglas alone dissenting, reached the conclusion that a compulsory Sunday closing statute is not unconstitutional as a "law respecting an establishment of religion." It was conceded, as it had to be conceded, that Sunday closing legislation was religious, specifically Christian, in its *origin*. In fact, the very Maryland statute challenged in the *McGowan* case refers to Sunday as the "Sabbath Day" and as the "Lord's day," describes the offense proscribed as "Sabbath breaking," and expressly prohibits persons to "profane the Lord's day" by bodily labor, business activities, fishing, and the like. Chief Justice Warren's opinion for the Court in *McGowan*, and Justice Frankfurter's sixty-three-page concurring opinion in all four cases, include detailed and elaborate accounts of the history of Sunday laws from their origin in England in 1237, when Henry III forbade the frequenting of markets on Sunday, through the Act of 29 Charles II (1677) which required Sunday closing in the American colonies for the stated purpose of securing "the better observation and keeping holy [of] the Lord's day" and the "repairing to church thereon," further through the adoption of increasingly more stringent Sunday laws in the United States, largely under the influence of such groups as the Lord's Day Alliance, and finally to the comprehensive although exception-riddled Sunday closing laws of today.

Whatever their religious origin, however, the Sunday laws, so the Court rules, are not *now* religious in aim or effect. This is the crucial step in the Court's reasoning: Sunday closing legislation has taken on a secular, public welfare character. Government, says the Chief Justice, is properly concerned with the "health, safety, recreation and general well-being" of its citizens, and a general requirement that business activities be suspended on at least one day in seven contributes toward "the good life for all" and bears "no relationship to establishment of religion as those words are used in the Constitution of the United States." But is it consistent with the First Amendment to choose the specifically Christian day of rest as the day which all storekeepers must observe for themselves and their employees? Would it not be enough that the state require simply that a business close one day a week, on whatever day the proprietor may choose? Here is the Court's answer:

> The state's purpose is not merely to provide a one-day-in-seven work stoppage. In addition to this, the State seeks to set one day apart from all others as a day of rest, repose, recreation and tranquility—a day which all members of the family and community

have the opportunity to spend and enjoy together . . . a day in which people may visit friends and relatives who are not available during working days.

Obviously a state is empowered to determine that a rest-one-day-in-seven statute would not accomplish this purpose.

And so, the Court concludes:

The present purpose and effect of most of [the Sunday closing laws] is to provide a uniform day of rest for all citizens; the fact that this is Sunday, a day of particular significance for the dominant Christian sects, does not bar the State from achieving its secular goals. To say that the States cannot prescribe Sunday as a day of rest for these purposes solely because centuries ago such laws had their genesis in religion would give a constitutional interpretation of hostility to the public welfare rather than one of mere separation of church and State.

A certain paradox emerges here, as so often in church-state constitutional adjudication. The Court's result in *McGowan* and the other Sunday closing cases is certainly pleasing to religious traditionalists. Members of the Lord's Day Alliance, for example, were undoubtedly relieved to have this authoritative adjudication that compulsory Sunday closing is not an unconstitutional "establishment of religion." But the theory underlying the decisions may, when fully understood, cause some second thoughts. The state-enforced Sunday day of rest is saved from unconstitutionality, but explicitly not on any such theory as that a religious majority is entitled to employ state power as a means to compel others to refrain from conduct offensive to prevailing religious sensibilities. Sunday closing is sustained only as a means of achieving the state's "secular goals." Sunday, in the Court's view, has been secularized. What was "the Lord's day" is now, as the Chief Justice's opinion characterizes it, a day "for family activity, for visiting friends and relatives, for late-sleeping, for passive and active entertainments, for dining out and the like." The moral and warning are inescapable. Only at the price of secularization may specifically Christian practices be made compulsory rules of conduct for the community as a whole.

One cannot but reflect on the relevance of the Sunday closing decisions to current discussions in many churches about the erosion of the religious significance of Christmas, of ways and means whereby, as the objective is usually expressed, "we can put Christ back into Christmas." To the extent that the several Christian denominations undertake to persuade and inspire their own memberships toward a more reverent observance of the Christmas holy day, they are, of course, acting within the best of their traditions. But when they seek to enlist the powers and the agencies of the state, as by calling for Christmas observances in the public schools, they run grave risk of undermining their own purposes. If Christmas observances in the public schools are constitutional, it can only be on some such theory as that Christmas has become a secular community holiday and, to paraphrase the *McGowan* opinion, no longer has the religious meaning which was its "genesis" "centuries ago."

The Supreme Court's reasoning in the Sunday law cases points—inevitably, it seems to me—to a conclusion that a secularized Christmas observance is permissible in the public schools but that a distinctively Christian observance is unconstitutional as "an establishment of religion." I would not be understood as taking an absolutist view on the constitutional question presented. I cannot really conceive of a court holding that the singing of familiar Christmas carols at a public school assembly is "an establishment of religion" in the constitutional sense. My sense of proportion, and perhaps my sense of humor, restrain me from any such unqualified professional prediction. But carol-singing and other forms of Christmas observance in the public schools are constitutional, if they are, only on the theory that such celebrations are now without distinctively religious significance and have become part of a common, essentially secular, cultural heritage, shared by Christians, non-Christians and unbelievers alike.

Church leaders and other religious people eager to add quasi-religious ingredients to public school programs—Christmas observances, Bible readings, morning prayers, and the like —should look before they leap. If they want public schools and other public agencies to proclaim a specifically religious witness, that is precisely what they cannot have, for that is clearly an unconstitutional "establishment of religion." Conceivably, even Bible readings in the public schools might survive court test, if the passages to be read are meticulously selected. If Bible readings are sustained, however—and most of the better-reasoned court decisions are against the constitutionality of the practice in the public schools—it can only be on some such theory as that the Old Testament, at least, is part of our historical and literary heritage, our *secular* heritage, and that the passages chosen for school reading in the case at hand were without distinctive religious significance. But a secular *prayer?* In terms of the Sunday-law decisions, it is clearly not enough that the morning prayer in the schools be "nonsectarian"; it must be "nonreligious." I have been cautious about my prophecies in church-state cases since I guessed wrong on the Supreme Court's decision in *Zorach v. Clauson*, so I venture no flat prediction as to what the Supreme Court's ruling will be in the Regents' Prayer case argued before the Court April 3, 1962.[39] Conceivably, so innocuous a petition will be characterized as without distinctive religious significance and therefore not unconstitutional. But how I would hate, as a believing if not very good Christian, to argue the case for the Regents on any such ground! Will anyone deny that a "secular" prayer, constitutional or not, would be an abomination before the Lord?

Thus far we have considered only the first, "no establishment," problem in the May 1961 "never on Sunday" cases. We return now to the second, "free exercise," issue and specifically to *Braunfeld v. Brown*, the case from Pennsylvania in which the "free exercise" point is presented most sharply. Mr. Braunfeld, the appellant, is an Orthodox Jew, who operates a retail clothing and home furnishings store in Philadelphia. His Orthodox faith requires that he abstain from all manner of work from nightfall on Friday until nightfall on Saturday, and he does, in fact, keep his store closed throughout the Jewish Sabbath. For a time, he had kept his store open for business on Sundays, but the Pennsylvania statute was amended in 1959 so as to make it unlawful for anyone to sell clothing or home furnishings on Sunday. In the argument before the Supreme

[39] Engel v. Vitale, *supra*, discussed in Part 1 of this chapter as "The Case of the Regents' Prayer."

Court, the application of the statute to Mr. Braunfeld was challenged as an unconstitutional impairment of his right to the free exercise of his Orthodox religion. Mr. Braunfeld's case, simply put, was about this: (1) I am bound in conscience to refrain from business on Saturday, and that forbearance is an exercise of my religion; (2) State law now compels me to remain closed on Sunday, too, and this puts me at an impossible competitive disadvantage, five days a week against the six days of my competitors; (3) Thus I am penalized for the exercise of my religious conviction, and the Orthodox Jewish faith is itself put at a disadvantage which can hinder its chance of gaining new adherents and even cause it to lose present members to other denominations less strict about Sabbath observance. Manifestly, the same essential arguments might be, and actually have been, made by members of the Seventh Day Adventist Church.

The Supreme Court found the *Braunfeld* argument far more troublesome than the pure "no establishment" contention advanced by the challengers in *McGowan v. Maryland* and *Two Guys v. McGinley*. Four members of the Court joined in an opinion, this one, too, written by Chief Justice Warren, in which Mr. Braunfeld's "free exercise" argument was rejected on substantially the following grounds:

1. Pennsylvania's Sunday-closing law does not directly impair Mr. Braunfeld's "free exercise" of his religion—as it would do, for example, if it compelled him to keep his store *open* on Saturday—but operates merely so as to make the practice of his religious beliefs more expensive to him; and

2. A state might provide an exemption from Sunday closing for persons who, by religious conviction, observe a day of rest other than Sunday, but the administrative problems involved in drafting and enforcing such an exemption are so difficult that a state is under no constitutional obligation to grant the Sabbatarian exemption.

Justice Frankfurter, in a concurring opinion in which Justice Harlan joined, reached the same essential conclusions. Indeed, the Frankfurter opinion placed even greater emphasis on the practical problems of law administration that are raised inevitably when a special exemption from the Sunday closing laws is given to Orthodox Jews, Seventh Day Adventists and others similarly situated.

Thus we have six of nine Supreme Court votes against Mr. Braunfeld's "free exercise" contention. The three dissenters were Justice Douglas, who had dissented also on the "establishment" issue of the *McGowan* and *Two Guys* cases, and Justices Brennan and Stewart, who had joined the majority in rejecting the "establishment" argument. Justices Brennan and Stewart, however, were convinced by the Braunfeld "free exercise" contention, and they expressed the view that a Sunday law containing no exemption for persons observing a day other than Sunday as a religious day of rest cannot constitutionally be enforced against such persons. Justice Stewart's dissent is short and crisply to the point:

> Pennsylvania has passed a law which compels an Orthodox Jew to choose between his religious faith and his economic survival. That is a cruel choice. It is a choice which I think no State can constitutionally demand. For me that is not something that can be swept under the rug and forgotten in the interest of enforced Sunday togetherness. I think the impact of this law upon these appellants grossly violates their constitutional right to the free exercise of their religion.

Braunfeld v. Brown is a hard case and, for this reason, a profoundly instructive one. We Americans should be clearer than we usually are as to just what it is that a court decides in a constitutional case. In a litigated church-state controversy, the Supreme Court decides only what a state or the Federal government can or cannot do constitutionally. It does not decide what government, through its political departments, should do as a matter of policy within the bounds of the constitutionally permissible. It is not the Court's function to decide that some other way of handling a problem might have been better, from the point of view of public policy, than the way actually chosen by the state's elected representatives.

The legislative problem suggested by *Braunfeld v. Brown* illustrates my point perfectly. Six of the nine justices of the Supreme Court have ruled, simply, that a state is not under constitutional duty to grant Saturday religious observers an exemption from the Sunday closing laws. Three of the nine feel so strongly about the hardship and injustice suffered by the Saturday observers that they believe the state cannot constitutionally withhold the sought exemption from them. But it is manifest from the Warren and Frankfurter opinions that the majority six, too, are sensitive to the competitive plight of the Orthodox shopkeeper in a dominantly Sunday observing community. Thus we reach the question of legislative policy: should not the Sunday closing statutes now be amended to grant the exemption unsuccessfully sought as a matter of constitutional right by Mr. Braunfeld and those in his situation? Several bills designed to grant the exemption were introduced, but failed of enactment, in the 1962 session of the New York State Legislature.

As in the *Ballard* case and elsewhere in church-state matters, we encounter again the distinctively legal problem: how can a workable solution be devised? Granting, as I think we will all grant, that Sunday closing laws bear harshly on the Orthodox or Seventh Day Adventist merchant, can a way be found to give him the relief to which the spirit of the First Amendment, if not its direct mandate, entitles him? No one will suggest, I take it, abandonment of the requirement that stores and industrial establishments close one day a week. Is the workable compromise, then, an amendment of the Sunday closing laws that will require one day's closing but allow the proprietor to choose his closing day, any day in the week, according to his own preferences or ideas of business advantage? Talk a moment with any trade union leader, and you will discover at once how unacceptable that solution would be. The Supreme Court majority is quite right on this point; Sunday has become a day when families and friends get together. It is important that the day off be the *same* day off. Community recreational schedules are made up on that basis, and the "social welfare" day of rest becomes something far different if members of the social group are free from work only on different days.

Thus we are brought to the next suggestion, which is essentially the view of Justices Brennan and Stewart: make Sunday the compulsory closing day for most members of the community, but grant a special exemption to those who, as a matter of religious identification or affiliation, are required to refrain from work on a day other than Sunday. I like this, too, at first impression, but reflection discloses that we may now have an even harder question of public policy and constitutional law. In most communities, the majority of storekeepers would then be required by law to remain closed on Sunday, and that could make Sunday opening a measurable and distinct competitive advantage. If there are ten retail clothing stores in New Bloomfield, nine of them operated by owners who are Catholics, Protestants, Reform Jews or secularists, a special statutory exemption will, retail experience demonstrates, enable the Adventist or Orthodox Jewish storekeeper to do two or three times as much business on Sunday as he would have done had his store been open on Saturday. If mere church affiliation qualifies an applicant for the exemption, we might, as Justice Frankfurter's *Braunfeld* opinion suggests, witness an astonishing conversion of Protestant storekeepers to Seventh Day Adventism and of Jewish storekeepers to the Orthodox version of Judaism.

Shall we then, as proponents of the Sabbatarian exemption will say at last, restrict the exemption from Sunday closing to those who have an honest, individual religious conviction that they must not work on Saturday or some other weekday? We are brought full circle, back to *United States v. Ballard.*[40] As now qualified, the proposed Sabbatarian exemption takes on the character of a religious test, involving inquiry by a state official, here a mere licensing officer, into the inner, subjective integrity of an individual's religious professions. If this long discussion of the constitutional law of church-state relations has made any point at all, it has at least furnished warning against this last proposed solution to the troublesome *Braunfeld v. Brown* problem.

I close with this difficult and involved task of practical problem-solving largely as an offset to my own preferences, which are, as my readers will have observed, the views of one who thinks it good public policy to keep the respective provinces of church and state as nearly separate as possible. To speak of "absolute separation" is, of course, nonsense and has been since the common law, hundreds of years ago, abolished

[40] 322 U.S. 78 (1943), discussed at length in Part 2 of this chapter.

the privilege of benefit of clergy. My personal inclinations are strongly with those who favor Sabbatarian exemptions from the Sunday closing laws but, at least so far, I have not been able to see a workable solution. And that is what courts and legislatures and lawyers must do, that is, devise solutions that are both workable in life and consonant with constitutional principle.

We can and should criticize the decisions of our courts, particularly when matters of profound constitutional principle are involved, as they are inevitably in church-state relations. But let us understand the task of those who are charged with judicial responsibility. Unlike pure social scientists, who need not announce their findings and conclusions until all the returns are in, judges cannot wait. Judges have the duty to decide and to decide now. If there are imperfections in the craftsmanship of the Supreme Court and other courts in church-state cases, it must be borne in mind that this nation of religious diversity would be far more strife-torn without the religion clauses of the First Amendment, and that the First Amendment might be meaningless in our society without the institution of judicial review. There is always far more to the part of the iceberg that is concealed beneath the surface of the sea. Perhaps now my readers can reconstruct some of the judge-to-judge deliberations that went on in the Supreme Court building between December 8, 1960 and May 29, 1961, the six months that passed after the argument and before the Court finally announced its verdict, "Never on Sunday."

TO POINT A MORAL . . .

The constitutional problems in American church-state relations are not easy ones. Too many writers on religion and the Constitution address themselves to the subject as if they were doing nothing more than describing what the "law" is, that is, predicting what the Supreme Court will surely decide if and when a case comes to it for judgment. In a certain lawyer's sense, that is what constitutional law is: "a prophecy of what the courts will do in fact and nothing more pretentious," as Justice Holmes once characterized it. But we must not confuse our preferences with our predictions. We must not read the

First Amendment, or any part of the Constitution, as if it embodied our own deeply felt notions as to some ideal pattern of church-state relations.

In constitutional law, as elsewhere in the world of ideas, dogmatism is not enough. I am under no illusion that my views on the policy issues of church-state relations are the only permissible views, the only intellectually respectable interpretations, for one who reads the First Amendment in the light of its history and its purposes. I detest the occasional suggestion, in church-state discussions, that anyone who disagrees with the particular writer's view on this or that constitutional question is an enemy of religious liberty, or a tool of special denominational interests, or an appeaser willing to compromise away some asserted doctrine of absolute separation of church and state. When the Supreme Court divides from case to case—five to four as in *Everson*, six to three as in *Zorach* and *Braunfeld* —it is a poor constitutional lawyer who will claim that his is the only authorized version of some First Amendment revelation and that those who do not bow to his interpretation are uninformed, misguided, or worse. The spirit of civil liberty is, above all, a spirit of regard for the other fellow's honest point of view. One stands up and is ready to be counted for what he believes, but the libertarian is always mindful of Learned Hand's warning that "the spirit of liberty is the spirit which is not too sure that it is right."

There is an affirmative side to this. As a matter of constitutional morality, we respect the authority of the Supreme Court's decisions, but we are not to be too sure, either, that the Court is always right, or that one of its decisions, right in the conditions of its time, is immutably right, right forever, no matter what changes may come about within our national community. For the ten years after 1950, Sunday closing laws were said to raise no substantial federal question. In 1961, they are sustained, as to Orthodox Sabbatarians, by a vote of but six to three. Who is rash enough to claim absolute verity for his prediction of what the Court may decide in the matter ten years from now? And so it is with other constitutional issues in the church-state area. To deny the Supreme Court's continuing right to re-examine its own past decisions, to bring the judicial exegesis on the constitutional text more closely into line with the felt necessities of a later time, is to deny the possibility of judicially enforced constitutional government and so to endanger the ultimate guarantee of American liberty.

Church-state controversies will always be with us. Difficulties of adjustment and accommodation are forever recurrent when two great institutions, the church and the state, occupy the same territory and draw on the allegiance of the same people. One thinks of Robert Frost's line, "Something there is that doesn't love a wall," and this is as true of Mr. Jefferson's wall of church-state separation as of any other. But our difficulties become less intractable, I believe, when we think of the "no establishment" clause of the First Amendment not only as one of the articles of peace that narrow interdenominational rivalry in a religiously pluralistic society, but also as the best guarantee of the independence and vigor of the churches themselves. Our political and social order needs continuing criticism —castigation, when the situation demands that—from those who see the urgent issues of our day in the timeless and uncompromising dimension of the Judeo-Christian tradition. Churches beholden to Caesar for support and financial aid are, to that extent, less free to proclaim for society the things that are God's.

John Kennedy and the Catholic Issue: 1960-1964

JOHN WICKLEIN

IN polite society fifty years ago there was a cliché about what should, and what should not, be discussed at an afternoon tea. The young women of Miss Clinch's classes heard it over and over again—which is really the test of a good cliché. "Girls," Miss Clinch used to say, "it's better not to talk at all. But if you *must* talk, remember this: *never* discuss religion or politics."

If a Clinch girl had been required to stick to that nicety during the last presidential election, she would have snapped a stay. Through much of the campaign there wasn't anything to discuss but religion *and* politics. And the discussion, in altered form, is troublously with us today.

As a reporter for *The New York Times*, I spent the greater part of 1960 covering one running story: the so-called religion issue in the presidential election. Most people referred to it that way when they talked about it. But it is probably more accurate to call it the "Catholic issue." No one who mentioned religion to me in the 1960 campaign meant he was concerned because Richard M. Nixon was a Quaker. In fact, one Republican told me that Nixon didn't believe in pacifism and Quaker things like that. "Heck," he said, "the people don't have to worry about Mr. Nixon being influenced by his religion if *he's* elected President."

So far as the people were concerned, it was the fact that John F. Kennedy was a Roman Catholic that created the "problem," and nothing else. And although many Catholics voted for Kennedy who had not voted for Adlai E. Stevenson, Kennedy became President despite his religion, not because of it. The Gallup and Harris polls showed that nearly two-thirds of all Protestants had voted against him. His popular vote would have been much higher if he had not been a Catholic. There were several reasons for this, including Kennedy's charm. But one reason alone would have done it. Nixon was just not a popular candidate, even among the people of his own party. For many people he had only one outstanding qualification: he was Protestant.

In the primaries and the election campaign itself there was an outcry among conservative Protestants against letting *any* Catholic become President—ever. The issue, they said, wasn't so much the candidate, but the Roman Catholic Church. Throughout history, they insisted, the church had used intimidation and force to impose its religion on countless people, and they just didn't want to "take a chance" that it would happen here. The really swinging ones, such as a cowboy evangelist I talked to out West, said they thought Kennedy would turn right around and hand the country over to the Pope. This was the typical argument that was used against Al Smith in the 1928 campaign. Nothing Kennedy could say or do would convince these believers that he could remain free from ecclesiastical pressure.

More rational Protestants among the "antis" said they knew Kennedy would not take dictation from the Catholic hierarchy. But they said his election would "open the door" to the election twenty-five years from now of another Catholic candidate who was not so firmly committed to separation of church and state.

Liberal Protestants who supported the Senator said the election should be decided on the men and issues of the day, not on a hypothetical situation a generation from now. The Roman Catholic Church, they contended, was not standing for election any more than the Religious Society of Friends.

And that was true, at the time. The election did not turn on the Roman Catholic Church, but on the two men who were running for President. Yet in a sense, today, the Catholic Church *is* standing for election. Even before the inauguration, the Catholic issue, knocked down in the Democratic victory, was revived in a new form and thrown once more—this time by the American Catholic Bishops—into the political path of John F. Kennedy.

The American hierarchy, after carefully assessing the new political and social climate, deliberately put the church at the center of the most controversial question involving the separation of church and state. In demanding Federal aid for parochial schools, it called on Kennedy and Congress for a country-changing decision—asking in effect to be made a partner with the Federal government in educating the nation's school children.

Symbolically, through the school issue, the hierarchy is asking the President, the Congress and the public to recognize that the Catholic Church is a basic and legitimate force in American life, co-equal with the Protestant culture group. No other tactic of the church could have solidified Protestants so quickly for a rearguard defense of their "era" in the United States.

During the election campaign, because a liberal candidate, and not the church, was the focus of the Catholic issue, only conservative Protestants seemed to be standing against the church. But now that the hierarchy, by forcing the parochial school debate, has become the focus, liberal Protestants as well as conservative have joined the opposing line-up. Because many liberal Protestants, although they respect and admire the Catholic position on segregation and some other social concerns, do suspect that the hierarchy itself is an illiberal force in its approach to government and politics.

It has been fascinating to watch the way Kennedy has countered the two major challenges in the religious sphere: the first from Protestants in the 1960 election campaign, the second from Catholics in the long Congressional debate. And it is fascinating to speculate on how he will parry these competing forces when they have at him from two sides in the 1964 election. Because it seems certain, when you take into account the determination of the hierarchy and the implacability of the Southern Baptist preachers, that the Catholic question will become a major campaign issue again next time.

In the 1960 election, conservative and fundamentalist Protestants staged organized drives to defeat Kennedy because he was a Catholic. An official of the National Association of Evangelicals admitted to me afterwards that he and a lot of others in his group—all of them political conservatives—would not have voted for Kennedy in any case, because of his liberalism.

So the motives of the "antis" were mixed. Some religious and political conservatives obviously used the religious issue cynically to try to defeat a political liberal. Others had a deep conviction that if Jack Kennedy were elected, the country would, as they put it, "begin going down the road to Rome."

The theme question on the rational side of the discussion was posed by James A. Pike, Protestant Episcopal Bishop of California, in a magazine article in December 1959. Bishop Pike said there were two traditions in the Catholic Church: (1) the European, which does not support separation, and (2) the American, which does. The question, then, he said, is this: Does this particular Catholic candidate support the American tradition, which adheres to the United States Constitution?

This question on religion, concerning public policy, could legitimately be asked in a political campaign; a question concerning a man's personal faith could not.

It is *not* bigotry to say to a man, "I don't agree with your views on religious liberty, and so I won't vote for you."

It *is* bigotry to say to a man, "You are a Catholic, and I don't like Catholics, and so I won't vote for you."

This is the distinction that Bishop Pike wanted to make.

Senator Kennedy gave a definitive answer to the Bishop's question in a speech to the American Society of Newspaper Editors in Washington on April 22, 1960. He pointed out that he had often stated his complete support of the Constitution, including specifically its clauses on religious liberty and separation of church and state. He declared he would not "in any way be responsive to ecclesiastical pressures or obligations of any kind" in his conduct of the Presidency. He went further in supporting rigid separation than did Alfred E. Smith, the only previous Catholic who had received a major party's endorsement for the office. Some Catholic bishops and editors thought Kennedy had gone *too* far. As early as March, 1959, he had stated in an article in *Look* magazine: "There can be no question of Federal funds' being used for support of parochial or private schools. It's unconstitutional under the First Amendment as interpreted by the Supreme Court."

The diocesan press criticized him for this. The editors, who are spokesmen for their bishops, declared there could be more than one interpretation of the religious clause in the Constitution as it concerns parochial schools. This is the clause in the First Amendment that says: "Congress shall make no law respecting the establishment of religion, or prohibiting the free exercise thereof."

The American Catholic position on separation has not yet been resolved within the hierarchy itself. Its members have, however, tried to assuage Protestant fears about its view of the church-state relationship. In 1948 the late Archbishop John T. McNicholas, speaking as chairman of the bishops' administrative board, said this:

"We deny absolutely and without any qualification that the Catholic bishops of the United States are seeking a union of church and state by any endeavors whatsoever, either proximate or remote. If tomorrow Catholics constitute a majority of our country, they would not seek a union of church and state. They would then, as now, uphold the Constitution and all its amendments, recognizing the moral obligation imposed on all Catholics to observe and defend the Constitution and its amendments."

Yet during the campaign, Cardinal McIntyre of Los Angeles told me in an interview that, theologically, separation of church and state is impossible. A man cannot separate himself from his religion when he assumes a public office, he said. And for good measure, he added this: "You cannot separate God from the state and be a Christian country. And we are a Christian country—and all the people in the United States would approve of that."

Then in March of 1961, and again that November, the Catholic bishops declared that their parochial schools should receive financial support from the Federal government. They had a right to receive such support, the bishops said, because the schools were performing a service to the public in educating 13 per cent of the nation's children. The bishops vowed they would work to defeat any legislation for Federal aid to education that did not include aid to private and parochial schools.

Now, this, of course, was not meant to shore up the "wall of separation" first proposed by Thomas Jefferson. But then, many bishops have been critical of this "wall" metaphor ever since Jefferson uttered it.

During the campaign, liberal Protestants were interested in what the Catholic bishops thought about separation, but their main concern was what Kennedy thought about it. His statement to the newspaper editors satisfied Episcopal Bishop Pike and most other liberal churchmen. But it did not mollify Protestants of the ultraconservative school.

They began putting their mutterings down on paper, then preaching them as sermons and issuing them as statements to the press. "Nuns will be lighting candles in the East Room of the White House!"

The proving ground for the antibigot weapons Kennedy was to use in the big war was the West Virginia primary. There, conservative Protestants flailed Kennedy with his Catholicism as soon as he set foot in the state. Kennedy struck back, and the fight that resulted proved to be the decisive one of the spring campaign.

Senator Hubert H. Humphrey of Minnesota was in that Democratic go-round, too. But the real contest was between the "Catholic candidate" from Boston and the fundamentalist preachers.

West Virginia is about 96 per cent Protestant, with the Catholic population isolated in the northern panhandle around

Wheeling. Many of the Protestants in the southern part of the state are Primitive Baptists who think the Catholic Church split off from Baptist Christianity in the year 254 A.D. Most of the others are pretty conservative about their religion, too, and they have an inbred suspicion of the Church of Rome. By the time the primary campaign began, everybody knew Kennedy was a Catholic and Humphrey was some kind of a Protestant.

On Easter Sunday I stood with some people on a riverbank, watching a young preacher baptize five of his flock by total immersion. I asked a white-haired woman standing next to me whom she was going to vote for in the primary. "I can't say as I've made up my mind yet," she said. "But I wouldn't want to see a Catholic in the White House."

Both candidates went into West Virginia with qualms about the religious question. Humphrey, a liberal Congregationalist, was sick at the thought that the race might be decided on that issue. He felt it would be indecent for him or any of his staff to refer to religion in any way. Every reference, even one that deplored the issue, would tend to crystallize it as the decisive factor.

Kennedy didn't want to mention it either, although he knew if he started poking around in the Protestant hollers for votes, he was bound to stir up a bear or two. Still, with the odds seeming to be heavy against him, West Virginia appeared to be a fine place to prove he could win by a lively performance on the stump. But the religious sniping was worse than he had expected—the preachers threw his faith up to him repeatedly, and he was questioned about it by the citizens in every town he went to. To these Protestants, there seemed little to choose between the policy positions of the two liberal candidates. So religious kinship appeared almost certain to be a factor in making up their minds.

In late April, against the advice of his managers, Kennedy came to the decision that was to make his campaigning so different from that of Al Smith in 1928. Al Smith avoided replying to his religious critics from the platform. Jack Kennedy decided that not only would he reply to all of them, but he would volunteer some remarks about religion on his own. This decision, and its follow-up in the campaign, probably saved him from the defeat that Protestant voters handed to Al Smith in 1928.

Kennedy began telling people at every stop, even before they asked him, that he would "not take orders from any Pope, any Cardinal, any Bishop or any priest."

From then on, the feeling began to grow in West Virginians' minds that it would be bigotry to vote against this personable young man just because he happened to be born a Catholic. Most people don't like to be thought of as bigots, even though they are bigots.

If they voted for Humphrey, their neighbors might point. So in many minds, a vote for Kennedy became a vote that showed they were tolerant.

As for campaigner Humphrey, himself he could not save. Hubert Humphrey usually has something trenchant to say about most issues. But he couldn't say a word in his own defense against this idea. You just can't knock tolerance.

By the end of the contest, Humphrey was fit to be tied. And the Kennedy people obliged him.

On May 8, two days before the balloting, Kennedy threw his most effective punch at the religion argument, as far as the voters in West Virginia were concerned. He went on statewide television and declared he thought that a candidate would "sin against God if he broke his Constitutional oath to defend separation of church and state."

Two days later he won by a margin of 60 per cent to 40 per cent. Jubilantly, he told the country: "I think we have now buried the religion issue once and for all."

The statement was overly optimistic, but understandable in the circumstances. In sixty-one interviews of West Virginia Democrats, from the coal mining camps in the south to Wheeling in the north, I found only one man who said he was for Humphrey because he thought Humphrey was better qualified. Every other person who said he was for Humphrey said it was because Kennedy was a Catholic.

In this particular primary contest, only Democrats could vote. If you assume, conservatively, that 25 per cent of the Democrats voting turned Kennedy down because of his religion, then it was a good bet that religion would be a factor nationally, if Kennedy got the nomination. The presidential election might easily be decided by the defection of, say, 5 per cent of normally Democratic Protestants to the Republicans.

Kennedy went on to win all seven primaries that he entered. Religion showed up to some degree in each.

His strategists had now proved to the big-city Democratic leaders that he was an effective campaigner. But many of these leaders were Catholics themselves, and they still believed it would be hard to break the jinx against a Catholic candidate nationally.

So, to try to nail down the nomination, they brought in an argument that considered the other side of the religious coin.

At the convention, they circulated a memo which said that a party that ran a ticket with a Catholic at the top could expect a 20 per cent switch of Catholic voters to that party's standard. And Catholic voters, they pointed out, were concentrated in fourteen swing states with 261 of the 269 electoral votes needed to win. In order of "clout," these states were: New York, with 45 electoral votes; California, 32; Pennsylvania, 32; Illinois, 27; Ohio, 25; Michigan, 20; New Jersey, 16; Massachusetts, 16; Wisconsin, 12; Minnesota, 11; Maryland, 9; Connecticut, 8; Rhode Island, 4, and Montana, 4.

If Catholic switches provided the margins needed to tip most of these states to the Democrats, they argued, then Kennedy would have to add only a few states from the traditionally Democratic South to carry the Electoral College.

Catholic citizens who would vote *for* Senator Kennedy because of his religion, his backers contended, were much more strategically placed, as far as electoral votes went, than were the Protestant citizens who would vote *against* the Senator because of his religion. For instance, New York, with the largest number of electoral votes—45—has the largest Catholic population of any state. There are nearly 6,000,000 Catholics in New York State, or about 35 per cent of the population. All the other big electoral-votes states averaged out to about 30 per cent Catholic with the exception of Texas, which had 19 per cent.

To win a national election, the Democrats have to carry most of the big-population states of the industrial North—this is axiomatic. The Kennedy camp predicted that with their man heading the ticket, the party would pull back the bulk of normally Democratic Catholics in these states who had shifted to Eisenhower in 1952 and 1956. And, they said, he would also pull across some Catholic Republicans, which would be helpful.

The conservative Protestant, anti-Catholic voters are concentrated in the Midwest and South, the Kennedy memo pointed out. The midwesterners could be expected to vote Republican in any case, and any southern defections from the normal Democratic pattern would be more than offset by the big northern states that would be swung to Kennedy by Catholic voters.

Catholics in the North are crowded into the larger cities, where the Democratic organizations could be counted on to get them out. And this would supply the needed counterweight to the traditional "upstate" and "downstate" votes for the Republicans.

This reasoning, plus Kennedy's showing in the primaries, did much to convince the big-city politicians. The convention went to Kennedy, despite some remaining doubts among liberal Democratic leaders, including Adlai Stevenson, that the nation had reduced its prejudice enough to elect a Catholic President.

Once the hurrahs of the July convention died, the first sniping shots of the running religious battle began. In the South there appeared a piece of literature that was destined to be big with the "ultra" Protestants. This was an anti-Kennedy, anti-Catholic statement that had been made in the pulpit of the biggest all-white Protestant church in the world—First Baptist in Dallas. In a sermon delivered July 6, the Rev. Dr. W. A. Criswell declared: "Roman Catholicism is not only a religion, it is a political tyranny."

And Kennedy, he asserted, would not be able to stand up to the political pressures of his church.

Dr. Criswell told me later that his sermon had not been intended for use against Senator Kennedy in the election campaign, but rather as a pre-convention argument that might help Lyndon Johnson get the presidential nomination. But when that Catholic Kennedy was nominated, he said, he and most of his congregation had no recourse but to support Richard Nixon.

One member, H. L. Hunt, the oil millionaire, paid for the anonymous distribution of 100,000 copies of the Criswell sermon. By the time the campaign ended, this piece had been reproduced in many hundreds of thousands of printed copies and sent by direct mail to people in every part of the country.

Other conservative Baptist preachers beat their pulpits into stumps with political orations against a Catholic for President. Kennedy as a Catholic became the talk of the South. Liberal southerners called their conservative neighbors bigots. The conservatives retorted that this wasn't bigotry at all, but just the acceptance of hard, cold fact that a Catholic in the White House was not going to be able to do as much to preserve separation of church and state as a Protestant could.

One Roman Catholic priest remarked wryly that he wasn't sure the conservative Protestants believed in separation. Hundreds of Baptist preachers in the South were taking the national election into their sanctuaries, he said, but not one Catholic priest had done so.

What he said about the Catholic clergy was true: throughout the campaign, as far as I know, not one preached a political sermon supporting the idea of a Catholic for President, or Kennedy in particular as a candidate who happened to be a Catholic.

There were good reasons for this. No matter what the logic of the situation, any comment on the election by a Catholic priest would have been taken by many Protestants as an unwarranted interference by the Catholic Church in affairs of state. Perhaps the rationale for this was that Protestants generally think that a priest, whenever he speaks, is speaking directly for his church—or at the direction of his hierarchy. They consider that a Protestant, on the other hand, is speaking only for himself.

In any event, it would have been bad public relations for Catholic clergy to take sides openly in an election in which a Catholic was seeking to be the first man of his faith elected President.

Another reason is that it was likely that most of the Catholic cardinals, bishops, and priests did not want to see Kennedy elected. Some in the hierarchy felt that Kennedy was not as doctrinaire a Catholic as they would like to see making the race. Many of the bishops thought he had yielded too much to political expediency in dissociating himself from ecclesiastical authority. To them, he did not represent the main line of Catholic thinking on the roles of religion and government. To them he sounded even farther out on the question of separation than Father John Courtney Murray, the most liberal interpreter of the church's doctrine as applied to state concerns.

Then there were misgivings among the clergy, and leading laymen, that the country was still not ready to receive a Catholic as a candidate. They feared that the discussion of religion would stir all the antagonisms that had boiled up in the 1928 campaign and spilled over into the years that followed. They believed that any such partisan religious battling would only lead to a setback for the church, as well as for peaceful relations among the major faith groups.

Finally, there were some who thought the American Catholic Church would fare better under a Protestant President than it could under a Catholic. The first Catholic President, they reasoned, would be in a terribly exposed position. He might feel compelled to turn down requests from the church that a Protestant President might grant without hesitation.

The church had flourished under Protestant Presidents. Eisenhower, for instance, had come much closer to endorsing the American bishops' stand against birth control in foreign-assistance programs than had Senator Kennedy. Franklin D. Roosevelt and Harry S. Truman sent special envoys to the Vatican; Senator Kennedy said he opposed appointment of a special envoy or an ambassador.

And in the campaign itself, Henry Cabot Lodge, a Protestant (Episcopalian) and the Republican nominee for Vice-President, said he favored giving *some* Federal aid to parochial schools; Kennedy declared flatly that this could not be done under the Constitution.

Several Catholic publications commented that the church would obtain "more equal" treatment through the election of another Protestant in 1960 than it would through the election of a Catholic with a suspicious electorate criticizing every dealing that involved a position of the church.

But in the more rabid areas of the South, any evidence that the church itself did not want a Catholic in the White House went unheeded. The only conclusion the super-Protestants could draw from the fact that a Catholic was in the contest was that the Catholic Church had put him there, in an effort to take over the country.

They fanned the fires that they themselves had set, and the campaign got a little meaner. In Texas the Nixon Democrats, the Republicans, and the Masons used political jokes against Kennedy that were based on his religion. One of these was that if Kennedy got elected, the Protestants were going to have to ride in the back of the buses.

For liberals the joke seemed to be a Freudian admission of guilt over treatment of Negroes in the segregationist states. Not all the jokes were *fraught*, however. Some merely reflected the absurdity of basing a noisy campaign against a presidential candidate on one emotional issue alone. The silliest one I heard said that if ever a Catholic got into office, the Masons and the Knights of Columbus were going to merge—and call themselves the Masonites.

Local Democratic leaders in the South and elsewhere began saying that local Republican leaders were using the religion issue quietly to work up Protestant support for Nixon. "They wouldn't be human if they didn't," one Democrat told me in Dallas.

But at the very start, Vice-President Nixon had issued a directive to his workers that religion was not to be mentioned in any official statements or pamphlets put out by any Republican organization in the country. And throughout the campaign he stuck to his vow not to discuss the issue in any public utterance. Nixon went so far as to say he did not think either candidate should discuss religion. This the Democrats considered not so much idealism as a political ploy. Nixon, at the start of the campaign, had nothing to lose by keeping quiet about the religious issue, since it seemed to be working for him. Kennedy had the election to lose. So he ignored Nixon's challenge and continued to state his position on religion whenever he thought he had to. As a consequence, the Republicans countercharged that the Democrats were fostering the religious issue themselves, to incite Catholic voters in the cities to storm the polls for Kennedy. But at this early stage, Democratic leaders didn't have to lift a hand to rouse Catholic voters—the conservative preachers were doing the job for them.

By August the preachers appeared to be gaining the effect they desired in the overwhelmingly Protestant South. The polls showed more strong Nixon sentiment running there than anywhere else in the country. Billy Graham, the best-known Southern Baptist, told a press conference that he considered religion a major issue, but he wasn't going to comment on it, and he would express his convictions privately in the polling booth. He made no secret of his personal commitment to Vice-President Nixon, however, and later appeared on the same platform with the Republican candidate, in South Carolina.

By now the Democrats in Washington had got the Baptist jitters. The atmosphere at National Headquarters reached the gloomiest point of the whole campaign. Politicians and staff people began to think that Kennedy was already finished, and that the thing that had finished him was the religion issue.

Robert F. Kennedy, managing the campaign for his brother, remarked to me in an interview that he thought religion was "the biggest issue in the South and in the country." He said he hoped that as the campaign progressed the people would get their minds off religion and onto more important issues, such as the country's relations with the Soviet Union. But by then the Kennedys had learned that religion arouses irrational fears and that those fears had to be combated directly.

The grand strategy had already been fixed. The Senator recognized from the start that a majority of the country's Protestants were going to vote against him. The Protestants in the Midwest and in the northeastern suburbs had long traditions of voting Republican. And in every section of the country there were hard-core Protestants who would vote against any Catholic. Interviews by Louis Harris, the New York public-opinion research analyst who worked for Kennedy throughout the campaign, indicated that "marked religious concern" about a

Catholic President was higher than many of Kennedy's backers had believed.

In the least affected state, New York, strong prejudice was found in 15 per cent of all Protestants interviewed. In California and Ohio, it ran to 30 per cent. And in the State of Tennessee, 53 per cent of those interviewed said they did not want to see a Catholic in the White House.

Kennedy strategists could hope for, and even count on, the kinship vote of a large percentage of Catholics. But they could not try to "mobilize" the Catholic vote nationally. For every one Catholic vote Kennedy went out openly to win, he stood to lose three Protestant votes.

In the nation, people of Protestant tradition formed the voting base of the electorate. To win, Kennedy had to cut to a minimum the religious majority that was foreordained to be against him. So his basic appeal would have to be aimed at the Protestant voters.

To carry out one part of the strategy, the Democrats set up a bureau with the euphemistic title "Community Relations Committee." Its chief tasks were to single out and discredit the anti-Catholic extremists and to dispel fears of a Catholic President among those Protestants who would listen to rational argument. (The emotional "antis" would be against the candidate no matter what he said or did, the Democrats realized.)

In staffing the committee, they cleaned out half the public-relations department of the National Council of Churches. The Council is composed of twenty-seven major "main line" Protestant denominations and six Eastern Orthodox communions—which altogether have a constituency of about 40,000,000 members.

Kennedy took the Council's top public-relations executive, James A. Wine, and installed him full time as head of the Community Relations Committee. Once it got organized, this group hit the positive and negative sides of the Catholic issue simultaneously. They saw to it that the candidate's statements in favor of separation and religious liberty got out across the country, in brochures and through the press. And they began collecting and analyzing every piece of anti-Catholic, anti-

Kennedy literature that Democrats from New York to Los Angeles found in their areas. They wanted to track down the sources, and find out whether political interests were paying for the mailings. The anti-Catholic "angels" remained concealed, however, because there was no law that said the conservative religious groups—the primary source of the hate mail—had to disclose the names of their supporters.

So the committee was more successful in this informative function—projecting the image of a Catholic who believed in separation of church and state—than it was in the investigative. In any event, the Kennedy people must have been satisfied with the work—Jim Wine was named United States Ambassador to Luxembourg.

As Labor Day and the formal kick-off of the campaign approached, the clamor from the conservative preachers increased. Bobby Kennedy began looking for some way for his brother to deal the issue a body blow, as he had done in West Virginia. It was suggested to him that Senator Kennedy go right into the heart of the "anti" country and ask for a meeting with the very preachers who had been criticizing him. Most of these pastors were respected in their communities, it was pointed out, and they could not in honor refuse to meet an opponent who wanted to give his side of the story. And Jack, as anyone knew who had seen him campaigning in West Virginia, could be mighty persuasive when he got close to a group of prospective voters.

The right forum was found, and in an appropriate state—Texas. Kennedy agreed to go before the Greater Houston Ministerial Association on September 12, give his views on church and state, and submit to any questions the ministers wanted to ask him.

Some of the Houston ministers had spoken from their pulpits against a Catholic for President. Most of them were conservatives, and most of them were suspicious of Kennedy both as a Catholic and as a liberal. But these were responsible men, who could sit still and pay attention to rational exposition. And Kennedy gave it to them, in his clearest and sharpest style.

The so-called religious issue, he told them, was properly the chief topic of the meeting. But there were far more important ones in the 1960 election: the spread of Communism abroad, for instance; the lack of adequate public schools for children and the lack of adequate medical care for older people.

These and similar problems, he said, were the real issues facing the country, not the religious issue. But he added that because he was a Catholic, and no Catholic had over been elected President, the real issues had been obscured—perhaps deliberately by some groups less responsible than the Houston association.

And then he went on to define his position on religion and the Presidency. It was an excellent statement, one that should be a guide for any Protestant, Catholic, Greek Orthodox, Jew, or Mohammedan who might have to face the issue in the future. Its credo was this:

> I believe in an America where the separation of church and state is absolute—where no Catholic prelate would tell the President (should he be a Catholic) how to act and no Protestant minister would tell his parishioners for whom to vote—where no church or church school is granted any public funds or political preferences—and where no man is denied public office merely because his religion differs from the President who might appoint him or the people who might elect him.
>
> I believe in an America that is officially neither Catholic, Protestant nor Jewish—where no public official either requests or accepts instructions on public policy from the Pope, the National Council of Churches or any other ecclesiastical source—where no religious body seeks to impose its will directly or indirectly on the general populace or the public acts of its officials—and where religious liberty is so indivisible that an act against one church is treated as an act against all. . . .
>
> Finally, I believe in an America where religious intolerance will someday end—where all men and all churches are treated as equal—where every man has the same right to attend or not to attend the church of his choice—where there is no Catholic vote, no anti-Catholic vote, no bloc voting of any kind—and where Catholics, Protestants and Jews, both the lay and the pastoral level, will refrain from those attitudes of disdain and division which have so often marred their works in the past, and promote instead the American ideal of brotherhood.

The Houston ministers, persimmon-faced when the talk began, broke into applause when the Senator sat down. The speech and his answers to their questions probably did not convert many in that room politically. But Kennedy had won their personal sympathy, and damped down their fears about what might happen if this particular Catholic should be elected President.

The Houston speech, parts of which were seen on national television, became the most important single campaign piece used by Kennedy workers in the two months that led to his election. The Community Relations Committee had scores of film prints made, and sent it out to be shown over and over again throughout the country. How many people it convinced, no one could say. But the speech certainly ranks with the television debates in instilling confidence in wavering voters. And it stood alone in holding many Democrats who might otherwise have gone into the polling booth and—instinctively—pulled the "Protestant" lever.

Political polls indicated that just after the Houston speech—which was followed by the first television debate—Kennedy reached the peak of his popularity in the campaign. The Harris poll then stood at 52 per cent for Kennedy, 48 per cent for Nixon.

Around the time the planned strategy of the Houston meeting was being carried out in the South, Kennedy was handed a fortuitous piece of assistance by his religious opponents in the North.

A group of 150 conservative Protestant ministers and laymen came together at a secret meeting in Washington on September 7. They formed a National Conference of Citizens for Religious Liberty. This group was never identified by its founders as a religious campaign organization against Kennedy, but it was patently that.

After the meeting, the group issued a statement to the press that warned against the election of a Catholic. A Roman Catholic President, it declared, would be under "extreme pressure from the hierarchy of his church" to align the foreign policy of the United States with that of the Vatican. The gathering got national attention because the chairman of one of its sessions had been the Reverend Dr. Norman Vincent Peale.

Immediately it became known as the Peale group, although this was a misnomer. The conference had been conceived by officials of the National Association of Evangelicals, a group of conservative Protestant churchmen not affiliated with the National Council of Churches. They were given support by leaders of Protestants and Other Americans United for Separation of Church and State, a tax-exempt organization that draws heavily for leadership on preachers of the Southern Baptist Convention.

The campaign group and their statement, although not extreme in anti-Catholicism, nevertheless betrayed enough poor logic and emotion to make them objects of ridicule from moderate and liberal newspapers. The 150 ministers and laymen were assailed for bad taste and lack of responsibility. The group, the newspapers pointed out, had emphasized the religious phase of the campaign at a time when community leaders were trying to do what they could to keep down frictions between the faiths.

(I tried to reach Dr. Peale in the spring of 1961, to ask him how he thought President Kennedy was carrying out his pledge to support strict separation. Dr. Peale's secretary, after conferring with the minister, said, "Dr. Peale is absolutely out of politics—he thinks he can do more good by sticking to religion in the church.")

From the time the religion issue first drew public notice, many newspapers and civic organizations, led by men of conservative, moderate, and liberal beliefs, spoke up for fair play and rational discussion. Among the most active citizens' groups were the National Fair Campaign Practices Committee and the National Conference of Christians and Jews.

The Fair Campaign group had dedicated leadership from Charles Taft, a Protestant church executive who is a moderate Republican, as chairman, and Bruce Felknor, a Presbyterian layman who is a liberal Democrat, as executive director. They worked hard and conscientiously to throw the light of publicity on persons, religious groups, and political organizations that tried to use prejudice as a campaign weapon.

The Conference appealed to the whole nation to consider the consequences of a campaign of hate. This interreligious group had been formed by leaders of three major faiths right after the disastrous 1928 campaign. Its aim was to reduce the bitterness that grew out of that angry fight, and to work for increased harmony among the country's several religious communities. Throughout the 1960 election its president, Dr. Lewis Webster Jones, its Protestant, Catholic, and Jewish co-chairmen, and its regional directors in sixty-five cities pleaded publicly and at private community meetings for men of good will to work for a decent, unprejudiced contest.

The efforts of these groups did help to keep the religion issue within rational bounds. But in the temper of 1960 it was not reasonable to expect that they could be totally successful.

Understandably, Senator Kennedy, as the target of the prejudiced, was angry at first when he found people saying that he should be deprived of the Presidency because he had been born a Catholic forty-three years before. But as the campaign went on, he became philosophical about the attacks, and was even able to turn the issue as a joke on himself. At the annual Al Smith Dinner in the middle of October, he noted wryly that Harry S. Truman had declared that anyone who voted for Mr. Nixon ought to go to hell. And then he said:

"However, I would not want to give the impression that I am taking former President Truman's use of language lightly. I have sent him the following note:

" 'Dear Mr. President: I have noted with interest your suggestion as to where those who vote for my opponent should go. While I understand and sympathize with your deep motivation, I think it is important that our side try to refrain from raising the religious issue.' "

The protest in the nation against the Citizens for Religious Liberty practically ended the overt, public campaign to defeat John F. Kennedy because of his religion. As the criticism rose, Dr. Peale reconsidered, and withdrew from the organization. The Citizens dispersed to their homes, leaving behind a small office in Washington to distribute "If-a-Catholic-gets-elected,-watch-out" sermons by one or two of the group, plus the warning tracts of P.O.A.U. From that point on, except for an outbreak of anti-Kennedy preaching on Reformation Sunday, October 30, the religious-political forces went underground.

The silent campaign—the anti-Catholic literature campaign—reached its most devastating stage.

My favorite person among the hate mailers was a little old lady in San Francisco. She told me she did all her own work. She was over eighty years old, and she lived in a tiny, one-room apartment halfway up one of the Twin Peaks. It was a shock to see her when she opened the door—she was only about four and a half feet high, and she looked sweet and wrinkled as my own grandmother. She told me she was very happy to see me, because she loved to have someone come in and talk to her about her work.

Her work, basically, was a printed letter that said in part: "If we were to get a Catholic Commander in Chief in the White House in control of thousands of bases all over the world . . . the world-wide massacre of non-Catholics could be accomplished simultaneously. . . . The murdered Protestants' property would become Catholic property."

The rest of the letter explained how the Catholic hierarchy had turned every Catholic high school into a military academy, in preparation for Der Tag. It ended with the ringing admonition: "Remember Ethiopia!"

The little old lady told me she was being watched constantly by Jesuit spies, and that one night about midnight, she had heard a scratching noise outside, and when she opened the door, there stood Cardinal Spellman, dressed all in black, looking up at her.

She confided that she didn't *really* think John F. Kennedy was such a bad person. But she said she thought that Kennedy *did* believe in his religion, and so she felt it was her duty to write letters against his election.

It was almost incredible, as I sat watching her rock gently in her rocking chair, to think that this deluded woman could become a factor in a presidential election campaign. Yet she was.

She had a note in her broadside that it was not copyrighted, and that anyone was free to copy it and send it out. Lots and lots of good people did, apparently. I found that the letter was being circulated in every section of the country that I visited.

I asked the old lady where she got the money for the copies she mailed out directly.

"Oh," she said, "people just send me money in the mail, they don't even say who it's from, lots of times. I sit up every night till one A.M. addressing these letters. One morning I went outside to do my morning exercises, and there were fourteen boxes of envelopes, sitting right on my doorstep. I guess people must think I'm doing a good job."

My little old lady is still active out on the coast. Just the other day, while I was looking through a collection of anti-Catholic literature at the Fair Campaign Practices Committee headquarters in New York, I ran across a new letter she has put out, warning against the *re*-election of a Catholic President.

Another piece of mail that was big in the election was one that had been revived from the Al Smith campaign: the fraudulent and scurrilous "Knights of Columbus Oath," supposedly taken by members of that Catholic fraternal order. Here is an excerpt that particularly whets the imagination:

> I will wage relentless war secretly or openly against all heretical Protestants, as I am directed to extirpate them from the face of the earth, and that I will spare neither sex, age, or condition and that I will boil, flay and burn these infamous brutes. . . .
>
> That when the same cannot be done openly, I will secretly use the poisonous cup, the strangulation cord, the steel of the poiniard, or the leaden bullet, regardless of honor, rank, dignity or authority of the persons, directed to do so by any agent of the Pope or Superior of the Brotherhood of the Holy Father.

Now, this was not calculated to be used as an ice-breaker for an evening of good talk on "Open End." It was put out in quantity by several fundamentalist tract houses, and distributed by small, ultraconservative church groups. As early as 1928 the courts held that it libeled the Knights of Columbus, and various chapters of the Knights have been suing and collecting on it ever since.

Surprisingly—or rather, hearteningly—the bulk of the "religious" literature in the last campaign was not so wildly irrational or hate-rousing as the "K. of C. Oath" and similar pieces used against Al Smith in 1928.

The most effective pieces used against Kennedy were the

reasoned ones that took up questions of church and state. They aimed their arguments at undecided Protestants who had vague worries about a Catholic for President. The blows were not directed so much against "that Catholic," as in the time of Al Smith, but against "that church," or "that Pope."

They were mailed out in bulk by the "church-and-staters"—people and organizations that had fought for separation not just in this campaign, but over the years. They were inspired, of course, by Protestants and Other Americans United for Separation of Church and State, which has been the core organization for the drive since its founding in 1948.

The mailings from these and the more emotional sources were timed to reach their peak at the end of the campaign. A final drive was kicked off by sermons against Kennedy on Reformation Sunday, October 30. This particular effort was sponsored by the National Association of Evangelicals and joined by Southern Baptist ministers and other conservative Protestant preachers. Some of them were professional anti-Catholics, willing to fight on this ground until the last vestige of good will was gone.

The suspicion persisted that, while many conservative Protestants honestly believed that the election of a Catholic would be a blow to Protestantism, many others used religious feeling to try to defeat Senator Kennedy because he had expressed liberal convictions on social and economic issues.

An appeal to religious chauvinism doesn't have to be explained; it has a fine, clean emotional ring. Economic and social arguments, on the other hand, have a disturbing rationality about them that is harder to put across.

While campaign literature that raised religious antagonisms could be deplored, in almost no cases could it be prosecuted. All the religious campaign literature fell within the Constitutional guarantees of free speech. About the only Federal law dealing specifically with the mailings was a statute that says no campaign material may be sent out without identification of the source. But almost all of the religious literature, with the exception of the Criswell sermon distributed by H. L. Hunt, was signed.

To a man, the anti-Catholic, anti-Kennedy distributors refused to identify their chief financial backers. They all said the mailings were financed by many small contributors. But their own estimates, and those of the Fair Campaign Practices Committee, indicated that the volume ran to tens of millions of pieces and the cost at probably more than a million dollars. The committee has catalogued 264 different publishers who had pamphlets in the campaign. The publishers' mailing lists were compiled chiefly from conservative Protestant church rolls.

Obviously, church groups themselves could not have put on such an extensive campaign on their own. They obtained quiet, and sometimes clandestine, help from political organizations, economic groups, and individual conservatives of great wealth.

There were dark suggestions from the Democrats that the Republican National Committee had a secret national director of anti-Catholic literature, who told state and local directors where they could "get the stuff." The Republicans weren't printing the material themselves, the Democrats said privately. But they were sure the money was going circuitously to the printers from various Republican groups, and that some people in the G.O.P. were secretly helping with the distribution.

One day while I was in Washington in the middle of the campaign, a Democratic staff man said he had a hot tip from someone inside Republican National Headquarters that the Republicans had 100,000 pieces of anti-Catholic literature stacked up in the basement of the headquarters, ready to go.

I walked around to the Republican National Headquarters, took the elevator down to the basement, and toured the mailing rooms where people were working away, whistling while they worked. I talked to some pleasant girls who were stacking boxes of Nixon stickers. No, they said, they hadn't seen any shipments of church-and-state literature, but would I like a Nixon sticker?

For a clandestine operation, I thought Republican National Headquarters had very poor security.

A little later, out on the west coast, I ran across two Democratic campaign workers with their heads together, attempting to dream up some "fresh and new" church-state arguments for a handbill they were going to try to palm off on the Republicans. *They* had got a hot tip that there was a man working secretly out of a coast Republican headquarters, buying up religious literature for distribution in the area. The two Democrats thought it would be a delightful idea if they could sell this Republican a pamphlet they had got up themselves, then expose him with a blast in the press. When I flew home four days later, they were still writing, and still making phone calls to make contact with the enemy.

I went to Richard Guylay, public-relations director for the Republican National Committee, and asked him about the general charges being made by the Democrats that the Republicans were responsible for the literature that was blanketing the country.

Guylay wrinkled his brow and ran a hand over his graying cap cut. "Certainly we have no responsibility for this literature thing," he told me. "We've disavowed anybody sending out the stuff who could be remotely connected with the Republican Party. But we don't exercise responsibility for 180,000,000 Americans and what they want to say."

An election analyst who has since checked into the "national director" charge told me he is convinced there was no such person. Throughout the campaign, no one produced evidence that the Republican Party had a hand in the hate mail. Some P.O.A.U. church-and-state literature was found in local headquarters in New York City, Darien, Connecticut, and elsewhere. And there were isolated instances in which local committees handed out pamphlets on the religious argument. In each case the instigators were found to be low-echelon zealots, and usually they were repudiated by their Republican state chairmen. No formal charges of direct Republican support of the literature drive were filed with the Fair Campaign Practices Committee, nor did the Committee find such evidence on its own.

But if there was no evidence of Republican Party complicity in the distribution, neither was there evidence that the Republicans did much to discourage it. In fact, about the only time the Republicans complained officially about literature was when the United Auto Workers paper ran a cartoon and an article that suggested that a vote for Nixon would be a vote for bigotry. Walter Reuther, embarrassed, disavowed the piece and ordered the issue withdrawn from circulation.

The incident set off more Republican charges that the Democrats were trying to stir the religious issue to promote bigotry in reverse—in other words, to "firm up" the Catholic kinship vote for Kennedy. There was evidence, from Pittsburgh and Chicago and other cities, that local Democratic ward leaders went out and lined up a Catholic vote. There were more reports of Democratic workers promoting the idea of "tolerance" as an aid to the Kennedy cause. The candidate himself avoided set public statements on the issue after his Houston talk.

However, with G.O.P. clearance, an eastern industrialist who was a Catholic—Mortimor J. Moriarity of the Good Humor Corporation—took full-page ads in sixteen newspapers to warn Catholics that Kennedy was trying to use them as stepping stones to the Presidency.

Toward the close of the campaign, Nixon strategists urged him to make a public statement on the religious issue. He refused. Baptists from the South swarmed into Republican headquarters, asking if they could work "in the political arena" to defeat a Catholic for President. These offers, too, were turned down.

Despite Senator Kennedy's fight to establish himself early in the campaign as a candidate independent of his church, any increases he had earned among Protestants dropped off toward the end. The anti-Catholic literature was certainly a factor in making some of them forget the conclusions they had come to about Kennedy's independence after his speech before the Houston Ministerial Association.

It was impossible, as a practical matter, for the Kennedy team to counteract this literature. It was silent, it was deadly, it reached directly into the homes of millions of Protestants. There wasn't enough time or money left for Kennedy backers to mount a direct-mail counterdrive, even if they thought this might be effective. And there was nothing Kennedy could say then that would have the dramatic impact of the Houston speech. Anything he could say about his belief in religious liberty he had said before.

Besides, by this time, many people in the Kennedy entourage had become convinced that the Senator was going to "win big," despite the conservative Protestant attacks. They thought that no further statement on the religious issue would be necessary, or proper.

But then they got a jolt that showed they were wrong. On October 21, in Puerto Rico, an American commonwealth, the island's three highest-ranking bishops issued a pastoral letter forbidding their people to vote for the Popular Democratic Party of Governor Luís Muñoz Marín.

This was a great shock to moderate and liberal Protestants who had decided to vote for Kennedy. It gave the conservative Protestant preachers a wonderful chance to say, "See, I told you so—the Catholic Church wants to dictate to their people on how they should vote."

The Puerto Rican bishops caused consternation in Catholic circles in the mainland United States. Cardinal Cushing, Cardinal Spellman and the Apostolic Delegate in Washington all made statements to the effect that the action taken in Puerto Rico (a missionary diocese not reporting to the Church through the American hierarchy) was completely out of step with Catholic tradition in the United States. It appeared to some Catholics here that the Puerto Rican bishops, noted as conservatives, had intervened not only to influence the island election, but also to cause Protestants on the mainland to vote against Senator Kennedy. The Kennedy people certainly were afraid that would happen. They reacted quickly with one final statement on religion:

"Senator Kennedy has stated on many occasions that he considers it wholly improper and alien to our domestic system for churchmen to tell the members of their church for whom to vote or for whom not to vote."

But the damage had been done. Kennedy lost countless Protestant votes because of the Puerto Rican bishops, who, when challenged, reaffirmed their pastoral order in even stronger terms. Louis Harris, who did Kennedy's private polling, estimates that in the last three weeks of the campaign, more than a million Protestants shifted to Nixon. He attributes this to two things: the last-minute anti-Catholic literature crescendo, and the pastoral letter of the Puerto Rican bishops.

In both the Kennedy and the Nixon camps, the bishops focused attention again on the Catholic issue. The Nixon camp, which had fallen into a despondent state, now began openly counting on the "downstate" fundamentalist votes to pull the election out of the bag for them. The Kennedy camp, jarred out of its cockiness, began counting again those electoral votes that Catholics in the Northeast were going to win for the Senator.

In the grand finals on November 8, John F. Kennedy won by a margin of 112,000 votes in a total of 68,000,000 cast for the two major party candidates. It was a margin that could have been blown away by any of the quixotic turns of the religious issue. It is clear from an analysis of the returns that many more Protestants voted against him because of his religion than Catholics voted for him because he was a co-religionist. But he did win.

And this is the biggest lesson learned, the biggest question answered in the 1960 election: that a Roman Catholic can be elected President in this country whose people have an overwhelmingly Protestant background.

Despite the fact that nearly two-thirds of all Protestants voting voted against Kennedy, Protestants accounted for more than half of his 34,000,000-vote total. By appealing primarily to the country's Protestant majority, Kennedy had succeeded in his strategy of keeping the prejudice vote down to the point where a combination of the Catholic vote, the Jewish vote, the Negro vote, and the labor vote could put him over.

To the mathematicians of American politics, analysis of the voting by states suggested another lesson: With the electoral-college system, in which the winner in each state takes all that state's electoral votes, it may just have been to Kennedy's advantage to have been a Catholic, from the standpoint of his electoral score. This was 300 to 223, a much safer margin than his hair-breadth popular plurality. In this kind of mathematics, Catholic-bloc voting appears to count more heavily than Protestant-bloc voting. The prediction of the Kennedy planners—that a Catholic candidate would bring enough of the big-city Catholics back to the Democratic Party to carry most of the key Northern industrial states—proved correct.

The Gallup and Harris polls showed that about three-quarters of all Catholics voting in the national election voted for Senator Kennedy. That this was a dramatic return to the Democratic fold can be seen from the fact that in 1956, only 51 per cent of Catholics voted for Adlai E. Stevenson. Not only did normally Democratic Catholics return to "normal," but some Republican Catholics crossed over as well.

In contrast to the outspoken Protestants, Catholics did not admit religion was a factor in their decisions. A taxicab driver in downtown Pittsburgh told me he was a Catholic of Italian extraction and a Republican. "I think Kennedy's the better man," he said. "I'd feel safer with him in the White House than I would with Mr. Nixon. I haven't seen any of the television debates—it's just the way I feel about it."

Allegiance of Roman Catholics to the Democratic Party had not reached such proportions since the first terms of Franklin D. Roosevelt. In the industrial states of the Northeast the percentage of Catholics who voted for Kennedy went above 80.

Looking at the Catholic "kinship" vote one way, we find that the Democratic candidate carried eight of the twelve states with Catholic populations of 30 per cent or more. The Kennedy convention memo, looking at it in a slightly different way, had figured that Catholics were concentrated in fourteen swing states with 261 of the 269 electoral votes needed to win.

The people in these states, incidentally, were found by Harris interviewers to have less prejudice against a Catholic President than those in most other states.

In the end, Kennedy carried all of these states with the exception of California, Ohio, and Wisconsin.

California had no massive, organized Catholic bloc voting in the cities. The conservative Protestant cultists were strong in Los Angeles and the fundamentalist "antis" stretched northward through the Central Valley. So there was no well-defined city-versus-country religious voting formula.

In Wisconsin and Ohio the equation existed, but this time it went against the Democrats. In each of these states the country Protestant polling against a Catholic for President was stronger than the city Catholic rally to put the first of the faith in the White House.

Anti-Catholicism seemed to be the major reason for Kennedy's loss of Oklahoma, Tennessee, and Kentucky. It was a contributing factor in Florida and Virginia, and it came very close to costing him South Carolina.

The inroads of the Republicans in the traditionally Democratic southern and border states seemed directly attributable to the Catholic question.

Throughout the campaign, most of the pulpit work against Kennedy had been done by preachers in these southern and border states. And many of their flock were receptive to their pastor's words. "Being a Mason," one man said to me after a Sunday service in Charlottesville, "I could not vote for a Catholic."

Across the country, conservative Protestants came out strongly to vote against a Catholic except in areas of heavy unemployment. There the pocketbook issue carried more weight than the religious issue. For instance, Kennedy carried heavily Protestant West Virginia, which he had put first in his "depressed areas" book, by 442,000 to 395,000.

Noting this, one of Kennedy's top advisers remarked to me the day after the election, "Where they're hungry, they think of their stomachs and the Democrats. Where they're not, they think of the Pope."

An anti-*Protestant* vote, it appeared, gave Kennedy the surprise upset of the election—Texas, with a bonus of 24 electoral votes. In the campaign, protests against a Catholic for President had been heard earliest, loudest, and oftenest from Baptist preachers in Texas. Toward the end, there appeared to be a reversion among Protestants against this. And after all, Texans couldn't forget that Lyndon Johnson was running on that Democratic ticket, too. So an anti-Catholic vote failed to solidify. But Catholic voters in San Antonio and El Paso had heard what those Baptists had said. They came out heavily and mad, and tipped the state to Kennedy. Ironically, the Baptist preachers had defeated their own cause.

In balancing the electoral votes that Kennedy won because of partisan religious feeling against the electoral votes he lost because of partisan religious feeling, it would appear that he gained more than he lost.

Nixon, for example, would rather have had New York than Tennessee.

Nationally, it was the sharpness of the swing of Catholics back to the Democratic side that drew politicians' attention to the Catholic factor in the election. Because, apart from this big switchback, in such a close election, the Jewish group, the Negro group, and the labor group each could have claimed equal billing with the Catholic group as the "faction that put Kennedy over." The Jewish group, for instance, gave Kennedy an 82 per cent vote of confidence.

In drawing conclusions for the future about the religious content in elections, one of the questions national politicians have had to ask themselves was this:

Why had John F. Kennedy, a Roman Catholic and a Democrat, fared so much better with the electorate in 1960 than Alfred E. Smith, a Roman Catholic and a Democrat, had in 1928? Smith lost to Hoover by a landslide: 444 to 87 in electoral votes, 21,000,000 to 15,000,000 in the popular vote.

Several answers suggest themselves. Kennedy had a firmer grasp of the meaning of separation of church and state than Smith did. His stand on this was stronger than Smith's. And he knew how to make it known to a suspicious public. He addressed the religious issue directly, while Smith, disgusted at the bigotry being shown against him, refused to admit religion was an issue until it had forced him to the wall.

Kennedy, of course, proved to be a popular campaigner. He did not have to fight the Prohibitionists, as Smith did, and he didn't face a provincial distrust of him as a cigar-smoking, big-city politician.

And in the thirty-two years between the two campaigns, there had been marked changes in the situation of Catholics in the United States. In 1928 there were 19,000,000 Catholics in the country, making up only 16 per cent of the population. By 1960, their numbers had increased to 40,000,000. The proportion had reached 24 per cent—nearly one quarter of the population.

From this, a candidate who was a Catholic in 1960 derived benefits two ways: one was that there were more people to vote for him out of religious kinship. The other grew from the sociological axiom that in areas containing a higher percentage of Catholics within a Protestant majority, prejudice against

Catholics tends to decline. It's always easy to hate "the Catholics" in the next county. But when one of them is your neighbor, lending you his power mower every time yours breaks down, he doesn't seem like quite such a devil.

A Gallup poll published right after the election showed that prejudice against the idea of a Catholic in the White House had been dropping steadily over a twenty-year period. Voters had been asked this question:

"If your party nominated a generally well-qualified man for President, and he happened to be a Catholic, would you vote for him?"

In 1940, 31 per cent of those questioned said, no, they would not.

In 1958 the percentage of no's had dropped to twenty-four, and by 1960, to twenty.

The comparatively low figure may mean that people are aware that it isn't cricket any more to show they are prejudiced, and so they give the "nice" answer to the poll-taker. Nevertheless, the number of the prejudiced does seem to be diminishing, and this trend will probably continue.

Another fact from the Gallup polling was that younger voters showed the least amount of prejudice. Thus in 1960, while 27 per cent of the sample who were fifty years old and older said they would not vote for a Catholic, only 13 per cent in the twenty-one-to-twenty-nine age group said they would not.

All these things seem to say that if Kennedy were to do nothing more than maintain his standing with those who voted for him last time, the religious equation should be even more in his favor in 1964 than it was in 1960. By then there will be more Catholic voters, and four new classes of younger, less-prejudiced Protestants will be graduating into the electorate.

With the Kennedy victory and the current Catholic equation in mind, national Democratic leaders will consider the possibility that in the future another Catholic might give them a better chance to win than a non-Catholic. A candidate who is a Catholic does seem to provide the insurance for holding those big-electoral-vote states the Democrats need in a national contest.

The Republicans too are beginning to think they ought to

pay more attention to the Catholics than they have in the past. If the Democrats continue to need the northern industrial states, there will be a temptation to nominate a Catholic Republican from the Northeast, to try to neutralize the Democratic base.

At the least, I think it is likely that the Republicans will nominate a Catholic for the vice-presidential slot when they go in against Kennedy again.

It may be that we are coming to a time when the idea of a balanced ticket will be adhered to at national conventions as rigidly and cynically as the balanced ticket is in New York City. Except that in New York a Protestant can't get a look-in for one of the three top offices, no matter how good a man he may be. There the formula is: one Irish Catholic, one Italian Catholic, and one Jew. This formula does not guarantee that the city will get good men to run it. But the politicians have not yet worked up the courage to nominate a well-qualified Buddhist, say, and test whether the people can rise above ethnic and religious-bloc voting.

It is just possible, of course, that religious prejudice and religious chauvinism will diminish in the nation to the point where the convention delegates won't have to work out the Protestant-Catholic equation. But that time hasn't arrived yet.

It would be unlikely that Richard M. Nixon, if he runs next time, would let the campaign slide by without some overt gesture to Catholic voters. Already Governor Nelson A. Rockefeller of New York, a northeastern Republican Baptist, has shown that the role of northeastern Catholics in the Kennedy victory was not lost on him. In the spring of 1961, at the height of the Catholic hierarchy's drive for Federal aid to parochial schools, he announced he favored state grants to students in sectarian colleges. At least twenty-one of these in New York State are run by the Catholic Church.

Church-state groups pointed out immediately that under this plan, religious colleges would be allowed to raise their tuitions an amount equal to the grants, thus making the grants practically direct subsidies to sectarian institutions. And this is prohibited even more specifically under the New York State Constitution than it is under the Federal Constitution—where the prohibition is clear enough.

Governor Rockefeller backed off. But he gave his approval

to another proposal that would have helped Catholic institutions. This one would have amended the state Constitution to permit state grants and loans for construction of facilities of higher learning, including religious schools.

Protestant groups in the state, and newspapers and civic groups concerned about separation, fought hard to kill this amendment. As a result of their publicity campaign, it was defeated in the November election. But Rockefeller had made points with Catholic voters. It remains to be seen what effect his divorce will have with this group, so strongly opposed to divorce.

Paradoxically, at the time the Governor was beginning to improve his position with Catholics, Kennedy, by saying no to Catholic demands for school aid, gained the support of some of his bitterest enemies of the election campaign.

Nothing scares the southern Baptists and other church-state separatists more than the thought that the Catholic Church might, as they put it, get its hand into the Federal till to finance their parochial schools. These people see such assistance as a first step toward state subsidy of the Catholic Church itself.

Kennedy had said during the campaign that he believed Federal aid for parochial schools violated the Constitution. But somehow the Baptists just couldn't believe he meant it.

Just before the inauguration, a Kennedy task force came in with a plan that proposed extensive Federal aid to public schools, but nothing for private or parochial schools.

Cardinal Spellman immediately threw down the gauntlet to Kennedy. In a speech in the Bronx three days before the new President was to be sworn in, the Cardinal assailed the Kennedy team's proposal in the strongest terms. In denying aid to Catholic pupils, he said, the plan "blatantly discriminated" against them.

Then, on March 2, the Council of American Catholic Bishops met in Washington and declared that any legislation for Federal aid to public schools that did not include Federal aid to parochial schools would be discriminatory. They said they had no choice but to oppose such legislation.

At this time President Kennedy stood firm. In a press conference he repeated his assertion that direct aid to sectarian schools was ruled out by the Constitution.

Shortly afterward I called up the Reverend Dr. Ramsey Pollard, then head of the Southern Baptist Convention, who had been among the most outspoken preachers against Kennedy's election. "What do you think of Kennedy now?" I asked him.

Dr. Pollard said he thought Kennedy was making a real effort to live up to his campaign promises regarding separation. "However," he added, "they don't reflect the thinking and purposes of the Roman Catholic Church."

And it is true that the American Catholic Church is not nearly so concerned that acceptance of subsidies from the government might break down this separation. American Protestants are very much afraid that it would, and would lead eventually to state control of the church, or the establishment of a state church. To them, these ideas are equally abhorrent.

In May the entire Southern Baptist Convention passed a resolution in St. Louis praising the new President for his stand in support of religious liberty and separation. "Jack Kennedy is making a pretty good Baptist President," one of the delegates said to me. Governor Rockefeller, I thought, had better watch out.

A private poll showed then that Kennedy's stock with Protestants had risen considerably over what it had been on election day. But then, as the bishops' campaign to include parochial schools in any Federal aid began to make things hot for the administration, some of the Baptists began to have doubts again.

On July 18, Representative James J. Delaney of New York, a Democrat and a Catholic who had normally voted with the Kennedy administration, cast the deciding vote (the tally was 8 to 7) to block the administration's education aid bill in the House Rules Committee. Representative Delaney announced he would not vote to clear any bill that did not include aid to parochial schools. At this point it seemed to conservative Baptists and liberal Protestants who were fighting to maintain the principle of separation that the administration wavered on the issue.

In his press conference, President Kennedy had argued the

case against aid to church schools on strictly legalistic, not philosophical, grounds. During the school bill fight, it appeared to some liberals within the administration itself that perhaps Kennedy, despite his statements of the campaign, did not have a philosophical conviction that strict and absolute separation should be upheld to the last shot—at least where aid to parochial schools was concerned. But to yield on this, the symbolic point, they said, was to lose the war along with the battle.

Privately, they accused Secretary Abraham Ribicoff of the Department of Health, Education and Welfare of adopting almost the Catholic point of view in the matter. Ribicoff, who had been Governor of Connecticut, a state that is nearly 50 per cent Catholic, is quite aware of the Catholic voting potential. With Kennedy's approval, he tried to negotiate a series of compromises with the Catholic bishops. In the end, the hierarchy indicated it would go along only with a simple extension of the National Defense Education Act, because the act did provide loan funds that could be used by parochial schools in building science and mathematics classrooms. Kennedy signed the bill reluctantly, saying he would be back in the 1962 session with another school aid proposal.

Early in December, Secretary Ribicoff, then out for the Democratic senatorial nomination in Connecticut, floated a trial balloon. The administration, he said, was thinking of introducing a plan to grant education aid directly to the states, and let each state decide for itself whether to use the funds to support parochial schools. Under such a plan, because Catholic legislators have working control of several state legislatures, some Federal assistance would be certain to go to religious schools.

This arrangement might appear to administration advisers to finesse the problem, mollifying its Catholic critics and keeping the President in good standing with his new-found Baptist friends. But that notion reckons without the Baptist rigidity on the issue of separation. To the Baptists, any such proposals would be the first blow of the ram against that sacred wall of theirs. If Kennedy gives in on schools, some of them are saying, the next thing you know he'll be going along with the Catholic groups that want to knock the separation clause out of the Constitution.

It is true that Kennedy has not yet made it clear what he feels about the philosophical rightness of the doctrine of separation. In this, he has placed himself in somewhat the same stance that President Eisenhower held for so long on the issue of segregation. Eisenhower said repeatedly he would uphold and enforce the Supreme Court's decision on desegregation, but it was years before he stated, in answer to a query from *The New York Times*, that public segregation is morally wrong.

In February of 1962 the Kennedy administration came back with the same school aid program it had offered in 1961—excluding funds for parochial schools. Cardinal Spellman fired a shotgun blast at it, predicting that if Federal aid for public schools ever got past Congress without a subsidy to religious schools, it would mean the end of religious schools. Next day President Kennedy made what might almost be construed as an apology to Catholic parents. He was sorry, he said in effect, but this bill, limiting aid to public schools, was just as far as he could go under the current interpretation of the religion clause of the Constitution by the Supreme Court. "So," he told his press conference, "I am going to continue to take the position I now take—based on Constitutional grounds—unless there is a new judgment by the Supreme Court."

All of which was disheartening to people who believe that separation has been good for both church and state. They had been waiting—and, hopefully, are still waiting—for a declaration from the President that he supports the concept in principle as well as in law.

Government aid to parochial schools is, of course, the overriding question in religion-and-politics today. In general, Catholics and Protestants stand on opposite sides on some other political questions. To name a few, these include public policy in support of birth control (Protestants for, Catholics against), legalized gambling (Catholics for, Protestants against) and liberalization of the divorce laws (Protestants for, Catholics against). More often than not, Jewish groups find themselves aligned on these and other political and social questions with the Protestants, rather than with the Catholics.

But the "Catholic issue" in politics is being kept alive chiefly by the determined ground campaign for Federal aid being waged by the Catholic hierarchy, and the counterattacks being thrown at it by Protestant groups.

Some voices within the Catholic Church have doubts that the political pressure for Federal aid is worth the antagonism it will raise within the Protestant community. Richard Cardinal Cushing of Boston said in November of 1961 that Catholics, if they believe that state support of parochial schools is right, should work hard to have their views accepted. But they should not oppose all Federal legislation to aid the public schools if they do not get their way, he said.

At least through the 1964 election, and probably beyond, the school question is going to be the one that divides Protestants and Catholics politically as no other does. It is likely to have its expression in state and local contests, as well as national, in instances where the Protestant groups support bond issues and increased budgets for public schools, and the Catholic groups oppose them.

Politically, no issue is more important to Kennedy. By adopting and maintaining an unequivocal position on schools, and thus symbolically on separation, he would do more to improve his standing with the Protestant majority than he could through any other pronouncement he could make.

The inroads the Republican Party made in the South in 1960 were due largely to Southern doubts about a Catholic's ability to stand up to pressure from the church. If Kennedy satisfied the South that he has remained independent of the hierarchy, the bolt to the Republicans might very well end in 1964.

The religion issue will still exist, of course, in the next election, no matter what the bishops decided to do, because of diehard Protestant preachers and their followers. But the appeal to Protestants to holy war will have become hollow, especially if the opposing champion keeps flying the banner of separation. The President, if he falters in his stand against Federal aid to parochial schools, will lose his post-election converts among the southern Baptists. And he will probably lose the allegiance of many moderate and liberal Protestant voters as well.

Kennedy's political tacticians, looking to 1964, are undoubtedly worried because the President has been caught in the middle of this tug of war between the Catholic bishops and the

Protestant separatists. For the pragmatists among them, if not indeed for the philosophers, the better course must seem to be: Keep pulling with the separatists. They are aware that the cultural ratio of Protestant voters to Catholic voters in 1964 will still be about 3 to 1, and that religious partisanship has not died. To keep or gain one Catholic vote by outright support of a distinctly Catholic position that is opposed by Protestants will mean the loss of three Protestant votes. And the American voting base, despite the "clout" of Catholics in the swing states, remains Protestant.

Churches, Education, and Politics[1]

ROBERT LEKACHMAN

In the American tradition great issues of public morality and institutional readjustment are frequently resolved according to the rules of trial by political combat rather than by the severe canons of rational argument. I shall take this observation as the fundamental premise of my discussion with you of the relationships between churches, education, and politics. The central questions upon which we shall linger are two: how do churches act in the public arena on those occasions when their vital interests are involved, and how *should* churches act? I shall preface my reflections—*answers* would be an exaggeration—on these two questions with a tale of a legislative conflict which has only just terminated: the sad story of the latest attempt to

[1] In revising these lectures for publication, I have naturally corrected errors which I identified, converted incomplete sentences into complete ones, and made numerous verbal changes. However, I have retained the tone and manner of the lecture and I have allowed the time to remain December, 1961—the month during which the lectures were delivered.—R.L.

enlist the Federal government in the financial support of public education.

TWO MEASURES . . .

On February 20, 1961, Representative Frank Thompson of New Jersey introduced on behalf of his long-time friend and associate, the President of the United States, the administration's Aid to Education Bill. This amounted to either the third or the fourth time—there is some doubt about the seriousness of the attempt in one of the instances—that a President had tried to secure passage of some kind of Federal assistance to public education. On two previous occasions, one house of Congress had actually passed such a bill, in the confidence—fully justified by the sequel—that the other house would kill it. Possibly this is an illustration of what is known as "co-ordinate function" in Congress.

But on this latest occasion President Kennedy proposed both the most substantial and the most diversified program of aid to education that has thus far been advanced as a Federal responsibility. Let me briefly outline the three major divisions into which this program fell.

The first was aid to public elementary and secondary schools. *Aid* as defined in the bill extended to construction, operating expenses, and teachers' salaries. In the course of the tangled Congressional history of the debate teachers' salaries became an important subissue. Speaker Rayburn, for example, opposed application of Federal grants to teaching salaries even though he favored general aid to education. His was not a unique position. The bill proposed to appropriate $666,000,000 for the first year after Congressional approval, $766,000,000 for the second year, and—as momentum might imply—$866,000,000 for the third year. The three-year program assumed an expenditure of some $2,300,000,000.

The distribution of the aid represented another complex issue and another complex problem of legislative drafting. In Representative Thompson's original proposal, every state was guaranteed at least $15 per school child per year, but the poorer states were promised more. The promise implied that the state of Mississippi, which is poor in almost any meaning of the word, would have received under this particular formula $29.67, or nearly double the minimum amount. States like New York and Connecticut would have received something very close to the $15 minimum.

The second major heading of the President's program covered aid to higher education. In part this aid was a simple expansion of the existing College Housing Loan Program to a five-year subsidy of $250,000,000 per year to *both* public and private colleges in aid of dormitory construction. A new feature was an additional $300,000,000 a year for classrooms, libraries, and laboratories. This new program also extended to private colleges and universities.

The third and last important category in the President's proposals was scholarship assistance. The actual legislative device took the shape of a new program tacked onto the National Defense Education Act of 1958. The new program offered four-year college scholarships to 212,500 students—a fairly generous number. It was estimated by the experts that the stipends paid to the students would average $700 a year, according to need, and that the maximum which any student might receive as a grant should not exceed $1,000. It was expected that the college would make matching contributions to those students who participated in the Federal scholarship program.

In short, the President's educational policy seemed to many, including this writer, a fair-minded and only moderately expensive measure. In many respects its design was extremely sensible. It promised more aid to the states and the students who most required help. Since it takes time for a new program to get into action, the schedule of appropriations contemplated annual increases. And while aid was denied to private elementary and secondary schools, something substantial was made available to church-related colleges and universities.

So much for presidential aspiration. Let us now shift the scene. On October 3, 1961, Mr. Kennedy signed the only education legislation which Congress was ultimately willing to approve. Congress contented itself with the extension of two existing programs. It continued in precisely or nearly precisely its present version the National Defense Education Act of 1958, complete with the loyalty oath and affidavit which have protected American higher education against the danger of subversion. And, as all observers had predicted, Congress endorsed the program which grants special Federal aid to what are horribly called the "Federally impacted areas." These deserve a word to themselves. "Federally impacted areas" are defined by the presence of defense installations. Local communities do their best to attract Army bases, out of both patriotism and profit. Nevertheless, for purposes of Federal subsidy, communities and their Congressional representatives prefer to describe these defense installations as a tax burden, and particularly an unfair expense to be borne by local school systems because of Federal activity. So eloquent has this argument been and so numerous are the congressmen in Federally impacted areas that the Federal government has been extending aid for some years to the school districts that are afflicted. This program is very dear indeed to the hearts of many congressmen who are otherwise unalterably opposed to Federal aid to education. Since substantial sums flow to their districts, they cheerfully make this particular exception to their general principle. Such, one might note, are the normal operations of political pragmatism.

But this was all that the President got from his unco-operative Congressional partner. Not to labor the point, he got nothing that he had asked for back in February. In consequence, he signed what Congress offered him, to quote his own comment, "with extreme reluctance." But he did sign the bill into law.

. . . AND THEIR PROGRESS

It appears to be one of the articles of contemporary American faith that education is underfinanced. Teachers' salaries are too low. Money for school construction is inadequate. Teaching is a low-status occupation. Hence people of the best abilities are reluctant to become teachers. Because able young people won't enter teaching, the profession continues to suffer from a low public estimate. So it goes. Everyone recognizes these conditions. In the last few years we have even enjoyed co-operation from the Russians in emphasizing our national need to strengthen scientific education. It has even been intimated that it would aid the national defense if the population at large learned to read and write English. This last was an extreme recommendation, regarded in some circles as a trifle unpatriotic.

How, then, did it turn out in the presence of national need and apparent national consensus that Congress failed to do its manifest duty? How did the President's bold program of February turn into the dismal negation of October? The life and death of the administration's school aid program is an interesting example of how politics actually operates in our land. It is worth the telling for its own sake. In addition, it indicates something about what happens when religion, education, and politics are entangled.

I have referred to the chronology of defeat as extending from February to October. Properly the story ought to start a month earlier. In January 1961 Mr. Kennedy's task force on education made its report to him. When Mr. Kennedy was elected in November, he speedily appointed a whole covey of special study groups—task forces—which were charged with the missions of analyzing specific issues and offering to the President proposals for legislative action. This procedure on the President's part conforms faithfully to the conventions of American politics. First a man expends his energies in securing his party's nomination to public office. Then he redoubles his activities in order to win election. Then he frantically tries to discover what it is that he wants to do in the office he has so eagerly sought. Thus it was that between November and January President Kennedy set his array of experts to work in order that they might help him find out what the people's November mandate really meant.

The educational task force was not the only group which reported to the new President in January but it is the one which here concerns us. The program which this truly distinguished group proposed was substantially the same as the measure which Representative Thompson introduced a month later in Congress. We are now familiar with its major components. But what starts our story in January is the fact that the educational task force flatly excluded any form of aid to private and parochial schools. Here began the fight which the President was to lose. It is not entirely clear who won.

The religious reactions to the task force report were rapid. Let us begin with Cardinal Spellman, the most influential Catholic voice in the United States. On January 17 the Cardinal said: "It is unthinkable that any American child be denied the federal funds allocated to other children because his parents chose for him a God-centered education." The next day, January 18, the Reverend Oswald Hoffman, who is public-relations director of the Lutheran Missouri Synod, which operates its own system of Protestant parochial schools, registered the opposition of his group to Federal aid for parochial schools. Taking direct issue with Cardinal Spellman, he said: "Let Cardinal Spellman speak for himself. He does not speak for Lutherans." Even thus early in the argument the note of acerbity was to be heard in the land.

Other reactions were not lacking. The Reverend W. Huber Porter, Associate General Secretary of the American Baptist Convention, also opposed any Federal aid to church schools and added that the use of tax revenue for any sectarian purpose would be "a violation of a basic liberty." As you know, Baptists have been possibly the sturdiest supporters of the wall of separation doctrine. Then there were the Jewish groups. On various grounds which may include a general suspicion that when governments intervene, Jewish interests suffer, most Jewish organizations oppose government meddling in education. It was entirely in character, therefore, for the American Jewish Committee, the Jewish War Veterans—both lay groups—the Union of American Hebrew Congregations (a Reform body) and the United Synagogues of America (a Conservative body) to join in opposition to the Catholic statement.

It is worth interpolating parenthetically that as the argument developed, one Jewish group at least did ally itself with the Catholic position. This was an extremely Orthodox organization which, in language that paralleled the Catholic statement, declared its belief in the justice of aid to parochial schools of all varieties.

Thus it is fair to say on the basis of these statements, which are representative of a great many others, that the blood of controversy had begun to flow even before February, in anticipation of the legislation which the President had promised to introduce. But the temperature began to rise still higher when the President actually sent down to Congress his message on education. This message stated firmly that private elementary and secondary schools could not be aided, "in accordance with the clear prohibition of the Constitution." How "clear," in fact, was this "prohibition"? On this point, as on almost every other aspect of aid to education, controversy raged. To note the view of one distinguished authority, whose views are expressed in a preceding chapter—Harry W. Jones of the Columbia Law School faculty—it is actually very difficult to identify in the Constitution itself a clear prohibition of this kind of aid to private schools.

An official Catholic reaction came on March 2. The hierarchy declared that Congressional assistance to education should include loans, at the very minimum, to private and parochial schools. If such support were not forthcoming, it was the judgment of the Catholic bishops that aid to education should be defeated. Here, then, was the first unequivocal statement from authoritative Catholic sources that unless assistance reached the parochial schools, Catholics should work for the defeat of all aid to education.

On March 8 our Catholic President took public issue with the hierarchy of his own church. At his press conference he reaffirmed his judgment that "across the board loans as well as grants" were unconstitutional. At this juncture he seemed to say that he could not accede even to the minimum Catholic terms—some system of loans to private and parochial schools.

Actually, the situation was not that simple. It seldom is in politics. His comment really held the door at least ajar. We must go back one week to the President's news conference of March 1 to justify this inference. Let us quote a bit of that conference in illustration of the distinctions that were beginning to be made:

Question: In view of the criticisms that have occurred could you elaborate on why you have not recommended federal aid to private and parochial elementary and secondary schools?

The President: The Constitution clearly prohibits aid to the school, the parochial school. There is no doubt about that.

And the President went on to add that in the Everson decision, which he had obviously read carefully, both the majority and the dissenting opinions had been very clear in their prohibition of aid to religious schools. This, argued the President, was now settled constitutional fact and law.

But the reporter was persistent. Probing the President's position, he said: "But you are free to make the recommendation which you have made which will affect private and parochial colleges and universities?" While this is not the best-phrased of questions, the reporter obviously wanted to know how it was possible for President Kennedy to favor aid to church-connected colleges and universities, at the same time that he insisted that aid to church-supported secondary and elementary schools was clearly unconstitutional. The President's answer read in part as follows:

The aid that we have recommended to colleges is in a different form. We are aiding the student in the same way that the GI Bill of Rights aids the student. The scholarships are given to students who have talents, and they can go to the college that they want. In that case, it is aid to the students, not to the school or college and not to a particular religious group.

This passage should recall Professor Jones's remarks about the theory of pupil benefit as a rationale for granting subsidies to church schools. The President's comment amounts to an informal statement of this doctrine. But we must observe that he confined its application to college and university students, and excluded from its ambit both elementary- and secondary-school pupils. I can see no reason in logic why he could not have gone on to these categories of education, although there were many compelling political reasons for his refraining.

About this same time in March—it is important to keep the

chronology straight—Mr. Abraham Ribicoff, Secretary of Health, Education and Welfare, did his best to ward off still another threat to the bill. He indicated that the administration would not, indeed could not withhold school aid funds from segregated school districts. We must not forget that this very issue had in past aid conflicts seriously contributed to the defeat of proposed legislation. In the past it was entirely predictable that any declaration of the Ribicoff variety would have stimulated Congressman Adam Clayton Powell to attach to the proposed legislation his famous Powell rider. This rider—a simple statement—prohibited the use of Federal funds to aid schools which had failed to comply with the 1954 Supreme Court desegregation decision in Brown vs. Board of Education. In the earlier battles for school aid, Congressman Powell began the charade by attaching his amendment to whatever measure was before the Congress. Most Republicans solemnly joined him in voting for this amendment. Northern Democrats from areas which contained large minority groups also voted for the rider. Then once the rider was firmly joined to the bill, the same Republicans who had supported Powell's amendment cheerfully voted against the entire measure which contained it. In their vote enough southern Democrats would join them safely to bury school aid for another session of Congress. The device is familiar to all devotees of *Robert's Rules of Order:* one simply votes for a provision which is likely to damage the ultimate prospects of passage of a measure which one personally opposes. So it had occurred during two of the earlier trials by combat.

This occasion was fated to be different. True enough, Congressman Powell grumbled, but he did not threaten to attach once again his famous rider. For this change of front there was a good reason. This time Congressman Powell, noted in the past as a maverick, was on the team. In fact, he was and is chairman of the critically important House Education and Labor Committee, into whose hands the school legislation was originally consigned. So this issue at least was apparently scotched. And in fact it did not arise significantly during the entire controversy, although much northern response to Secretary Ribicoff's statement was decidedly acid and many angry voices found objectionable a new flow of Federal funds to school boards which were in defiance, covert or overt, of the Supreme Court's decision.

Then the pace of events began to slow. In fact, at the end of March and the beginning of April, nothing seemed to be happening. The appearance was deceptive. In politics, when public comment is stilled, it is a fair guess that much is being settled, or at least argued, privately. Which is to say that people are caucusing at most likely places at most times during the day and the night. There was no real mystery about the apparent pause: the administration was trying desperately to find some way of handling the religious question. For to any political leader there was an obtrusive, intractable fact, the presence of approximately 45,000,000 American Catholics. Although some of these Catholics oppose aid to parochial schools—the excellent lay Catholic journal *Commonweal*, for example, has taken at the least a qualified position on the issue—most Catholics, and certainly all official Catholic spokesmen, have favored aid to parochial schools in strong terms. If you are the President of the United States, what do you do with 45,000,000 citizens, most of whom vote and are perfectly capable of remembering your stand on this particular issue?

The President's methods in handling this hot potato were instructive to observe. We must not forget that on at least four important public occasions the President had firmly stated his conviction that aid to parochial schools was unconstitutional. The first occasion was when he addressed his famous remarks to the Houston Ministerial Association during the campaign itself. He had underlined his position in his Education Message to Congress, and during the two press conferences to which we have referred. He could scarcely openly disavow so unequivocal a definition of his own attitude. The President, acting in that American tradition which makes each man his own constitutional lawyer, had rendered his decision and to all appearances he was stuck with it.

At first inspection, what the President did on April 26 did nothing to take him off the hook on which he had so neatly placed himself. On that date he sent to Congress legislation which expanded his original request for improvement in the

National Defense Education Act. He now asked financial assistance for the teaching of English and physical fitness in the *public* elementary and secondary schools. Why English and physical fitness? Well, naturally we must be physically fit if we are to compete with the Russians and, for similar reasons, we need to be literate in our language if not in theirs.

Thus the new legislative request simply reiterated the presidential refusal to support parochial schools. But there was a quiet corollary, the product of the anguished conferences of the preceding days and weeks. This was the tacit agreement that in the House Education and Labor Committee itself the grants would be expanded to include private and parochial elementary and secondary schools. For his part, it was made known, the President would not oppose this modification of his policy. Thus while the President was preserved from public inconsistency, he was offered a face-saving opportunity to modify his previous, firm position. Thus, if all went well, private and parochial schools would secure funds to build the classrooms in which English and physical fitness might be taught. After all, parochial school students could aid the national defense just as effectively as their public school colleagues.

All of this, once it reached the committee, caused more delay and more argument. Although the story of this legislation is mostly confined to the House of Representatives and the President, the Senate made itself felt on May 25 when it passed a bill, Senate 1021, which authorized $2,500,000,000 in grants, or slightly more than the President had sought. These grants were liberal in their purposes, for they covered construction of new buildings, maintenance and operation of existing schools, and increases in teachers' salaries. In fact, the senators had given their former colleague just about what he had asked. In defiance of stereotype, the Senate had acted smoothly, and, given the normal rate of Congressional action, fairly expeditiously.

Much less could be said for the House of Representatives. Finally, on June 1, the House Education and Labor Committee reported a similar bill to the one that the Senate had passed. This was House of Representatives 7300. Now the House fight entered a still rougher phase. House Majority Leader John

McCormack (now Speaker) is a devout Roman Catholic. He is also an old political enemy of President Kennedy's, a survivor of many dangerous Massachusetts skirmishes. Nor was their relationship improved by another circumstance, the battle between the President's brother Teddy and the Majority Leader's nephew Edward for the Democratic senatorial nomination in Massachusetts. Teddy's ambition is quite comprehensible. Already thirty years old, he is not yet a senator. Naturally he feels left out in the contemplation of his distinguished brothers' exalted positions.

The Kennedys are a tightly-knit clan. On the other hand, Mr. McCormack, who has no children of his own, happens to be very fond of his nephew, at the moment State Attorney General in Massachusetts. Equally ambitious for preferment, young Edward McCormack would very much like to be the senator from Massachusetts. A difficult situation. Mr. McCormack, a devout Roman Catholic, undoubtedly feels very strongly that justice will not be done unless aid is extended to parochial schools. But the intensity of this conviction and its legislative effects can scarcely avoid enlargement by the ancient hostility of the two political families and the latest battle between them.

What Mr. McCormack did was this: he sought assurances that the National Defense Educational amendments, which included the physical-fitness and English-instruction provisions to which I have alluded, would be considered *before* the general aid-to-education measure. Thus, if his demand were granted, the House of Representatives would be compelled to commit itself to special grants to *all* schools before it permitted itself to adopt general aid to public education only.

As can be imagined, the battle was immediately joined. The situation confirmed everyone's doubts about the good faith of everyone else in this tangled argument. There were those who suspected that if the National Defense Education Act amendments were passed, the public school aid program would never be enacted. On the other side, there were those who suspected that if public school aid were once granted, then the National Defense Education Act amendments would be treated to speedy burial. Certainly no observer could declare that these mutual suspicions were utterly unfounded.

What with one thing and another, more delay occurred. Finally, on July 18, the "reformed" Rules Committee—the first major legislative victory which the President won had been the enlargement of this vital group so as to give administration forces a dependable majority—came unstuck. With truly massive impartiality, the committee tabled both bills: the National Defense Education Act amendments and the general aid-to-schools measure.

How did this deed get done? The vote was indeed close. In fact, a single-vote majority killed very probably for several years to come the chance to pass aid to education legislation. That vote belonged to Representative Delaney, a liberal Democrat from the borough of Queens. Representative Delaney is a Roman Catholic who represents a constituency which includes a large number of other Roman Catholics. He voted against consideration of either one of these bills because in his judgment even the National Defense Education Act amendments extended too little assistance to parochial schools.

So the struggle ended or all but ended in bad temper and inaction. But there was still an untidy epilogue, a ritual anticlimax, to be experienced. The Kennedy administration made a second attempt to secure some kind of an act on August 29. On that date, the House Labor and Education Committee introduced a stripped-down, poor cousin of the original Thompson measure. It simply offered $325,000,000 a year for school construction. No supplement to teachers' salaries was included. Also dropped was the scholarship program and much of the remainder of the original proposals. The dollar cost of this program was less than half the amount of the original. But it was too late. Even this so-called compromise measure was defeated on August 30 by a vote of 242 to 170. Thus it was that what the President described as the most important single piece of domestic legislation which he had offered the Congress met complete defeat.

PERSUASION AND POWER

So much for the condensed chronology of events. How can these events be interpreted? Let us start with a platitude. The political process is extraordinarily untidy. In part, a very small part, it advances on the basis of rational discourse and temperate argument. In part, a very large part, the political process reflects the play of conflicting interests. When it works best it soothes or resolves these interests. In short, the stuff of politics is only slightly rational. It is very substantially a matter of pressure and power. Hence I want to speak about the manner in which both arguments and pressures so collided as to result in an utter fiasco.

Let's dispose of the arguments first. Much of the controversy was constitutional. In the school fight everybody deployed constitutional arguments. Doing his best to reduce the emotional temperature, the President studiously avoided taking sides on the social merits of aid to parochial schools and concentrated on their unconstitutionality, according to his own interpretation. Constitutional argument was no presidential monopoly. Jewish and Protestant bodies, and secular organizations like the American Civil Liberties Union, advanced what have been called standard "wall of separation" arguments, which, according to the preference of the group, were deployed to bar all aid, some aid, some varieties of aid and not others, and so on.

Nor were the Catholics constitutionally naked in the debate. I would judge that Catholics relied upon three major constitutional claims. One was based upon the "free exercise" portion of the First Amendment. The wall-of-separation proponents tended to concentrate upon the second part of the First Amendment's religious guarantee, the bar against the establishment of religion. Let me illustrate the way that the free-exercise argument can be put. A recent letter in *The N.Y. Times*, signed by a Father Daniel S. Hamilton, will serve our purpose. He rhetorically asks, "Can that freedom," by which he means the freedom to send children to religious and private schools, "be taxed out of existence? Can the numerous religious schools be rendered hopelessly inferior and ultimately extinguished by considerable federal aid to public non-religious schools only?" Father Hamilton's argument is exceedingly simple. Parochial schools are indispensable elements of Catholic religious observance. If the state's fiscal measures make it impossible for Catholics to support these schools and educate their children in them, or even to maintain these schools in inferior condition, then it follows for Father Hamilton that Catholics no longer may freely and fully exercise their religion.

Take next a second and stronger constitutional argument, the pupil-benefit theory, to which I have already referred. This is a rationale full of pitfalls, but again it is easy to state. Under the theory of pupil benefit, aid is considered to apply to the pupil, not to the school or the church. Thus if local authorities transport a parochial school pupil in a school bus at public expense, the aid is appropriately regarded as applying to the transported student rather than to the school to which he is carried. Again, if public funds purchase the parochial school pupil's textbooks in secular subjects, the same argument applies.

Of course, as in many constitutional arguments, the problem is one of limits. Where does pupil benefit end and where does aid to a church begin?

Finally, let us mention a third constitutional claim which was fully made only this month. In an 82½-page memorandum prepared by Catholic attorneys on behalf of the National Catholic Welfare Conference there occur at the outset these three sentences:

> Education in church-related schools is a public function which by its nature is deserving of governmental support. There exists no Constitutional bar to aid to education in church-related schools in a degree proportionate to the value of the public function it performs. Such aid to the secular function may take the form of matching grants or long term loans to institutions or scholarships, tuition payments, or tax benefits.

In short, here is a claim for unlimited assistance, for a public purpose.

I shall make only two passing observations on this position. The proposition that education in a parochial school is in some sense and in some degree *public* education depends on the public desirability of training all children up to some minimum standard of spelling, reading comprehension, computational skill, and historical appreciation. Wherever this training occurs, the benefits are public, regardless of the organizational form which the educational arrangements may assume. But the claim is, after all—and this is my second point—smaller than full support of parochial school education. The brief identifies a secular function of the religious school and separates that secular function from the religious function. It seeks public support only for the secular activities of the religious school.

Not all the Catholic arguments were constitutional. There was also a much more complex set of propositions derived from older sources than the American Constitution. These older sources are distributive justice and natural law. Here, ran the argument, the right to educate a child is a parental right, based on the very nature of man. The right has nothing to do with the state. Rather, the parent delegates the right to educate his child to the state. Therefore, the Catholic parent suffers injustice whenever the state arrogates to itself the right to subsidize only schools in which no religion is taught. That is to say the Catholic parent suffers injustice if he wishes to delegate his parental right to a parochial school. This is an argument which you will find well expressed in Father Murray's book,[2] as well as in William Gorman's essay in one of the Fund for the Republic pamphlets.[3]

Still in the realm of more or less rational argument, there was also some discussion of the relative merits of parochial and public education. But here the debate tended rapidly to deteriorate into emotion, in part because amazingly little is known about the operations and merits of parochial schools. Finally, much argument was heard on the importance of the relation between democracy and public schools.

No doubt it would be well for the republic if reasoned argument—constitutional and otherwise—decided public policy. But a realist must observe that what counted more than persuasion was pressure. Each Congressman was the focus of intensive efforts by his constituents, individually and organizationally, to vote the proper way. Let us look at these pressures, first, the pressures to aid public education only, and second,

[2] John Courtney Murray, *We Hold These Truths,* Sheed & Ward, 1960.

[3] *Religion and the Schools,* Fund for the Republic Pamphlet, 1959.

the pressures to aid parochial schools only, and third, pressures to give no aid to any schools whatsoever.

Who wanted to aid public schools only? By all odds, the biggest lobby was the National Education Association, which represents—or at least speaks in the name of—a constituency of 750,000 teachers and school administrators. (It is an odd alliance of teachers and their natural enemies, the principals and the supervisors.) In the first half of 1960, in preparation for the battles of 1961, the National Education Association expended $77,913 on lobbying, or to use the dignified euphemism, "public representation."

That's a lot of teachers and officials, 750,000, scattered all through the community. A congressman simply must listen to an organization of this kind. Moreover, the National Education Association had many allies. The AFL-CIO, the National Farmers' Union, Americans for Democratic Action, the American Civil Liberties Union, and the American Library Association were among them. There was even a service group, the American Veterans Committee, which is composed of liberal veterans and is therefore very small. With some differences of tone and emphasis among themselves, all of these groups favored aid to public schools only and made their views heard. I shall speak separately a bit later of the Protestant and Jewish religious groups who took similar stands.

Who were the President's opponents? They fell into two categories: those who wanted no federal aid of any variety, and those who wanted the provisions of the legislation extended to parochial and private schools. To some degree they were allies in opposition to the legislation which the administration sponsored. It is easy to identify among the opponents of any aid organizations whom anyone would expect to take this position: the Chamber of Commerce, and the National Association of Manufacturers, for example, who fought the President's bill partly out of fear that the budget would be unbalanced, and partly on the ground that local control would be menaced. Concerning the latter reason, it is permissible to suspect that their apprehension was that the acquired right of business groups to dominate local boards of education would be menaced. They were joined by the American Medical Association.

My guess is that the A.M.A. fought aid to education out of consistent principle, its automatic opposition to any measure which smacks of public altruism.

The dreary list included the American Legion and the Daughters of the American Revolution. As we know, the D.A.R. is an active defender of American institutions. It has unmasked Communist infiltration into the United Nations Children's Fund and advised refusal to purchase UNICEF Christmas cards. It has guarded our gold in Fort Knox. These are only two examples of the constructive role these latter-day revolutionaries have taken in our national life.

The groups that wished to extend the legislation rather than kill it were almost entirely Catholic. The National Catholic Welfare Conference, representing Catholic bishops, carried much of the brunt of the battle. A small Orthodox Jewish group adhered to the Catholic position. And a scattering of prominent individuals, either Jewish or Protestant in affiliation, also endorsed the principle of aid to parochial schools. Will Herberg, and Charles Silver, at the time Chairman of the New York City Board of Education, are examples.

Thus the motley coalition of opponents of the administration bill included conservatives, Catholics, numerous segregationists, and militant patriots. Frequently these categories overlapped, sometimes they did not. Alliances were temporary and partial among partners so diverse in temper.

HOW DID THE CHURCHES BEHAVE?

What can we now say about how the churches acted? What can we say about how they should have acted either from their own standpoint or from the standpoint of the wider public interest?

Let us start with the first and easier of these two questions. In detail, church behavior was extremely complicated but in general it is easy to summarize. The churches acted approximately like other legal, responsible, voluntary bodies in our community. This is to say, they employed, within the limits set by their conscience and the law, any serviceable technique which was adapted to the success of the particular objective which they sought, whether this objective was aid to parochial schools or no aid to parochial schools.

What are these techniques? Among them are argument, letter-writing campaigns, visits from old friends to their congressmen, anxious inquiries from campaign contributors, and hurt letters from priests to Catholic congressmen asking them to examine their consciences and see whether it was consistent with conscience to vote for an aid-to-education bill which excluded parochial schools. These are familiar devices. So also was organized letter writing in school classrooms. There were letters received in Washington which read, in one version or another, "My name is Rose Marie. I'm 7 years old and I am in parochial school here in ——— and I would like the federal government to give money to my school because I like my teachers and my classes." This is no parody. There were masses of such letters and it is only fair to say that the technique is a venerable one which in this instance was used largely by Catholics.

And such letters are designed to appeal to the sympathies of congressmen, and what may be more important, their instinct of self-preservation. For while seven-year olds don't vote, their parents do vote and so may the teachers in religious schools. The pressure of these dictated letters was unmistakable.

This leads us to the major pressure, derived not alone from Catholic sources but from Protestant, Jewish, and secular ones as well: this was the threat, overt or covert, of electoral retribution. This threat might take the shape of a guarantee to a congressman in a substantially Catholic district that if he voted against aid to parochial schools, he would be free to enjoy the delights of peaceful retirement to private life come the next election. Now, whatever may be the burdens of public office, it is notable that most officials are willing to bear them for some time into the future. Not for a moment are such threats ineffective. It is not only that partisans threaten not to vote for the delinquent congressman in the next primary or the next election, but also that they withhold accustomed contributions and tell their friends all about it. What these people say to their Congressman amounts to this: "Vote my way out of conviction, but vote my way in any event, or it's going to be the worse for you in the next election."

It does not take a close analyst of electoral statistics to know that the voting pattern in the school aid struggle followed the religious composition of the districts from which the congressmen came. Let me offer you a local illustration. The congressman who represents the area from 110th Street north to the very borders of the Bronx is Representative Herbert Zelenko. Mr. Zelenko is Jewish. He has been in Congress now for three terms. On the whole he has been typical of big-city northern Democratic legislators. He votes for housing, social welfare, and civil rights measures. Otherwise he is a quiet, inconspicuous figure whose good deeds have won him little publicity or newspaper mention. Until recently. For in the last session of Congress, Representative Zelenko blossomed out somewhat startlingly as a proponent of aid to parochial schools. How does it happen that Mr. Zelenko, neither a Catholic nor an alumnus of parochial education, suddenly achieves identification as the spokesman in Congress (for a brief period) of His Eminence, Cardinal Spellman?

The mystery has a ready political solution. The Twentieth Congressional District contains in its northern portion, the Inwood area, a large number of Catholics. Anticipating a strong primary fight in the next election, Representative Zelenko apparently calculated that the chances of offending his Jewish constituents in the Washington Heights area were smaller than the gains which he might derive from pleasing his Catholic constituents. Hence he joined himself to a cause which in the past had won the support largely of Catholic legislators.

In other districts, Congressmen feared to oppose large bodies of active Catholics. I am describing naked pressure in operation. Those who exerted it were not entirely, perhaps not even predominantly Catholic. It is quite conceivable that there were Congressmen from the South and from the Midwest who, if they had dared to vote their convictions, would have been willing to grant some aid to parochial schools. But if you are a Congressman who comes from the hard-shell Baptist country, or from some sound midwestern fundamentalist rural constituency—where it is notorious that Rome threatens American democracy daily if not hourly—then you simply do not vote for legislation which seems to benefit Rome or its American agents.

Although the pressures seemed to come from both Catholic and non-Catholic sources, in one practical sense the pro-parochial-school side of the issue had the better of the argument. School legislation which would have aided only public schools was, after all, defeated. But even this conclusion must be qualified. For it is equally possible to interpret the outcome either as a victory for those who preferred no aid at all to aid which encompassed parochial schools, or as a triumph for reactionaries who opposed school aid at the Federal level without qualification. Perhaps what happened is best described as a breakdown of good will, primarily among Catholics, Protestants, and Jews. In effect, Catholics said: "If we can't have aid to parochial schools, then no aid for your schools either." Protestants, Jews, and a good many secularists said: "If the cost of aid to public schools is equivalent aid, or any aid to parochial schools, let's have no aid at all." As you observe, the common clause in both attitudes was: "Let's have no aid." And no aid there was.

Here in fact was one of the many political occasions where ends conflicted rather than converged. What do you say if you believe that the need for school aid is enormous and you also fear that aid to parochial schools will damage public education? Do you say: "Well, I don't want aid to parochial schools, but the public need is so overwhelming that I'll accept reluctantly some aid to parochial schools as the necessary price of this prop to public schools"? Or will you say instead, as in the end a large number of persons must have said, "I'd rather have no aid at all to public schools than include parochial schools in my program"?

Although I may have implied a contrary conclusion, I do not condemn out of hand Catholics, Protestants, Jews, or secularists. Indeed, how can I? For the tactics of the faithful were indistinguishable from the methods of trade unions when they lobby for amendment to or repeal of the Taft-Hartley Act, or when they seek improved minimum-wage legislation. These are the same tactics as the American Medical Association—the most successful lobby in our history—has employed. They are the tactics of corporations who seek favorable tax treatment. Dare I say it here, they scarcely differ from the methods of universities intent on the promotion of their special interests. In short, what the churches and their followers did was perfectly legal. As a skeptic, I rejoice to see the churches behaving no better than the remainder of society. But is this enough for their members? Let us examine next this question.

HOW SHOULD CHURCHES ACT?

When a church tries to influence public affairs, how *should* it behave, according to its own standards? Should it apply stricter criteria to its own acts than other institutions apply to theirs? Should churches refrain from the familiar techniques of trade unions, corporations, and other organizations which seek limited at best, and selfish at worst, aims? Does society have a right to expect better things from its churches?

We approach here a really difficult range of issues. Let us begin our explorations with a statement from *Religion in American Society*.[4] It goes like this:

> Almost all religious communities claim to have a special grasp of theological truth. Of course, some claims are more exclusive than others. Some groups put more emphasis than others upon their church's authority to interpret the law of God. The free society as such is neutral about all such claims, but so long as religious groups accept the basic charter of agreements that bind the American people into a civic unity, the nation has a right to expect religious groups, whatever their theological claims, not to impose their special truths on others by social coercion, by the use of economic pressure, political threats, boycotts, or blacklists.

And the same Fund for the Republic document goes on to quote something I had written in an earlier pamphlet: "As Robert Lekachman wrote in *The Churches and the Public*, the free society encourages the honorable expression of many beliefs. It is also a society in which the rules of the game are

[4] Fund for the Republic, 1961. The authors include Arthur Cohen, John Cogley, William Lee Miller, William Clancy, Robert Lekachman, Robert Gordis, William Gorman, Ernest Johnson.

themselves a shared value." The shared value in question can be put in this way: persuasion is the proper mode of action for those groups in American life whose overriding aim is the transformation of society. Direct or indirect coercion is properly held to be anathema.

Think for a moment of who the signers of the Fund for the Republic report are. With the single exception of myself, all of them are deeply committed to one of the three major American faiths. They concur in the conviction that churches ought to be different. Churches ought to distinguish themselves from other voluntary groups by the nature of their missions and their steadfast aim to alter their societies not in their own interest but in the social interest. Hence, runs the argument, just because the changes which they should seek are nobler than those of economic organizations like unions and corporations, they should refrain from the effective techniques of pressure and power which these other social agencies employ. It is best for the society which the churches aim to improve if the churches refrain from such techniques. And it is best for the religions which the churches preach. For, as the Fund report maintains, "A nation converted against its will remains unconverted still."

Does this sound like a pleasant, easy, even an obvious prescription? After all, if a church has in addition to its worldly aims a set of other-worldly objectives, then naturally it differs from other organizations which are essentially content with their society and wish only to readjust it marginally in their own advantage. Surely corporations and trade unions seek no more than the marginal adjustment by their lobbying.

Specific cases are the best test of general propositions. We do well to test this one by applying it to some particulars. If you are a Catholic, are you justified in personal opposition to a congressman whose general record pleases you, save that he has voted against aid to parochial schools? Go a step further. Are you justified in organizing others in opposition to this congressman? It seems a fair interpretation of the general prescription of the Fund for the Republic writer that you would not be entitled as a Catholic to vote against a congressman—whether he is Catholic, Jewish, or Protestant—simply because on this single issue he displeased you. What approach does a religious commitment justify? Essentially persuasion only. As a religious person, you would patiently endeavor to show him the merits of your position and the faults of his position. You should not threaten to vote against him, still less should you organize others in opposition to him.

The problem is not exclusively Catholic, although it has often been made to appear a specifically Catholic dilemma because of the high visibility of some Catholic actions and the tight organization of some urban Catholic groups. Imagine yourself a Protestant who believes that Sunday is sacred to God's purposes. It is your deep conviction that those of your fellow citizens who avoid religious observance should refrain at the least from distracting their believing and worshiping neighbors. Let them not drink beer, let them not shop in discount houses, let them not, in a word, pursue the disgracefully temporal activities which the profane tend to enjoy on Sundays as well as on other days of the week.

Suppose that you enjoy the representation of a good state legislator, a rarity almost anywhere in the United States. You admire his record. He is interested in many good causes of which you approve. But, on the Sunday-observance laws, he is excessively latitudinarian, in fact just plain wrong. It appears that he is prepared to countenance all kinds of frivolity on Sunday. As a religious Protestant, are you entitled to vote against him on this ground? Or should you try, after the fashion of peaceful persuasion, to convert him to a better sentiment?

This is far from a made-up issue. In fact, a Jewish variant of it can be observed in the Columbia University vicinity, to pick a single example. Daniel Kelly represents the Seventh Assembly District, in which Columbia University is located. An exceptionally independent legislator, Mr. Kelly was once called by the Citizen's Union "the conscience of the Assembly." In an undistinguished Assembly, Daniel Kelly has been a valuable man. He has blown the whistle on a great many scandals in Albany. He has earned himself vast unpopularity among his fellows and that, politically speaking, is usually a sign of an effective contribution. But, from the standpoint of many Jewish voters, he is wrong about the Sunday-closing laws. Here the issue is the wish of some Jewish groups to win legislative modifications in the present rules which compel almost all kinds of businesses to close on Sundays. These rules penalize Orthodox Jewish merchants who close their shops on Saturday because of religious conviction and lose Sunday as well because the law so decrees it. Mr. Kelly, who is an observant Catholic, opposes amendment of the Sunday closing laws. As a Jew, are you entitled to vote against Daniel Kelly and his excellent record on this single issue? Or do you try to convert him and if you fail, threaten him with electoral retaliation? Or do you content yourself with peaceful persuasion?

Are you entitled, still as a Jew, to vote for congressmen or senators largely on your judgment of the candidate's record on Arab-Israeli relations? Again the issue is real, not hypothetical. When President Kennedy was appointing his Cabinet, a leading prospect for Secretary of State was Senator Fulbright. A considerable outcry was heard from some Jewish groups against Senator Fulbright because he had made certain statements on Arab-Jewish relations which were considered "soft" on the Arabs and "hard" on the Israelis. Here was a use of a single issue as a touchstone of judgment. We should be clear that no one suggests among the Fund writers that you should not weigh a candidate's position on an important issue among his other public judgments. But if you take a single issue as your guide, then in effect you are preferring power and pressure to persuasion and argument.

A final specific instance will suffice. Many Catholics take the Legion of Decency pledge. If you are a believing Catholic, what are you entitled to do to a local film exhibitor who advertises a Brigitte Bardot movie, or some other film which has been categorized as morally objectionable by the Legion of Decency? What does the Fund for the Republic advise? Can you refrain from going to the film yourself? The answer is clearly affirmative. Here is a freedom of personal choice few would deny. Can you call up your Catholic friends and alert them to the morally offensive nature of the movie? All right so far? What about ringing your Jewish and Protestant friends and saying something like this: "You know, this exhibitor is showing the kind of movie which is bad for everybody. Children will eagerly attend and Lord only knows what this will do to stunt their moral growth, and damage their general attitude. Don't you think that we ought to boycott this film?" Is that all right?

Shall we continue one step further? Should you say: "There must be something morally wrong with the exhibitor who is willing to show this particular film. If he brazenly persists in his delinquency then we don't want to go to any of his movies and we'll see that no one else goes to them either. Let's boycott him and ruin his business." With belated charity, you may modify the decree of doom by this qualification: "Let's not boycott him forever, let's administer a trial boycott of three months, and see whether he isn't brought to a sounder moral frame of mind by his loss of revenues." And once again, Catholic boycotts of films are not unknown in real life any more than Jewish boycotts of movies like *Oliver Twist*. Some years ago Catholic groups compelled the withdrawal of *Martin Luther* from community theaters on the ground that the portrayal of Martin Luther was anti-Catholic. One can understand the Catholic feeling that the Reformation was a mistake to which as little attention as possible should be drawn.

What should the attitude of a religious Christian or a religious Jew be to such activities as actual and threatened boycotts? These are enormously powerful pressures. Their exercise tidily eliminates any need to convert or persuade movie exhibitors, bookstore proprietors, or newsstand operators. A movie exhibitor who is converted against his will may be unconverted still, but he is going to have to view the movies in the privacy of his own theater once an effective boycott begins to operate.

There is a range of issues of this variety in which the most effective techniques are the most temporal: power, pressure, boycott, economic retribution, and political retribution. The tools are not pleasant, the ends are short run, but their effectiveness cannot be questioned.

This is a long list of examples. What general principles apply? I'll start with an answer which is satisfactory to those who, like myself, are not religious believers. For us, or for some of us at any rate, a church is nothing special. It is simply another kind of voluntary organization, intermediate between the individual and the state. By virtue of legal exemption and traditional privilege, it is entitled to function in a number of community activities. Churches, therefore, are entitled to exactly the same public treatment as is extended to other voluntary groups in the community which by common consent serve benevolent or at least unharmful objectives. Thus, I would say for myself, and perhaps for some others of my general persuasion, that boycotts, electoral threats, and economic pressures are just as legal for churches as they are for trade unions or for corporations. Whether they are advisable or not is a question of prudence rather than of principle. And although these techniques in any hands may impede rather than improve the democratic process, I cannot in justice ban their use by one group more than by another.

Thus I find nothing reprehensible, or at least nothing especially reprehensible, in the activities of the Catholic hierarchy in the recent school aid fight. I anticipate that similar activities will be featured in the next round of the encounter. For I cannot require special behavior from churches if I am unwilling to accord them special privileges. As a good sound unbeliever, I am gratified rather than disheartened when churches behave no better than avowedly secular bodies.

But this answer can scarcely suffice for a religious person, anxious to conduct himself and regulate his behavior by the lights of his faith. Certainly for such a believer a description of churches as simply another kind of voluntary society—like the Elks or the American Legion—can scarcely fail to be offensive. If the churches are both different from and better than other voluntary organizations, it appears to follow that church leaders and church members cannot content themselves simply with doing nothing that is illegal. Legality is far too neutral an ethical guide. The means employed by churches shape their ends as infallibly as means shape ends in other spheres of human behavior.

Hence churches ought to choose their means with great care. After all, it is very well to say that a church has a mission beyond society and that its goals transcend the merely material aims of the remainder of society. But it is equally obvious that churches own property, administer schools, and tend a wide range of strictly economic interests. The churches, it might appear, can scarcely avoid trying to influence legislation which affects them as property owners, school administrators, book publishers, and charitable societies. Monk's bread baked by real monks and liqueur distilled by genuine members of the Benedictine order remind potential buyers daily that the church is within society as well as beyond society.

POWER OR PRINCIPLE?

Here at last is the church's dilemma. The church may say: "We shall employ only persuasion, education, and patience. When we educate and when we persuade we will take anxious care that our techniques are enlightened and aesthetic. We shall be wary of television and sparing even in our use of literature." A church may indeed take such a stand, but it risks something. To be brutal, the church stands in danger of being ineffectual. In this country it is the mass media which influence opinion. The mass media are distinguished neither by their taste nor by their intellectual scrupulousness nor by any genuine wish for intellectual conversion. Their function is entertainment. The generalization covers the pretentious mass medium like *Time* as well as the unpretentious mass medium like the comic book. In fairness I will concede that in its way *Time* is occasionally funnier by accident than the comic books are on purpose.

However, if the church's superior techniques are ineffective, what becomes of the church's message? Amid the clamor of the cynical will the voice of the responsible be heard? But suppose that the church does not refrain from the devices of the hucksters? There is the illustrative case of Norman Vincent Peale, an influential pastor whose volumes are best sellers. His columns are widely syndicated. His famous volume *The Power of Positive Thinking* must have retarded thought in hundreds of thousands of households. And he has his Protestant, Catholic, and Jewish rivals. Norman Vincent Peale is effective. Bishop Sheen is effective. That is to say, if effect is measured by notoriety and sales. But what becomes of the religious message? At best it is corrupted and at worst it vanishes.

The choices for the conscientious are grim. On the one side, there is the risk of impotence. On the other side, the price of being effective is becoming like the rest of society. A message which is merchandised is just as much a commercial as the plug for a product.

At the beginning, I promised some reflections, not a solution. I have none to offer now. I shall end with the comment that the problem of the churches is in its way the problem also of the university which lives within society but tries also to change it. It is the problem of any belief and any organization whose objectives transcend private gain. I am sincere when I wish the churches well in their attempts to grapple with it. I am honest when I say that none of them did very well in the battle over aid to schools which we have described.

About the Contributors

HAROLD STAHMER, graduate of Dartmouth College, Union Theological Seminary, and Cambridge University, is Associate Professor of Religion at Barnard College and Columbia University.

ARTHUR A. COHEN, founder of Meridian Books, and now Director of Religious Publishing at Holt, Rinehart and Winston, was consultant to the project "Religion and the Free Society" of the Fund for the Republic.

HARRY W. JONES is Cardozo Professor of Jurisprudence at Columbia University.

ROBERT LEKACHMAN, Associate Professor of Economics at Barnard College, was formerly a consultant to the project "Religion and the Free Society" of the Fund for the Republic.

REINHOLD NIEBUHR, formerly Professor of Christian Ethics and Vice President of Union Theological Seminary, has also been a consultant for the Fund for the Republic, and is currently Virginia Gildersleeve Visiting Professor at Barnard College.

WALTER J. ONG, S.J., Professor of English at Saint Louis University, was recently a Fellow at the Center for Advanced Studies at Wesleyan University, Middletown, Connecticut, and is the author of *The Barbarian Within*, *American Catholic Crossroads*, and *Frontiers in American Catholicism.*

WILHELM PAUCK, Charles A. Briggs Graduate Professor of Church History at Union Theological Seminary, is the author of *The Heritage of the Reformation.*

JOHN WICKLEIN, former religion writer for the New York *Times*, is now News Director at WNDT Television, New York City.